WHY NONCOMPLIANCE

WHY NONCOMPLIANCE

The Politics of Law
in the European Union

Tanja A. Börzel

CORNELL UNIVERSITY PRESS   **ITHACA AND LONDON**

This book is available in open access form as the result of a grant from the Freie Universität Berlin. Cornell University Press gratefully acknowledges this generous funding that made it possible to open this publication to the world.

First published 2021 by Cornell University Press

Library of Congress Cataloging-in-Publication Data

Names: Börzel, Tanja A., 1970– author.
Title: Why noncompliance : the politics of law in the European Union / Tanja A. Börzel.
Description: Ithaca [New York] : Cornell University Press, 2021. | Includes bibliographical references and index.
Identifiers: LCCN 2020013043 (print) | LCCN 2020013044 (ebook) | ISBN 9781501753398 (paperback) | ISBN 9781501753404 (ebook) | ISBN 9781501753411 (pdf)
Subjects: LCSH: Law—European Union countries. | Effectiveness and validity of law—European Union countries. | European Union countries—Politics and government—Philosophy. | Compliance.
Classification: LCC KJE5087. B67 2021 (print) | LCC KJE5087 (ebook) | DDC 341.242/2—dc23
LC record available at https://lccn.loc.gov/2020013043
LC ebook record available at https://lccn.loc.gov/2020013044

Contents

Figures and Tables

Figures

Tables

Preface and Acknowledgments

In March 2000, I went to Brussels for a European Commission meeting. I was desperate. For two years, I had been coding hundreds of individual cases in which the Commission had opened legal proceedings against member states for violating EU law. Those were the days before EUR-Lex, the official website of the EU that offers access to EU law, case law by the Court of Justice of the European Union, and other public EU documents. For large-N data on noncompliance in the EU, researchers had to rely on the Annual Reports on the Monitoring of the Application of Community Law. The Commission did not only publish total numbers of infringements in a given year by member state and policy sector. The annexes also listed the individual cases, with brief information on the legal act infringed and the stage of the proceeding. Yet the numbers simply did not add up. When I confronted a Commission official with the considerable mismatch between the aggregate numbers reported in the main part and the sums of the individual cases listed in the annexes, he asked me to come back the next day. I did, and obtained a complicated explanation that had something to do with reporting methods. Satisfied that there was no flaw or political strategy involved, I packed up my stuff. As I was leaving, the Commission official asked me what I was going to do. I told him that I would use "my" hand-coded data, of course, adding the explanation for the mismatch he had just provided. Nervously, he replied that I could not do this because it would undermine the credibility of the data published by the Commission. When I insisted, he asked me once again to come back. On my return a few hours later, his supervisor offered me a deal. I would not use "my" data. Instead, the Commission would give me a data set with the individual infringement cases drawn from its own database for the years 1978 up to 1999. This was the beginning of the Berlin Infringement Database (BID), which, thanks to EUR-Lex, I have been able to update until 2017. The data revealed the three puzzles that this book seeks to solve.

Coming up with a theory that explains variation in noncompliance with EU law across twenty-eight member states, eleven policy sectors, and more than forty years of European integration was a long journey in which many people took part. I am able to thank only some of my travel companions. With the financial support of the Robert Schuman Centre of the European University Institute, Charalampos "Babis" Koutalakis entered thousands of infringement cases into an access file, which became the "parent" of the BID. In 2002, Babis joined me at the Humboldt University as a Marie Curie fellow. Focusing on why some member states comply less with EU law than others, I had successfully applied for an Emmy Noether Research Group (BO 1831_1–2). I am grateful to the German Research Foundation (DFG), which provided four years of funding for three PhD students. Forged together by our struggle with quantitative and qualitative data on member state violations of EU law, Meike Dudziak, Tobias Hofmann, and Carina Sprungk followed me to the University of Heidelberg in 2004, where Diana Panke joined the team. Without the work and dedication to the project of these four, this book would have never been written. The collaborative project NEWGOV, funded for four years by the EU's Sixth Framework Programme (Project no. CIT1-CT-2004–506392), allowed me to extend eastward my research on member state noncompliance. The empirical research of Aron Buzogany and Sonja Guttenbrunner helped me establish the claim that noncompliance was not only not an exclusive problem of the southern member states. It had not become an eastern problem, either. The joint work with Frank Schimmelfenning and Uli Sedelmeier in the EU collaborative project EU-STRAT, funded by the EU's Seventh Framework Programme (Project no. 693382), corroborated the argument. The DFG enabled me to explore why noncompliance with EU law varied even more between policy sectors than between member states (BO 1831_6_1). Moritz Knoll did a heroic job in updating the BID between 2006 and 2010. Lukas Blasius took over in 2011. Together with Stephan Lutzenberger, Lukas turned the BID into an open access source. Stephan, Lukas, and Tobias Hofmann also helped me a great deal with the statistical analyses. Without their expertise, I would not have been able to make so much sense of the data. Their support was made possible, again, by DFG funding, provided by the Research College "The Transformative Power of Europe" (FOR 1026). Special thanks also go to Maria-Sophia Dellasega and Lukas Müller-Wünsch for their invaluable research assistance. Last but not least, I am very grateful to the professional team at Cornell University Press that helped me with the book throughout the production process. This includes Ellen Labbate, Brock Edward Schnoke, copyeditor Glenn Novak and indexer Ken Bolton. Special thanks go to Karen M. Laun for the excellent managing of the production process. Roger Haydon has been a constant source of encouragement and inspiration.

I had completed a first draft of the book in 2012. I cannot recall how many times I revised the manuscript in light of the fantastic comments I received by colleagues and friends, including Lisa Conant, Tobias Hofmann, Lukas Obholzer, Diana Panke, Thomas Risse, Frank Schimmelfennig, Susanne K. Schmidt, Uli Sedelmeier, Jonas Tallberg, and Asya Zhelyazkova. Given the long journey the book took, I simply do not have the space to list all the commentators on the many papers in which I presented different parts of the findings and arguments at numerous workshops and conferences. One of the very first occasions was the ECPR Joint Session of Workshops in Mannheim in 2001. I am grateful to Christian Joerges and Michael Zürn, the two workshop organizers, for nominating my paper for the Rudolf-Wildenmann Award. I also want to thank Rachel Epstein and Scott Siegel for organizing the "author meets critics" panel at the European Studies Association Meeting in Denver in 2019. The prospect of having my book discussed by a group of outstanding experts in the field kept me working during the year in which I struggled with serious illness. Being able to finish the book I had been working on for such a long time helped me get through those challenging months. Even more important, of course, were my family, friends, and colleagues. There are no words to express my gratitude to all those who stood by me. Diana, Nicole, and Kaja showed me what friendship is all about. Thomas did so much more than be there for me in sickness and in health. Without him, I could not have completed this book.

Abbreviations

ASEAN	Association of Southeast Asian Nations
BID	Berlin Infringement Database
CEAS	Common European Asylum System
CEE	Central and Eastern European
CETA	Comprehensive Economic and Trade Agreement
CPC	Consumer Protection Cooperation Network
CSN	Consumer Safety Network
DFG	German Research Foundation
DG	Directorate-General
EASO	European Asylum Support Office
EBCG	EU Border and Coast Guard Agency
ECB	European Central Bank
ECJ	European Court of Justice
ECN	European Competition Network
ECOWAS	West African Economic Community
EIA	environmental impact assessment
EMU	Economic and Monetary Union
ENVIREG	Regional Action Programme on the Initiative of the Commission Concerning the Environment
EP	European Parliament
ERG	European Regulators Group
ESSG	European Safety Assessment of Foreign Aircraft Steering Group
EU	European Union
FEIE	Forum of Exchange of Information on Enforcement
FFH	fauna, flora, habitat
GDP	gross domestic product
ICRG	International Country Risk Guide
IMI	Internal Market Information System
IMPEL	European Union Network for the Implementation and Enforcement of Environmental Law
INSO	Information Society & Media
IR	international relations
ISPA	Instrument for Structural Policies for Pre-accession
JAIN	Justice & Home Affairs

LIFE   Financial Instrument for the Environment
MEDSPA   Protection of the Environment in the Mediterranean Region
NAFTA   North American Free Trade Agreement
NATO   North Atlantic Treaty Organization
NGO   nongovernmental organization
OECD   Organisation for Economic Co-operation and Development
OLAF   Anti-Fraud Office
OPEC   Organization of the Petroleum Exporting Countries
PCP   power, capacity, and politicization
PHARE   Poland and Hungary: Aid for Restructuring of the Economies
POLCON   Political Constraints Index
Prosafe   Product Safety Enforcement Forum of Europe
QMV   qualified majority voting
REACH   Regulation on Registration, Evaluation, Authorisation and Restriction of Chemicals
SANCO   Health & Food Safety
SAPARD   Special Accession Program for Agricultural and Rural Development
SMEs   small- and medium-size enterprises
SRF   Single Resolution Fund
SRM   Single Resolution Mechanism
SSI   Shapley Shubik Index
TEU   Treaty on European Union
TFEU   Treaty on the Functioning of the European Union
tov   type of violation
TTIP   Transatlantic Trade and Investment Partnership
TTP   Trans-Pacific Partnership
US   United States
USMCA   United States-Mexico-Canada Agreement
UWWT   urban waste water treatment
WHO   World Health Organization
WTO   World Trade Organization

WHY NONCOMPLIANCE

INTRODUCTION

The Politics of Noncompliance

More than ten years after the collapse of Lehman Brothers in 2008, the European Union (EU) is still facing not one but multiple crises. The member states have managed to avert the breakdown of the euro. Yet Italy's expansionist budgetary policies could lead to its sovereign debt spin out of control and throw the eurozone into its next crisis. The historic influx of refugees into the EU, which brought the borderless Schengen area to the verge of collapse in 2016, may have subsided. But the EU has yet to agree on a common asylum and migration policy, by which all member states share responsibility rather than passing it on to a few. Even eastern enlargement, once celebrated as a success of the EU's transformative power, is called into question as Hungary and Poland, the former poster children of transition, contest the fundamental values of the EU. The Covid-19 pandemic, which struck Europe in early 2020, adds yet another crisis refueling and exacerbating the previous ones.

What the various crises have in common is that one of their main causes appears to be noncompliance with EU law. If Greece or Italy had complied with the legal rules governing the EU's common currency and the border-free Schengen area, they would not have piled up such record debts, nor would so many refugees and migrants have found their way into the EU but rather would have returned to their home countries. There is hardly any member state that has not violated the so-called convergence criteria, which are to keep in check state budgets. Likewise, virtually all member states have infringed on the EU's legal rules and procedures regulating the admission of refugees and asylum seekers. Finally, the EU initiated the Article 7 sanctioning procedures against Hungary and Poland for breaching fundamental values that are protected by Article 2 of the Treaty on European Union (TEU).

The extent to which member states have violated EU law during times of crises is exceptional. Rather than breaching selective legal obligations under EU law, Greece, Italy, Hungary, or Poland have gone against the core of norms and rules on which the euro, the border-free Schengen area, and the European Union as a polity are based. Moreover, noncompliance with EU law is usually about the scope of application. Member states usually contend that the law does not apply to the particular case at hand, or they disagree with the Commission as to what rule-consistent behavior entails. Italy, Greece, Hungary, and Poland, in contrast, have denied the validity of EU law, claiming that the EU has no authority to interfere with the sovereign right to spend their taxpayers' money, control their borders, and organize their political institutions.

At the same time, member state violations of euro and Schengen rules reflect those states' general noncompliance behavior. The laggards among the euro and the Schengen countries are also those who show the lowest levels of compliance with the more than thirty-four thousand pieces of EU legislation that regulate the quality of their drinking water, the equal treatment of men and women in the labor market, the admissibility of genetically modified food, or the rights of ethnic and sexual minorities. Whether it is their sovereign debt, the treatment of refugees, or the protection of wild birds, Greece and Italy outdo the other member states in their defiance of EU rules and regulations. They are joined by Portugal, France, and Spain. Denmark, Finland, Austria, the Netherlands, and Germany show greater respect for European asylum and refugee law, the Stability and Growth Pact, and the EU's environmental regulations. At the same time, there is significant variation within the two groups of compliance laggards and compliance leaders that defies any attempt to make noncompliance merely a "southern problem." Portugal and Spain have introduced comprehensive austerity measures and are praised by the European Commission for their reform efforts. Greece, by contrast, has only slowly been moving away from the edge of sovereign default. Italy used to show a strong commitment to reforms, but implementation is slow. The Commission opened an excessive-deficit procedure against Italy in November 2018. The populist government of the Five-Star Movement and the far-right League refused to back down in adjusting its budget plan for 2019, which violated EU fiscal rules by overspending on welfare. In that year, Italy's public debt ran at 131 percent of its gross domestic product (GDP) and was the second biggest in the eurozone after Greece. The EU's economic surveillance and disciplinary program could result in financial sanctions, amounting to fines of up to 0.2 percent of GDP and the suspension of some EU funds. After months of arm-twisting with the Commission, which saw Italy's credit ratings deteriorate, the Italian government finally settled at a compromise of 2.04 rather than 2.4 percent budget deficit.

France has largely managed to stay under the radar screen, despite posting the largest debt-to-GDP ratio among Europe's biggest economies and running a budget deficit of over 3 percent in 2019. Meanwhile, Denmark lives up to its reputation as the top of the class, whereas the UK and the Netherlands, which also belong to the group of compliance leaders, have been as reluctant as Spain, Italy, and Greece to abide with EU asylum and refugee law.

The euro, migration, and rule-of-law crises feature serious violations of EU law. This could lead to the conclusion that member states do not comply with EU law "when they view these rules as in conflict with . . . their myopic self-interest" (Keohane 1984, 99). US president Donald Trump's "America first" policy would simply be symptomatic for states reasserting their national sovereignty against the liberal world order. The period after the end of the Cold War saw the rise of multilateral institutions at the global and regional level with more authority than ever before, reducing the relevance of the consent principle in interstate decision making (Lake 2009; Börzel 2013; Zürn 2018). For states that commit themselves to international law, the growing scope of international authority in the attempt to advance peace, prosperity, and justice at the global level further limits their freedom of action domestically. In the absence of compliance, however, international authority will be futile in helping to tackle global challenges such as climate change, the proliferation of weapons of mass destruction, or massive human rights violations. EU norms and rules are superior to national law, do not require ratification to take effect at the domestic level, and can rely on an independent court for their enforcement. Identifying conditions under which states break the law in such a highly legalized context contributes to our understanding of when international law impacts the behavior and the policies of states (Simmons 2009; Risse, Ropp, and Sikkink 2013; Haftel 2012). It also offers important insights as to why the rule-based international order has been under increasing pressure since the turn of the millennium (Ikenberry 2018; Alcaro 2018; Lake, Martin, and Risse, 2021).

As for the EU, policy makers and EU scholars have been claiming for decades the EU is suffering from a growing compliance problem, which they believe to be systemic or pathological to the EU (Krislov, Ehlermann, and Weiler 1986; Weiler 1988; Snyder 1993; Mendrinou 1996; Tallberg 2003; Cremona 2012; Commission of the European Communities 2011); the more political authority the EU acquires, the less member states obey its laws. This book argues the opposite. First, there is no evidence that the EU has a problem with noncompliance. If anything, the functioning of the Internal Market suggests that almost all member states comply with almost all EU law almost all the time (paraphrasing

Henkin 1968, 47).[1] Second, the evidence that we have clearly indicates that non-compliance has been declining over the past twenty-five years. Violations of the euro and Schengen rules are extreme cases, which contradict this trend. Ever since the Maastricht Treaty sought to develop the Internal Market into a monetary, economic, and political union, noncompliance has decreased rather than increased, despite the substantive deepening and widening of European integration and a virtual doubling of the EU in size.

While not being indicative of a general compliance problem in the EU, the different extent to which member states have defied the EU's convergence criteria, Schengen rules, and fundamental values conforms to the general variation in member state noncompliance patterns. Moreover, as extreme cases, the euro, the migration, and the rule-of-law crises exemplify the role of politicization for explaining why some member states comply less with EU law than others do, and why noncompliance has declined since the 1990s. The different degree to which EU law spurs political conflict at the domestic level also helps to account for why noncompliance varies across policy sectors.

Three Puzzles

Noncompliance is defined as state behavior that is inconsistent with the obligations prescribed by domestic, international, or EU law (Young 1979, 104; Chayes, Chayes, and Mitchell 1998, 39; cf. Raustiala and Slaughter 2002). Placing the euro, the migration, and the rule-of-law crises into the broader picture of compliance in the EU gives rise to three puzzles that this book seeks to solve:

First, how do we account for the diverse patterns in member state noncompliance with EU law? Why does Eurosceptic Austria or the UK comply better with EU legal obligations than Europhile Italy, France, or Portugal? How is it that big and powerful Italy and France are almost as bad compliers as small Greece and Portugal? Why do centralized Greece and France have compliance records equally bad as those of regionalized Italy or Spain? As the book will show, none of the major compliance theories focusing on power, capacity, and legitimacy can fully capture these country-specific compliance patterns. They become even more puzzling when we bring eastern enlargement into the picture. Contrary to expectations of EU scholars and policy makers, the ten Central and Eastern European (CEE) countries, which joined the EU in the first decade of the 2000s, comply better on average than older member states whose domestic power and administrative capacity are equally limited and who show greater support for the EU. While the southern enlargement in the early 1980s had substantially increased noncompliance in the EU, eastern enlargement has had the opposite effect. This is hard to explain with standard accounts of the so-called southern problem (Pridham and Cini 1994) as the CEE countries equally struggle with authoritarian legacies and administrative capacities weakened by corruption and clientelism.

Second, noncompliance climbed steadily ever since the Commission began to report on violations of EU law in 1978. The trend reversed, however, in the early 1990s—despite an exponential growth in legal acts the EU had adopted in order to complete the Internal Market. Compliance research has been largely silent on temporal change focusing on explaining country variation. Existing compliance theories provide some potential explanations for why we might see a decline in noncompliance over time. Yet neither improvement in the EU's capacity to detect, punish, or manage violations of EU law, nor increasing socialization into EU law or changes in the public support for the EU, correlates with the decline in noncompliance since the 1990s.

Third, noncompliance with EU law does not only vary across time and member states. It also shows variation across policy sectors. All member states together infringe on EU law in some policy sectors more frequently than in others. Environment and Justice & Home Affairs (JAIN) are the most noncompliant sectors, while Competition and Agriculture have given rise to far fewer problems. The limited attention compliance research has paid to the policy dimension may be related to the lack of some clear or intuitive patterns as we find them with regard to time (decline since 1994) and member states (North v. South, new v. old). What do Environment and JAIN have in common, and what separates the two sectors from Competition and Agriculture? Policy matters, but the literature offers hardly any explanation for why.

Taken together, the three puzzles form the main research question this book seeks to answer: How do we explain the variation in compliance patterns in the EU, be it over time, between member states, or across policy sectors? Why has noncompliance in the EU decreased since the mid-1990s, despite a growing number of member states with weak compliance capacities and waning enthusiasm for European integration, and with EU legislation expanding in sectors that are particularly prone to noncompliance?

EU research has been rather eclectic in addressing noncompliance with EU law. It has identified a multitude of explanatory factors that provide a theoretical patchwork rather than a consistent theoretical approach (Toshkov 2010). This book develops a theory of compliance with international law that integrates major factors identified by various strands of the literature to account for variation across states, time, and sectors.

One Theory

The literature on compliance has focused on three different sets of factors to explain state compliance with international norms and rules: the preferences of states, along with their power and their capacity to act upon these preferences (Chayes, Chayes, and Mitchell 1998; cf. Raustiala and Slaughter 2002; Simmons 1998; Tallberg 2002). On a theoretical level, preference-, power-, and capacity-based arguments tend to be treated as competing or alternative explanations of noncompliance (Chayes and Chayes 1993; Downs, Rocke, and Barsoom 1996; Checkel 2001). Yet, empirically, a growing number of studies find that all three sets of variables are causally relevant (Mbaye 2001; Linos 2007; Börzel et al. 2010). The book corroborates these findings. Rather than merely adding their explanatory power, it integrates different explanatory factors into a theoretically consistent model dubbed the *power, capacity, and politicization* model (PCP). Conceptualizing the politics of noncompliance as a two-stage game played by rational actors across two levels within an institutionalist setting allows us to specify how power and capacity of member states connect with EU institutions in influencing the noncompliance behavior of states. Moreover, introducing politicization, which crucially affects the ability of states to shape and take compliance costs, helps account for why member state noncompliance varies across time and sectors.

Noncompliance becomes an issue only in the case that states are not willing or not capable to cope with the costs. Costs arise when compliance with EU law requires institutional and behavioral changes at the domestic level. As rational actors, states have an incentive to reduce such costs in the adoption of EU law. They differ, however, in their ability to shape EU law according to their policy preferences. Likewise, states are not equally able to take compliance costs. The PCP model integrates the taking stage, at which EU law is implemented and enforced, and the shaping stage, at which EU law is negotiated and adopted. Moreover, the PCP model assumes that power, capacity, and politicization are key factors that affect the ability of states to shape and take EU law and its costs.

Power refers to the ability of states to pursue their preferences against resistance at the EU and the domestic level. In light of the highly legalized framework in which states cooperate in the EU and their democratic systems, state power is largely institutional. At the EU level, their votes in the Council and their contributions to the EU budget should enable member states to reduce compliance costs by shaping EU laws according to their policy preferences. Moreover, if they fail to do so, they can resist taking the costs at the domestic level because they can afford EU sanctions or deter EU enforcement authorities from imposing sanctions in the first place.

Capacity relates to the resources member states are endowed with and the efficiency of their bureaucracies to use resources (staff, expertise) to shape EU law, on the one hand, and to change legal and administrative institutions, as well as the behavior of domestic actors targeted by EU law, on the other. The capacity to formulate a coherent bargaining position at the shaping stage and to bring together the public authorities with the competencies necessary to legally transpose, practically apply, and enforce EU law is not necessarily related to political and economic power a member state has in the EU. It allows small states, like the Netherlands or Denmark, to punch above their weight (Panke 2010a).

Politicization captures the extent to which compliance costs give rise to political conflict at the domestic level. It is not only a function of veto players, which have the institutional power to block compliance because they are not willing to incur the costs. Domestic actors have to be aware of the costs, and they have to care about them, being willing to politically mobilize against their governments imposing these costs on them. The compliance literature has largely neglected the public visibility of international and EU law and the public sensitivity to its costs. A higher propensity of politicization in the taking of EU law at the domestic level can increase the ability of a government to negotiate for less costly outcomes at the EU level. At the same time, politicization can seriously constrain the ability of a government to introduce the domestic changes necessary to achieve compliance.

The PCP model expects small member states like Denmark with weak voting and budget power, an efficient bureaucracy, and a Eurosceptic public, to be the best compliers. The likely domestic resistance against high compliance costs allows Denmark to shape EU laws despite its limited power. Should it fail at shaping, it still has the capacity to comply with costly EU laws and not enough power to resist enforcement power. On the other end of the spectrum, we find big countries, such as Italy and France, which have strong political and economic weight in the EU but inefficient bureaucracies and citizens who support the EU. They are less able to shape EU policies to minimize compliance costs. However, they have the power to resist enforcement pressure when their low capacity prevents them from taking the costs. As a result, France and Italy, as two of the largest EU economies, are as bad compliers as Greece, which has always been the poorest member state in the EU-15; while the UK and Denmark, as the two most Eurosceptic member states, are more compliant than Germany. Politicization also helps explain the counterintuitive finding that Eurosceptic member states are better compliers than their Europhile counterparts. Lower public support for the EU renders the politicization of compliance costs more likely. Governments can use their Eurosceptic publics to tie their hands (Putnam 1988) at the shaping stage, bargaining for EU laws that are closer to their policy preferences and entail lower costs.

By incorporating EU-level factors that are not country specific, the PCP model can also account for the time trend in declining noncompliance since the completion of the Internal Market. EU law has become less costly to comply with over the past twenty-five years, as it tends to amend existing rather than introduce new legislation. Amending legislation is less complex and requires fewer institutional and behavioral changes at the domestic level. Moreover, compliance costs are less likely to be politicized in the member states since large parts of EU law have been adopted and implemented with no parliamentary involvement. Finally, noncompliance is higher in sectors harmonizing national regulations, because the compliance costs of market-correcting policy are more likely to become politicized.

The PCP model offers four major benefits. First, it pulls together diverse strands of existing theory and empirical research on noncompliance in international relations (IR) and EU studies by integrating the bargaining (shaping) and the implementation and enforcement (taking) stages of EU law making. Drawing on the principal components of major IR approaches allows the PCP model to organize the multitude of explanatory factors empirically analyzed in EU research into three distinct theoretical concepts (power, capacity, politicization), thereby reducing the eclecticism and complexity of many approaches. So do the empirical testing of alternative conceptualizations and the operationalizations of power, capacity, and politicization.

Second, the PCP model moves beyond country variation. Both IR and EU research focus on explaining why some states comply less than others. EU scholars tend to assume that the EU has a growing compliance problem and argue about how to measure it (cf. Börzel 2001b). Likewise, IR scholars have debated whether compliance with international law has really deteriorated or to what extent this is an information effect (Clark and Sikkink 2013). Some EU studies have ventured into sector variation but identify selected variables that are related to individual legal acts rather than policy sectors. IR research has been reluctant to compare international institutions with regard to noncompliance because of the great differences between them.

Third, systematically exploring temporal and sectoral variation allows us to theorize how EU institutions and sector characteristics affect compliance costs and the power and capacity of states to shape and take them, adding politicization, which has been largely neglected in compliance research. The PCP model thereby provides a comprehensive explanation for why some member states comply less than others, why noncompliance in the EU has been declining, and why some policy sectors are particularly prone to noncompliance.

Fourth, since the PCP model draws on principal components of IR theories, it also travels outside the EU. International institutions, which do not pool and delegate political authority to the extent the EU does, still have an effect, albeit weaker, on compliance costs and the ability of states to shape and take them. These effects should also vary depending on the policy type and the regulatory logic of the issue area international institutions are tasked to deal with.

One Data Set

For the empirical analysis, the book draws on the European Commission's own infringement database, from which I received a data set covering the period of 1978 until 1999. I have been constantly updating the data set over the past twenty years. Unlike the data publicly accessible, the Berlin Infringement Database (BID) contains detailed information on the more than 13,300 violations of EU law the EU officially recorded between 1978 and 2019 (March). As the most comprehensive database on noncompliance with EU law, it allows for analyzing variation across time, member states, policy sectors, type of legal act, and type of violation. It encompasses all the cases in which the European Commission determined a violation of EU law. This may only cover the tip of the iceberg of noncompliance in the EU, and we have no way of knowing how big the iceberg is. Unlike alternative measures of noncompliance, however, infringement proceedings are less prone to bias and cover all possible types of violations of EU law, not only the transposition of directives into national law. While the BID does not allow us to measure the size of the iceberg, it includes all those cases that lie at its core and are central for the functioning of the EU.

Organization of the Book

Chapter 1 maps the variation in noncompliance across countries, time, and sectors. I outline the three puzzles the empirical chapters will explore in more detail. First, I tackle the methodological challenges of measuring noncompliance and introduce the BID. Weighing the strengths and weaknesses of the different indicators developed in the literature, I justify my choice of using the EU's official infringement proceeding to measure my dependent variable. Reasoned opinions are the first official stage of the legal action the European Commission can bring against the member states for violating EU law. Some caveats notwithstanding, I argue that they are the most comprehensive and reliable measurement of noncompliance with EU law. The chapter concludes with placing infringements into the wider context of noncompliance with EU law outside the Internal Market. I point to the risks of the EU trying to enforce compliance with its fundamental values and redistributive decisions, such as the relocation of refugees, the same way it does with regulatory policy.

Chapter 2 develops the PCP model that brings together power, capacity, and politicization in a theoretically consistent way. I start by integrating power and capacity within a rational institutionalist framework that conceptualizes noncompliance as a two-stage game played across two levels. This allows me to introduce politicization as a third principal component. The PCP model starts from the assumption that the costs of compliance determine the choice of member states to comply or not comply with EU laws. At the EU level, member states use their capacity and power to shape EU laws to make them less costly for their domestic constituencies. Member states have an advantage at the shaping stage when they can tie their hands to domestic constituencies that are likely to politicize EU law in the implementation at the taking stage. Capacity renders member states better shapers. It also enables them to take compliance costs in the implementation of EU law at the domestic level. Power, in contrast, allows member states to resist compliance with costly laws at the taking stage. Power, capacity, and politicization are country-specific variables that are rather stable across time and policy sectors. To account for temporal and sectoral variation, the PCP model brings in EU institutions. These institutions mitigate member states' power and enhance their capacity. EU decision-making rules at the shaping stage also influence the propensity of domestic politicization at the taking stage. Parliamentary involvement at the EU and the domestic level increases the public visibility of costly EU laws. Moreover, the compliance costs of EU laws and their propensity of politicization differ across policy sectors. Regulatory policy that aims at protecting citizens against market failure by harmonizing social and environmental standards incurs higher costs that are more likely to be politicized at the domestic level. Based on these propositions, I formulate expectations on which member states are more likely to violate EU law, on when noncompliance is likely to subside over time, and on which sectors of EU law are more prone to noncompliance.

Chapter 3 solves the first puzzle of the book related to the country variation: Why do some member states comply less than others? I argue that member state noncompliance is neither a purely southern nor an eastern problem. Neither the power nor the capacity nor the propensity of politicization varies systematically between the advanced industrial democracies forming the northern and western core of Europe, and its southern and eastern European periphery. Member state noncompliance in a deepened and widened EU is best explained by the combination of power, capacity, and politicization. Denmark and the UK are such good compliers not only because they have efficient bureaucracies; their Eurosceptic publics allow them to shape EU policies according to their preferences, reducing costs or seeking an opt-out. If they fail, both have the capacity to comply with costly EU law. Denmark's performance is even more exemplary, because, unlike the UK, it lacks the power to resist enforcement pressures. Europhile Italy and

Greece are such bad compliers because they lack the capacity both to reduce compliance costs by "uploading" their policy preferences to the EU level and to deal with the costs. What makes Italy the ultimate No. 1 noncomplier of the EU is its power to resist compliance. Unlike small and poor Greece, it can afford sanctioning costs.

Chapter 4 explains the second puzzle of the book regarding temporal variation: Why has noncompliance declined since the 1990s? Although compliance research has largely neglected time, many students of the EU assume that noncompliance has become worse amid a growing body of EU law and a rising number of member states that can violate them. Yet, while we have no data to evaluate how big the absolute noncompliance problem of the EU has been, I can show that it has not been growing. On the contrary, since the mid-1990s, we can observe a negative trend, which is driven by the more effective transposition of EU directives. In the absence of established explanations for temporal variation, the second part of the chapter uses the EU-level factors identified by the PCP model as affecting compliance costs and their politicization to explain why noncompliance has been declining. The decline in noncompliance is a secular trend that is related to changes in the nature of EU law. EU directives amend existing rather than set new legislation. Their adoption is (therefore) delegated to the Commission. Delegated legislation is less costly and less demanding on the capacity of the member states. I demonstrate that delegation has depoliticized EU law, despite the empowerment of the European Parliament and national legislatures in EU affairs. Policy without politics, however, comes at a price—it has fueled the politicization of the EU as a polity, undermining its democratic accountability.

Chapter 5 accounts for the third puzzle concerning policy variation: Why are some sectors more prone to noncompliance? I start with showing that to the extent the EU has a noncompliance problem, it is concentrated in four policy sectors. Following Theodore Lowi's famous dictum that policy determines politics, I use the PCP model to develop one of the first attempts to theorize sector-related noncompliance in the EU. I show that regulatory policy produces higher compliance costs than nonregulatory policy. (Re-)distributive policy is also costly, but the costs arise in decision making, not in implementation. Regulatory policy is particularly costly if it is market correcting rather than market making. Harmonizing national standards to protect EU citizens against failures of the Internal Market requires institutional and behavioral changes in the member states, which are costly and more likely to be politicized. The chapter concludes by arguing that the rise of populism in Europe renders noncompliance with regulatory policy even more costly, which has serious implications for the EU as a regulatory polity, particularly if it continues to transform redistributive issues into regulatory problems as it has done in the euro and migration crises.

The conclusion revisits the PCP model in light of the empirical findings of chapters 3–5. These findings allowed us to refine the model by specifying which factors affect the costs of compliance, their politicization, and the power and capacity of the member states to shape and take these costs. First, the most important EU-level factors lie in the nature of EU law. New legislation is costlier and more likely to be politicized because its adoption is not delegated to the Commission. Second, when it comes to country-related variables, it is neither the voting nor the budgetary power of member states but the Euroscepticism of their publics that matters for their ability to shape compliance costs. Governments tying their hands to their Eurosceptic publics account for the counterintuitive finding that greater public support for the EU results in more, not less, noncompliance. Third, power still matters for the taking of costly EU laws. Member states rely on their political and economic weight to resist compliance costs rather than to deter the European Commission from enforcing compliance. Fourth, rather than resources per se, the efficiency of national bureaucracies in using existing resources defines the capacity of member states to effectively shape and take EU laws and cope with their costs.

The concluding chapter also discusses the generalizability of the PCP model with regard to other regional and international organizations, particularly in light of the extraordinary degree to which authority is pooled and delegated in the EU. Since the PCP model draws on principal components of IR theory, the book offers some important contributions to the broader research on compliance with international law. It shows that power and capacity are not alternative or competing explanations of noncompliance but need to be combined to account for the empirical variation across countries, time, and policy sectors. Moreover, the politicization of international institutions and their decisions at the domestic level has a major influence on noncompliance that has been neglected in the literature so far. Finally, the nature of international law, rather than the rules and procedures by which it is adopted and enforced, deserves greater attention.

The chapter concludes by considering the implications of the PCP model of noncompliance for the effectiveness and legitimacy of the EU and international governance more broadly. If the costs of international regulatory policy, reaching from trade, to climate change, to nuclear arms control, become increasingly politicized at the domestic level, this does not only increase the risks of noncompliance. It also challenges the capacity and authority of international institutions to set such regulations in the first place. The rise of nationalist populism exemplified by Brexit, the democratic backsliding of Hungary and Poland, and the election of Donald Trump as US president show the limits of regulatory governance beyond the state.

INFRINGEMENT DATA AND NONCOMPLIANCE

For years, the European Commission has been complaining about a growing compliance deficit in the EU (Commission of the European Communities 1990, 2000, 2011, 2016). Some scholars have contended that the level of compliance with EU law compares well to the level of compliance with domestic law in democratic states (Keohane and Hoffmann 1990, 278; Zürn and Joerges 2005). However, many share the view of the Commission that noncompliance poses for the EU a serious problem that is "pathological" (Weiler 1988) and "systemic" (From and Stava 1993; cf. Krislov, Ehlermann, and Weiler 1986; Snyder 1993; Mendrinou 1996; Tallberg 2003; Cremona 2012). The contradicting assessments of member state compliance may at least partly be due to the absence of common assessment criteria and reliable data. Yet, this chapter shows that existing data provides no evidence that the EU has a compliance problem. EU scholars have to rely for their assessments on violations of EU law detected and reported by the European Commission. Some of them have compared noncompliance in the EU to an iceberg (Hartlapp and Falkner 2009). Only its tip is visible. However, how can we know how much of noncompliance remains under the surface?[1] We have no means to measure the actual size of the iceberg. Moreover, like icebergs in the age of global warming, noncompliance in the EU has been diminishing over the past twenty-five years. Time series data on violations of EU law does not tell us how big the iceberg is; but it shows that the iceberg has been melting.

Compliance and Noncompliance

Compliance is defined as behavior that is consistent with (international) norms and rules (Young 1979, 104; Raustiala and Slaughter 2002). It is a broader concept than implementation, which refers to the putting into practice of a norm, rule, or policy (Mazmanian and Sabatier 1981; cf. Treib 2008). At the same time, compliance is narrower than effectiveness, which relates to the impact a policy or law has on the socioeconomic environment in solving the problem it was adopted to address (cf. Levy, Young, and Zürn 1995; Nollkämper 1992; Bernauer 1995).

Since international and EU law is addressed to states, compliance refers primarily to their rule-consistent behavior. As in any other international organization, member states have to incorporate EU law into their domestic legal orders as well as apply and enforce it (Raustiala and Slaughter 2002; Simmons 1998). If they fail to do so, they are in noncompliance.

Research focuses on noncompliance rather than compliance as its *explanandum*. This may or may not have to do with scholars expecting compliance to be the default behavior of states. I suspect that it is more related to the available data. International institutions report on violations of their member states, not on their law obedience. Reported noncompliance is a common, if not the most common, indicator for noncompliance.

The European Commission reports on four types of noncompliance with EU law (table 1.1). The different types of violation are largely defined by the form EU law can take. EU law is divided into primary and secondary law. Primary law refers to the articles in the treaties, which are made by the member states. Similar to national constitutions, these articles set the ground rules for all EU action. They include the fundamental values on which the EU is built, such as human rights, rule of law, and democracy (Article 2 TEU). Secondary law is made by EU

TABLE 1.1 Types of EU law violations

EU LAW		
REGULATIONS, TREATY PROVISIONS, DECISIONS	**DIRECTIVES**	
Violations against directly applicable acts *Infringements of treaties, regulations, and decisions* *(tov_4)*	Delayed or incomplete transposition into national law *Nonnotification of (all) national implementing measures* *(tov_1)* Incorrect application *Infringements for bad application of directives* *(tov_3)*	Incorrect transposition *Infringements for (legal) nonconformity with directives* *(tov_2)*

Source: European Commission, Annual Reports on Monitoring the Implementation of EU Law, 1984–2012.

institutions according to the rules and procedures set by EU primary law. The treaties provide for five different legal instruments, which differ in their legal bindingness and scope of addressees. *Regulations* are legally binding and directly applicable in all EU member states. *Directives* are equally biding for all member states as to the results to be achieved; they have to be transposed into the national legal framework. They leave the member states discretion in choosing the means of implementation. *Decisions* are directly applicable but binding only for those to whom they are addressed. *Recommendations* and *opinions*, finally, are nonbinding, declaratory instruments. Treaty articles, regulations, and directives form the essence of EU law—they constitute legal obligations for all member states.

The first three types of violations (tov) refer to directives, which are not directly applicable but require transposition into national law.

First, member states may fail to notify the European Commission of all national measures taken in order to legally implement directives in due time (delayed transposition into national law, referred to by the European Commission as *noncommunication of national implementing measures*, tov_1).

Second, member states may incorrectly transpose directives. Parts of the obligations of the directive are not enacted, or national regulations deviate from European obligations because they are not amended and repealed, respectively (*nonconformity with directives*, tov_2).

Third, even if the legal implementation of a directive has been timely, correct, and complete, member states might still not practically apply and enforce it. Noncompliance involves the active violation of member states taking conflicting national measures or the passive failure to invoke the obligations of the directive. The latter also includes failures to enforce effectively EU law—that is, to take positive action against violators, both by national administration and judicial organs, as well as to make adequate remedies available to the individual against infringements that impinge on her rights (*bad application of directives*, tov_3).

Fourth, member states may not or only incorrectly apply and enforce treaty provisions, regulations, and decisions, which are directly applicable and therefore do not have to be incorporated into national law.[2] Noncompliance can also take the form of enacting, or not repealing, national measures that contradict EU law (*violations against treaty provisions, regulations, and decisions*, tov_4).[3]

The Methodological Challenge

Studies on compliance with international norms and rules face the methodological challenge of measuring their dependent variable. Many have developed their own assessment criteria and collected the empirical information in laborious case studies (e.g., Falkner et al. 2005; Zürn and Joerges 2005; Mitchell 2003a; Börzel 2003a; Finnemore and Sikkink 1998). This renders the comparison of empirical findings and theoretical claims difficult, particularly since some policy sectors (social affairs, environment) and some member states (UK, Germany, France, Italy, Greece) are more studied than others (Luetgert and Dannwolf 2009). Others, therefore, have drawn on statistical data provided by the monitoring bodies of international regimes and organizations (e.g., Reinhardt 2001; Mbaye 2001; Linos 2007; Perkins and Neumayer 2007; König and Luetgert 2009; Haverland, Steunenberg, and van Waarden 2011).

EU research has used different types of data published by the European Commission to measure noncompliance with EU law: statistics on transposition notification and on infringement proceedings (cf. Hartlapp and Falkner 2009).

Timely Transposition as a Proxy of Noncompliance

Since 1990, the Commission has reported the directives for which member states have notified transposition as percentage of the directives in force. In addition, the EU makes the notifications of national implementing measures and other information related to the transposition process publicly available in its EUR-Lex database (Sector 7 within the CELEX system).[4] A number of studies have used this data on the notification of national implementing measures as a proxy of noncompliance (Mastenbroek 2003; Steunenberg 2006; Kaeding 2006; Berglund, Grange, and van Waarden 2006; Toshkov 2007a; Thomson 2007; Haverland, Steunenberg, and van Waarden 2008, 2011; Steunenberg and Kaeding 2009; König and Luetgert 2009; Luetgert and Dannwolf 2009). Delayed transposition, however, is only one of four types of violation of EU law, and arguably not the most relevant one. Noncommunication (tov_1) only refers to directives and their timely (and complete) incorporation into the domestic legal order of the member states. Regulations, as the other major form of EU secondary law, do not require transposition into national law because they take immediate effect. Their number by far exceeds that of directives. Directives make up only 13 percent of the legislation in force (see chapter 4).

Moreover, the failure to transpose directives is low and has been diminishing. According to the data published by the European Commission, member states have always had more than 90 percent of the directives in force on their books. Transposition rates have improved over the years, from an average of 91 percent in 1990 to an average of 99.1 percent in 2010, and 99.4 percent in 2013—exceeding the EU's 2007 target of a transposition deficit of 1.0 percent of the total number of directives in force.[5] The range between transposition laggards and leaders, accordingly, is narrow, ranging from 97.8 percent of Belgium to 99.9 percent of Sweden. The EU's transposition scoreboards also testify to the exemplary performance of the new member states, which joined in 2004 and 2007 (cf. European Commission 2005; Dimitrova and Toshkov 2009). In other words, problems with timely transposition are limited and do not show much variation among member states. Arguably, transposition failures (noncommunication) cover only a very small and increasingly irrelevant part of noncompliance in the EU.

Studies that focus on the timeliness of transposition claim that transposition problems are more severe than suggested by the high percentage of directives transposed. Data collected at the national level shows that a significant number of important directives got transposed with serious delays, undermining the effective application of EU law and creating competitive disadvantages for industries in compliant member states (Haverland, Steunenberg, and van Waarden 2011; Haverland and Romeijn 2007; Steunenberg and Rhinard 2010; Borghetto, Franchino, and Giannetti 2006; Kaeding 2006; Mastenbroek 2003). The problem may be even more pronounced since notification data seems to underestimate the actual delay in transposition (Hartlapp and Falkner 2009). However, distortions between notified and actual transposition are greater for some member states, which points to a serious bias in the data (ibid.). Moreover, delays say little about whether transposition is correct (König and Mäder 2013; Hartlapp and Falkner 2009; Zhelyazkova and Yordanova 2015). Member states have substantial discretion when transposing EU directives. Even if they literally translate the letters of an EU directive into national law, they may fail to adhere to its spirit (Dimitrakopoulos 2001). Directives usually set framework legislation to allow accommodating country-specific context and conditions. Member states are left the choice as to the form and methods of implementation,[6] which provides substantial opportunities for incorrect and incomplete transposition.

Research on international law has shown that ratification is a poor indicator for compliance (Simmons 1998; Risse, Ropp, and Sikkink 2013). In the EU, there is evidence that speedy transposition indicates noncompliance rather than compliance. Notification data relies on the member states' self-reporting of the legal implementation measures they have taken to transpose a directive into national law. National governments may have an incentive to exaggerate their actual compliance, particularly if they anticipate problems. Thus, member states report *preexisting* national measures to notify the Commission of the transposition of a directive (Zhelyazkova and Yordanova 2015). Unless a member state was able to fully upload its domestic policy to the EU level (Héritier 1996; Börzel 2002a), the lack of any measures to adjust domestic legislation to a new directive is likely to result in problems of incorrect or incomplete transposition. The study by Falkner et al. (2005) on the implementation of EU social policy finds that some member states notify the Commission before they correctly transpose a directive. Notifying legal compliance helps a member state buy time to muster necessary resources and overcome domestic opposition to make the necessary adjustments (Zhelyazkova and Yordanova 2015; Zhelyazkova, Kaya, and Schrama 2017). The Commission routinely opens infringement proceedings if a member state fails notifying national implementing measures within the deadline specified by the directive. Notifying early or timely transposition, by contrast, may hold off the Commission by signaling that a member state is already in compliance with a new directive or at least prepared to comply. Not surprisingly then, timely transposition is associated with more rather than less noncompliance. The more timely the transposition, the less complete and correct is its legal implementation (Zhelyazkova and Yordanova 2015; Zhelyazkova, Kaya, and Schrama 2017).

Infringement Proceedings as a Proxy of Noncompliance

To work around the narrow focus and the bias of the transposition data, students of noncompliance have taken recourse to the European Commission's Annual Reports on Monitoring the Application of EU Law[7] (e.g., Mbaye 2001; Tallberg 2002; Sverdrup 2004; Börzel et al. 2010; Thomson, Torenvield, and Arregui 2007). Since 1984, the Commission reports each year on the actions it has taken against member states for all four types of noncompliance with EU law. Regardless of the type of violation at stake, Article 258 TFEU entitles the European Commission as the "guardian of the treaties" (Article 17.1 TEU) to bring legal action against member states for failing to fulfill their obligations under EU law.

From the very inceptions of European integration, infringement proceedings were to ensure compliance with EU law.[8] Many international organizations have dispute settlement procedures. They increasingly rely on courts rather than negotiated solutions (Alter 2014; Alter and Hooghe 2016). These developments notwithstanding, the EU still has the most elaborate compliance system at the international level. Infringement proceedings are an expression of the EU as a "community of law" (Hallstein 1972). They have been devised as an instrument to preserve and strengthen the rule of law, which has been constitutive for the EU, long before Article 2 TEU defined the rule of law as one of its "essential principles on which the EU is founded."[9] The main features of the infringement proceedings were already laid down in the treaty establishing the European Coal and Steel Community of 1951 (Articles 88 and 89). These included the prominent role of the European Commission (Higher Authority) as a sort of public prosecutor and the possibility to impose financial penalties.[10]

The infringement proceedings consist of several stages (figure 1.2). The first two stages, suspected violations (complaints, petitions, etc.) and formal letters, are considered unofficial. Suspected infringements refer to instances in which the Commission has some reasons to believe that a member state violated EU law. Such suspicions can be triggered by *complaints* lodged by citizens, corporations, and nongovernmental organizations (NGOs), or by *petitions* and *questions* of the European Parliament. The Commission can also start an investigation on its *own initiative*. Finally, the noncommunication of the transposition of directives results in the automatic opening of infringement proceedings. The formal letter of the Commission delimits the subject matter and invites the member state to submit its observations. Member states have between one and two months to respond. In contrast to what their name suggests, formal letters are considered by the Commission as a preliminary stage, which serves the purpose of information and consultation, affording a member state the opportunity to regularize its position rather than bringing it to account (Commission of the European Communities 1984, 4–5).[11] Nor has the Commission been willing to give public access to this information (Prete 2017, 350–352). It considers complaints and formal letters confidential, to enable "genuine cooperation and an atmosphere of mutual trust."[12] They are only accessible if they involve cases of delayed transposition (noncommunication). The European Court of Justice (ECJ)[13] has so far upheld the Commission's plea of confidentiality against transparency claims by complainants who wanted to access the formal letter the Commission had sent.[14] Letters of formal notice are listed in the annual reports, including information on both the member state and the legal act concerned. However, the actual content of the dispute remains confidential at this point, and it is only when a reasoned opinion is sent that the European Commission issues a press release and "goes public" with the alleged violation and the infringement proceeding.

The official proceedings (Article 258 TFEU) start when the Commission issues a reasoned opinion and ends with a ruling of the ECJ. The Commission sets out the legal justification for commencing legal proceedings. The reasoned opinion gives a detailed account of how the Commission thinks EU law has been infringed by a member state and states a time limit within in which it expects the matter to be rectified. The member states have one month to respond. The ECJ referral is the last means to which the Commission can resort in cases of persistent noncompliance. Before bringing a case before the ECJ, the Commission usually attempts to find some last-minute solutions in bilateral negotiations with the member state. The ECJ acts as the ultimate adjudicator between the Commission and the member states. First, it verifies whether a member state actually violated European law as claimed by the Commission. Second, it examines whether the European legal act under consideration requires the measures demanded by the Commission. Finally, the ECJ decides whether to dismiss or grant the legal action of the Commission.

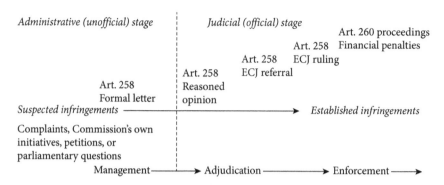

FIGURE 1.1. Stages of the infringement proceedings and compliance mechanisms

If member states still refuse to comply with a ruling of the ECJ, the Commission can open new proceedings (Article 260 TFEU). Article 260 TFEU proceedings consist of the same stages as Article 258 proceedings. Since 1996, however, the Commission can ask the ECJ to impose financial penalties, either in the form of a lump sum or a daily fine, which is calculated according to the scope and duration of the infringement as well as the capabilities of the member states.[15] The Lisbon Treaty simplified and accelerated the procedure for the imposition of financial penalties.

In sum, the Commission regularly publishes data on both notification and the official stages of the infringement proceedings. Unlike notification data, however, infringement data refers to all four types of violations, not only to the delayed transposition of directives.

Caveats and Challenges

Scholars have questioned the validity and reliability of infringement proceedings as unbiased indicators of compliance failure (Thomson, Torenvield, and Arregui 2007; Hartlapp and Falkner 2009; König and Luetgert 2009; König and Mäder 2014b). While it certainly has its limits, there is no evidence that infringement data contains systematic biases. So far, we have no other source for measuring noncompliance that is more comprehensive, valid, and reliable.

THE COMMISSION AS A STRATEGIC GUARDIAN OF THE TREATIES

Infringements are "the Commission's behavioral response to perceived compliance problems" (Thomson 2007, 993). For capacity reasons, the European Commission is not able to detect and legally pursue all instances of noncompliance with EU law (Hartlapp and Falkner 2009). The over 13,300 infringement proceedings officially opened between 1978 and 2019 (March) present only a fraction of all instances of noncompliance. Similar to the tip of an iceberg, they constitute the visible part of the problem. The sample could be biased. The Commission depends heavily on the member states reporting back on their implementation activities, costly and time-consuming consultancy reports, and information from citizens, interest groups, and companies, whose capacity and inclination to provide the Commission with information on noncompliance may vary (König and Mäder 2014b).

Moreover, for political reasons, the Commission may not choose to act upon all the cases in which it discovers violations of EU law. The Commission has considerable discretion in deciding whether and when to open official proceedings. Given its limited resources, the Commission strategically selects cases that are promising on legal grounds and serve its political and institutional interests (Conant 2002, 74–79; Steunenberg 2010; Toshkov 2010, 7; Carrubba and Gabel 2015, 134–135). The Commission itself has officially announced it would concentrate on "serious infringements" that refer to violations of EU law which "undermine the foundations of the rule of law" (e.g., breaches of the principle of the supremacy and uniform application of EU law or human rights violations), weaken the "smooth functioning of the Community legal system" (e.g., repeated violations of the same EU law), or which "consist in the failure to transpose or the incorrect transposal of directives" (delayed or incorrect transposition of EU directives into national law) (Commission of the European Communities 2002, 11–12, and 2007). In 2012, the Commission declared that it would primarily target timely and correct transposition with a particular focus on Internal Market directives (Commission of the European Communities 2012a). Such strategic prioritizing may be problematic for investigating policy variation, since some sectors or legal acts may be more likely to be targeted by the Commission than others. Internal Market directives may be in the sight of the Commission because they constitute more systemic and persistent instances of noncompliance than Common Agricultural Policy regulations. At the same time, Agriculture is among the most infringed sectors in absolute terms. When controlling for the amount of legislation that can be infringed in a sector, Justice & Home Affairs (JAIN) becomes the highest noncompliance sector. The Commission may strategically prioritize the enforcement of certain EU laws, but these legal acts do not seem to cluster in certain policy sectors (cf. Siegel 2011, 41–44).

Singling out or sparing certain member states could be more of an issue. Since the implementation of EU law falls into the responsibility of the member states, the Commission, which does not enjoy direct political legitimacy, is in a weak and "invidious position" vis-à-vis the member states (Williams 1994).

The Commission may treat some member states more carefully than others because they make significant contributions to the EU budget or wield considerable voting power in the Council (Jordan 1999; König and Mäder 2014b).[16] Even in the cases in which the Commission decides to take action, it may not necessarily report on it. The Commission values confidentiality higher than transparency, particularly at the early stages of infringement proceedings.[17] The ECJ has repeatedly confirmed the discretion of the Commission in disclosing information on infringements to the public (see above). The Commission may not only be deterred by powerful member states (see chapter 3). It may also be reluctant to prosecute Eurosceptic countries in order not to encourage anti-European attitudes by officially shaming their governments for violating European law (Jordan 1999; König and Mäder 2014b). Putting a member state on the spot may backfire, increasing domestic support for the offending government (Merlingen, Mudde, and Sedelmeier 2001; Schlipphak and Treib 2016).

There are good reasons to assume that the Commission is pursuing only a limited number of violations of EU law. Yet strategic prioritizing ensures that these include the most significant cases of noncompliance in the core areas of EU law (see above). It does not necessarily mean that the Commission is systematically biased toward particular member states or policies. The literature has yet to present evidence that infringement proceedings are biased. Nevertheless, to ensure that my data set provides an unbiased sample of noncompliance in the EU, I conducted a survey among the legal experts of the EU-15 member states' permanent representations to the EU in 2007. The expert survey analyzed the extent to which the infringement data collected by the European Commission reflects the member states' perspective and assessed whether and where national experts perceive a bias in the data. The questionnaire sent out to the fifteen permanent representations consisted of six questions, asking the experts of the Committee of Permanent Representatives (COREPER) how they would assess the level of compliance of their own country vis-à-vis other EU countries, which member state they perceived as performing best and worst, and whether they thought that the Commission's infringement data was biased toward certain member states. All but one COREPER expert replied, giving us a response rate of 93.3 percent. The most important findings were that more than two-thirds of the respondents did not think that infringement data contained any systematic bias toward certain member states. What is more, the experts' assessment of which member states violated EU law most and least was in line with the Commission's infringement data, with France, Greece, and Italy being considered the main laggards, and Denmark, Finland, and Sweden the compliance leaders. Another expert survey also conducted in 2007[18] focusing on a sector with serious compliance problems bolstered the confidence in the database. A total of 122 policy makers, civil servants, companies, interest groups, and scientific experts in fifteen EU member states assessed the level of noncompliance in their country in general and with respect to core norms and rules in environmental policy in particular. The response rate was 40 percent, but the non-responses were not biased toward particular member states (see also Schmidt and Wonka 2012, 344). The results corresponded to the relative distribution of infringement proceedings provided in chapter 3.

A group of scholars has supplemented existing data provided by the EU on noncompliance with national sources for selected policies and member states (Mastenbroek 2003; Berglund, Grange, and van Waarden 2006; Kaeding 2006; Haverland and Romeijn 2007; Haverland, Steunenberg, and van Warden 2011; König and Luetgert 2009; König and Mäder 2013; Zhelyazkova and Torenvlied 2009; Zhelyazkova, Kaya, and Schrama 2016, 2017). While national data tends to be more comprehensive, it generally finds a good match between EU infringement and national data. There appears to be no biased lack of information (Kaeding 2008; Steunenberg and Rhinard 2010). A recent in-depth analysis of a sample of twenty-one directives confirmed that the Commission effectively monitors and enforces compliance with EU law despite its strategic approach (König and Mäder 2014b).

The lack of evidence for a systematic bias in the infringement data resonates with arguments in the EU literature about a powerful organizational "logic of appropriateness" (March and Olsen 1998) that prevents the Commission from abusing its strategic discretion in enforcing EU law. The Commission's authority depends primarily on its credibility as an impartial adjudicator between competing interests. It has to avoid the impression of treating member states in an unfair way. Moreover, its identity as a truly supranational body makes it inappropriate for commissioners and Commission officials to block legal action against their own member state when it stands accused of violating European law (Egeberg 2001, 739; Egeberg 2006; cf. Börzel 2003a, 14–16). The opening of infringement proceedings is to be decided by the college of all commissioners, which helps ensure the neutrality of the Commission in guarding the treaty (Hauser 2004, 166). One of the few instances in which a commissioner openly objected to a decision of the college affecting his home country concerned the registration of a European Citizens Initiative to trigger Article 7 against Hungary in November 2015. Commission president Jean-Claude Juncker publicly rebuked Tibor Navracsics, Hungary's EU commissioner in charge of Education, reminding him that, as a commissioner, he had to remain neutral and could not represent the interests of his home country.[19]

DECENTRALIZED ENFORCEMENT

Infringement proceedings are the backbone of the EU's compliance system. The doctrine of supremacy[20] and direct effect[21] of EU law, which the ECJ established in the early 1960s, laid the foundation for a decentralized enforcement mechanism through national courts. The Treaty of Rome introduced the so-called preliminary ruling procedure, which allows the ECJ to establish rules for interpreting EU law in the context of specific cases. National courts have to use the guidelines when adjudicating disputes between EU and national law. With EU law having direct effect at the domestic level, Article 267 TFEU (formerly 177, 234) changed from a mechanism to challenge EU law into a means of controlling member state compliance with EU law. Citizens, groups, and firms obtained indirect access to the ECJ by litigating against member state governments or other public authorities in national courts for national law that does not conform to EU law (cf. Weiler 1981; Alter 2001; Conant 2002). The supremacy of EU law prohibits public authorities from relying on national law to justify their failure to comply with EU law. It requires national courts to resolve conflicts between national and EU law in favor of the latter. If in doubt about the compatibility of EU and national legislation, national courts are obliged to refer the case to the ECJ. Such Article 267 referrals involve noncompliance when member states interpret EU legal obligations in a way as to avoid costly domestic change. Like infringement proceedings, this may refer to incorrect transposition as well as flawed practical application of EU law. Yet not all cases originate with member states' noncompliance. In many cases, societal and economic actors use an alternative legal setting seeking to extend their rights under national law or advertise their general activities. They shop for a friendlier forum among national courts that will refer their case to the ECJ, whose dynamic interpretation of EU law is expected to expand EU requirements to a more ambitious level (Alter and Meunier-Aitsahalia 1994; Alter and Vargas 2000; Conant 2001; Cichowski 2007; S. Schmidt 2018). The ECJ's rulings on combating discrimination against women[22] and on age discrimination[23] are two prominent examples of how litigants may strategically employ the preliminary ruling procedure to push for "thickly evaluative norms" in the area of economic and social rights rather than monitor and enforce compliance with EU law (Chalmers and Chaves 2012, 31; cf. S. Schmidt 2018).

At the same time, decentralized enforcement requires the support of those actors who profit from EU law (Kelemen 2006, 2011). Preliminary rulings do not only rely on private litigants to bring cases before national courts. They also require the national judges to engage directly with the ECJ and to apply its rulings. Both vary considerably across member states because of different institutional, political, and cultural factors that substantially constrain the working of decentralized enforcement in national courts. Litigation by citizens, interest groups, and firms depends on their court access and their resources to make use of it (Conant 2002; Börzel 2006; Cichowski 2007). If litigants have legal standing and the person-power, expertise, and money to use it, national courts that do not have a tradition of judicial review, like those in Denmark, Sweden, or the UK, are reluctant to use preliminary rulings to solve legal disputes involving EU and domestic law (Conant 2002; Wind, Martinsen, and Rotger 2009; Wind 2010). Other courts have used ECJ precedent in adjudicating conflicts without involving the ECJ (Romeu 2006; Conant 2001, 81–84). Member state courts do not have to refer a case if EU law is sufficiently clear (*acte claire* doctrine; cf. Wind 2010). Drawing on a sample of 1,310 national court decisions, Carolin Hübner confirms that courts should not be generally expected to use preliminary proceedings as a "fire alarm" to alert the ECJ to noncompliant member states. Rather, they seek clarification with regard to the validity and interpretation of EU laws, which is particularly likely with regard to directives that leave member states more room for interpretation in implementation and are technically complex (Hübner 2018). Finally, courts have to be willing to rule against noncomplying member states. Carrubba and others have argued that the ECJ is sensitive to member state preferences and compliance costs (Carrubba 2005; Carrubba and Gabel 2015; Fjelstul and Carrubba 2018; Larsson and Naurin 2016; Blauberger and Schmidt 2017). The ECJ is more likely to convict member states for violating EU law when it expects them to abide with its ruling (Carrubba and Gabel 2015, 2017; cf. Staton and Moore 2011).

In short, unlike infringement proceedings, preliminary rulings are not per se about noncompliance. When they are, preliminary rulings appear to be biased toward member states where individuals and groups litigate because they lack access to policy-making venues and have the resources to resort to courts, and whose judicial review culture renders national courts more likely to refer their cases to the ECJ.

VIOLATIVE OPPORTUNITIES

Infringement numbers depend on the body of EU law (*acquis communautaire*) and the number of member states that have to comply with it. Between 1978 and 2012, the number of legal acts in force that the member states have to comply with increased almost four-fold, and eighteen new members joined. The control for changes in "violative opportunities"[24] is particularly important for comparisons of noncompliance over time. In 1978, nine member states had to comply with around four thousand articles, directives, and regulations. In 2012, twenty-seven member states faced nearly twelve thousand EU legal acts. The annual number of infringements reported by the Commission has to be put in relation to these growing violative opportunities. To do this, I multiply the number of EU laws in force in a given year by the member states that could infringe on them at the time. The relative infringements are calculated as the percentage of violative opportunities. Of course, member states can also differ in their opportunities to violate specific legal acts. Their landlocked geographical location prevents Austria and Luxembourg, for instance, from violating European law pertaining to deep-sea fishery. Because of the large number of EU legal acts and the wide range of policies they cover, determining and explicitly controlling for the individual violative opportunities of all member states and for all legal acts is virtually impossible. In the absence of any counterevidence, I assume that these varying opportunities are evenly distributed in the aggregate.

This is not to say that violative opportunities do not vary across policies. The sectors of EU law differ substantially with regard to their regulatory density. Internal Market or Agriculture have been among the EU's core competencies from its beginning in 1957, while it obtained the power to legislate on JAIN, or Information Society, only decades later. Moreover, the scope of the EU's legislative authority is much more constrained in Social Affairs or Taxation compared to Internal Market or Environment. Differences in age and regulatory scope largely explain why violative opportunities in Internal Market and Agriculture are more than five times greater than in JAIN. This is taken into account in chapter 6 when analyzing cross-sector variation in noncompliance with EU law.

While the number of member states is straightforward, calculating the legislation in force is tricky. The EUR-Lex database provides the number of adopted legal acts in a given year.[25] Yet many of them expire later or are replaced. The number of "outgoing" legal acts in a given year can also be obtained from EUR-Lex and be subtracted from the sum of legal acts adopted in the previous years. However, when I did the math, the results substantially diverged from the Commission's officially reported numbers. The *30th Annual Report on Monitoring the Application of EU Law*, for instance, states that "by the end of 2012, the acquis of the EU consisted of 9,576 regulations (2011: approx. 8,900) and 1989 directives (2011: approx. 900) in addition to the primary law (the Treaties)" (Commission of the European Communities 2013, 2). This amounts to 11,565 legal acts in force, which is less than a third of what I retrieved from the EU's own database. I counted 1,987 directives for 2012 but 1,980 for 2011, which makes a difference of almost 1,000! This might have been simply a typo. For regulations, however, the discrepancy is even bigger—9,576 to 34,949 (2012), and 8,900 to 33,738 (2011). I sent a query to the EU's Publication Office and asked for clarification. They kindly provided the data they used for Commission reports, which is accessible now as part of the code book of the Berlin Infringement Database, or BID.

Unfortunately, the data for legislation in force is not available by sector. I had to use a database on the legislative production of the EU compiled by Dimiter

Toshkov.[26] It covers directives adopted between 1967 and 2009 broken down by sectors. Adopted directives are an inflated proxy of the legislation in force, since the numbers contain directives that expired and were repealed or replaced. However, there is no reason to assume that this inflation introduces a bias toward certain sectors. Since there is an overall time lag of around three years, from the adoption of a directive to its entering in force (about six months) and to the expiration of the transition deadline (eighteen to twenty-four months), the period matches the time covered by the BID except for the last five years (1978 to 2012).

The Berlin Infringement Database

For the analyses in this book, I draw on the EU's infringement proceedings. The European Commission had kindly provided me with a data set comprising all the cases it had officially opened against the member states for violating EU law between 1978 and 1999. I updated the original data set with the help of EUR-Lex and the Annual Reports on Monitoring the Application of Community Law. The annual reports publish limited or aggregate data.[27] The BID, in contrast, contains detailed information on each infringement proceeding. This information includes the legal basis (CELEX number), type of violation, and the stage reached for all the 13,367 individual cases in which the Commission asserted a breach of EU law between 1978 and 2017 and for which it issued a reasoned opinion between 1 January 1978 and 7 March 2019.[28] Using individual infringement cases as the main unit of analysis allows us to make sure that each violation is counted only once, according to the highest stage it reached in the infringement proceedings. Moreover, infringements can be sorted by year, member state, policy sector, and legal act.

The BID extends existing data sets and is original in three ways. First, its scope is broad. It spans thirty-five years of violations of treaty articles, directives, and regulations committed by six to twenty-seven member states in twenty-three policy sectors. This allows for quantitative analyses and comparisons beyond a selected number of years, countries, sectors, or legal acts. Second, the data is compatible with different levels and units of analysis. The basic unit of analysis is the infringement proceeding, but at this level, the data provides for many possibilities of aggregation, allowing us to examine patterns of noncompliance across time, legal issue, member states, policy sector, and type of legal act. Third, each instance of an infringement is linked to supplementary data on characteristics of the violation, such as the offending member state, the legal act violated, the policy sector it pertains to, and the institutional context in which it was adopted. The data is drawn from a multitude of source databases, including EUR-Lex on EU legal texts,[29] Pre-Lex on EU preparatory documents,[30] and the database on the legislative production of the EU (see above).

Overall, the BID provides the basis for testing a wide range of theoretical expectations on factors driving noncompliance situated at different levels of analysis.

Reasoned Opinions as the Preferred Measurement of the Dependent Variable

The BID has data on all official stages of the infringement proceedings. I use reasoned opinions to measure my dependent variable for two reasons. First, they are the first stage of the infringement proceedings for which the Commission provides in-depth information. Second, reasoned opinions concern the more serious cases of noncompliance, namely issues that could not be solved through informal negotiations at the two previous stages (Mendrinou 1996; Tallberg 2002).[31] The number of infringements drops sharply at the later stages (figure 1.2; cf. Börzel, Hofmann, and Panke 2012). Of the 13,367 cases that entered official infringement

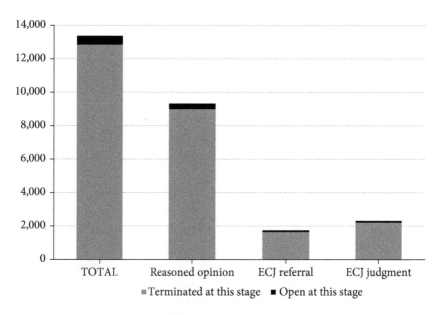

FIGURE 1.2. Number of infringements by stage, EU-28, 1978–2017
Source: Own compilation, with data from the Berlin Infringement Database. "Open at this stage" refers to the few cases that had reached the indicated stage and were still pending there in 2019. They could still move on to the next stage. "Terminated at ECJ referral" denotes cases that were referred to the ECJ but withdrawn by the Commission before a judgment was issued. Cases at the "ECJ judgment" stage include infringement proceedings having reached the second stage (Article 260 TFEU).

proceedings between 1978 and 2017, about one-third (30 percent) were referred to the ECJ. Of those 4,044 referrals, the Commission withdrew 40 percent (1,635) before a judgment was issued, while the ECJ ruled on 2,304 cases—in more than nine out of ten times (92 percent) against the member states. Fewer than one hundred cases were referred to the ECJ a second time because member states did not comply with a first judgment of the ECJ. In the majority of those cases, the ECJ imposed financial penalties.

The propensity of the member states to transform noncompliance into compliance across the stages varies. Sooner or later, however, they obey EU law (Panke 2007; Börzel, Hofmann, and Panke 2012). Most of them do so sooner rather than later, but on rare occasions it may take more than thirteen years.[32] With the exception of Italy and Belgium, member states usually cave in before the ECJ has to rule on the matter. While this book is concerned with the occurrence rather than the persistence of noncompliance, it is important to note that member state variation across the different stages of the infringement proceedings does not change. Only Portugal's initial poor performance improves significantly when entering the adjudication stage. The same applies to France, which remains, however, among the top laggards (cf. Börzel, Hofmann, and Panke 2012). The observed patterns of variation over time or policy sectors do not substantially change either when using later stages of the infringement proceedings.

To map the three puzzles of the book, I use the number of reasoned opinions related to all four types of violation to look at the absolute distribution of noncompliance across member states, time, and policy sectors. When controlling for violative opportunities, I have to drop infringements of treaties, regulations, and decisions (tov_4) at the sector level, since the only way to approximate the legislation in force by sector is to use the number of adopted directives (see above).

Introducing the Three Puzzles

Why Some States Comply Less Than Others

Some member states have a much larger share in EU noncompliance than others. The infringement data clearly shows significant variation among them (figure 1.3). Roughly speaking, the member states of the EU-28 can be grouped into three categories: leaders, laggards, and the inconspicuous.

The majority of the member states show a relatively moderate level of noncompliance. The three Scandinavian member states, the Netherlands, and the United Kingdom are especially good compliers and rarely violate EU law. The same is true for the newer member states, with the exception of Poland. While the leaders remain well below the EU average of infringements, Spain, Germany,

Austria, Poland, Luxembourg, and Ireland oscillate around it. The member states that display a consistent pattern of comparatively high noncompliance are Italy, Greece, Portugal, Belgium, and France. These five laggards account for about half of all infringements. They are led by Italy as the all-time undisputed no. 1. The performance of Greece, Belgium, and France is also poor and remains consistently bad. Belgium's performance even deteriorates with each stage. Portugal's, by contrast, improves significantly when entering the adjudication stage (Börzel, Hofmann, and Panke 2009, 2012).

The distribution of noncompliance between member states is puzzling because none of the three compliance approaches alone can provide an explanation that systematically accounts for the variation observed. Proponents of enforcement theories should ask themselves why France and Italy wield similar power in the EU as Germany and the UK, but are much less compliant. This becomes even more puzzling for management theories, since France and Italy comply as badly as or even worse than Greece and Portugal, which are the two poorest countries in the EU-15. In the EU-28, neither enforcement nor management can explain

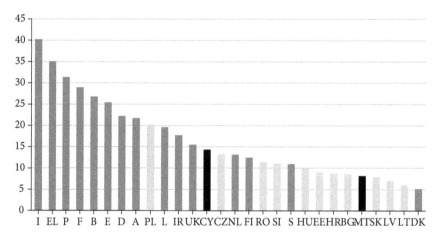

FIGURE 1.3. Average number of reasoned opinions per year and member state, EU-28, 1978–2017

Source: Own compilation, with data from the Berlin Infringement Database. For newly acceding member states, the first year of membership was omitted for the calculation of the annual average. The eleven post-communist countries of Central and Eastern Europe that joined in 2004, 2007, and 2013 are in light gray, Cyprus and Malta are in black.

Note: A = Austria; B = Belgium; BG = Bulgaria; CZ = Czech Republic; CY = Cyprus; D = Germany; DK = Denmark; E = Spain; EE = Estonia; EL = Greece; F = France; FI = Finland; HR = Croatia; HU = Hungary; I = Italy; IR = Ireland; L = Luxembourg; LV = Latvia; MT = Malta; NL = Netherlands; P = Portugal; PL = Poland; RO = Romania; S = Sweden; SL = Slovenia; SK = Slovakia; UK = United Kingdom.

why the thirteen states that joined the EU in the 2000s comply better than most of the EU-15 countries. Legitimacy approaches, finally, have a hard time understanding why Eurosceptical countries like the UK, Denmark, Sweden, or Finland comply much better with European law than states that are highly supportive of European integration, such as France, Italy, or Belgium.

Why Noncompliance Has Not Been Growing

Member state noncompliance varies significantly. At the same time, infringements of EU law have decreased since the mid-1990s when we control for the growing body of EU law and the rising number of member states (figure 1.4). In 1978, for every ten violative opportunities, two reasoned opinions had been sent. In 1994, the number had more than doubled and peaked at 5.5 reasoned opinions per ten violative opportunities. By 2012, however, it had dropped to a

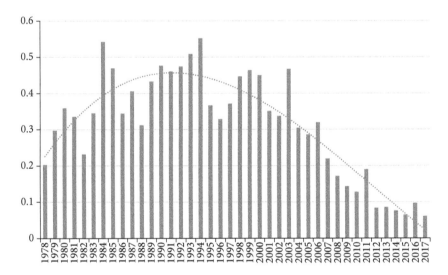

FIGURE 1.4.   Reasoned opinions relative to violative opportunities per year, EU-28, 1978–2017

Source: Own compilation, with data from the Berlin Infringement Database. The annual ratio is calculated by the number of infringements launched in a given year (having reached a reasoned opinion until 2019) divided by the violative opportunities in that year (number of directives, regulations, and substantive treaty articles in force multiplied by member states) and multiplied by 100.

Note: Because of continuous inconsistencies in the online database EUR-Lex with regard to "legislation in force" per year (see above), data on "incoming" and "outgoing" directives and regulations was retrieved directly from the European Commission on request in February 2017. The number of substantive treaty articles in force is based on Biesenbender 2011.

ratio of under one reasoned opinion. Neither the deepening of European integration through the introduction of a common currency, the liberalization of capital markets, and the increasing supranationalization of internal security, nor its widening by the doubling of member states, has resulted in the expected deterioration of law-abidingness in the EU.

This finding goes against a widely held belief that noncompliance has been growing precisely because the EU has deepened and widened. Compliance theories have largely neglected temporal variation. Enforcement, however, would have a hard time explaining why the growing diversity of member state preferences has not resulted in more violations of EU laws, which have been increasingly adopted by qualified majority voting (QMV) and with the European Parliament having an equal say. Rising compliance costs, at least for the powerful member states, could be balanced by strengthened enforcement powers of the EU. Monitoring and sanctioning have indeed improved; yet the decline in noncompliance had started well before. Nor can the decline be explained by a shift from centralized to decentralized enforcement (Hofmann 2018, 2019). Similar to infringement proceedings, the annual average number of preliminary rulings by member state declined in the second half of the 1990s and only picked up again in 2010 (cf. chapter 4), an increase that is not driven by the new member states (cf. chapter 3). As regards the EU's management capacity, its pre-accession capacity building may explain why eastern enlargement has not resulted in more noncompliance. Yet, again, infringement numbers had begun to drop ten years before, without the capacity of old member states substantially improving. Legitimacy would indeed expect an improvement over time due to socialization processes. These take time, which, however, is why eastern enlargement should have resulted in at least a temporary increase of noncompliance.

Why Noncompliance Is Sector Specific

Noncompliance varies not only across time and member states. It also shows considerable variation across policy sectors. All member states together infringe on EU law in some policy sectors more frequently than in others. Five of the total of twenty-three sectors into which EU law has been organized account for around two-thirds of all official infringement cases. Environment is the sector with the highest absolute number of reasoned opinions, followed by Internal Market, and, with some greater distance, Transport & Energy, Enterprise & Industry, and Agriculture (see figure 5.1 in chapter 5). The picture changes when we control for violative opportunities (figure 1.5).[33]

Environment remains the top noncompliant sector but is joined now by JAIN—and this even before the migration crisis started in 2015 and the European Commission opened more than sixty infringement proceedings against

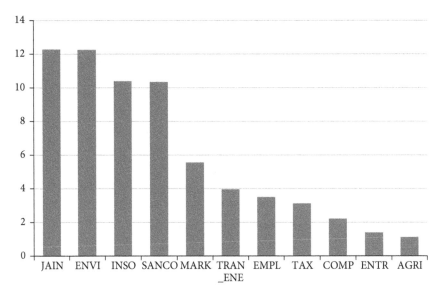

FIGURE 1.5. Annual reasoned opinions against directives relative to legislative production by policy sector, 1978–2012
Source: Own compilation, with data from the Berlin Infringement Database
Note: Policy sectors with more than one infringed directive in two years. AGRI = Agriculture; COMP = Competition; EMPL = Employment & Social Affairs; ENTR = Enterprise & Industry; ENVI = Environment; INSO = Information Society & Media; JAIN = Justice & Home Affairs; MARK = Internal Market & Services; SANCO = Health & Consumer Protection; TAX = Taxation & Customs Union; TRAN_ ENE = Transport & Energy.

member states for violating EU asylum law (Börzel 2016). For every violative opportunity (directives only) in JAIN, on average more than twelve reasoned opinions were issued. Internal Market, Agriculture, Enterprise & Industry, and Transport & Energy, by contrast, drop dramatically in the ranking. They make up for more than two-thirds of the *aquis communautaire* but feature only a third of its violations, which places them among the better-performing sectors. Next to Environment and JAIN, the two other top noncompliers are Information Society & Media and Health & Consumer Protection. How do we account for this variation in sector-specific noncompliance? What have the creation of an area of freedom, security, and justice and a digital single market in common with environmental, health, and consumer protection, and what distinguishes them from the regulation of network utilities, the protection and the promotion of workers' rights, and the harmonization of product standards?

EU infringement proceedings provide unbiased insights into member state noncompliance with core areas of the *acquis communautaire.* The latter covers about fifteen thousand laws—the famous eighty thousand pages that accession candidates have to have on their books before joining the EU—that regulate everything from water quality, to climate change, to work safety, to gender equality, to net neutrality, to foodstuffs, to asylum. Again, the more than 13,300 infringements constitute the "tip of the iceberg" (Hartlapp and Falkner 2009); we do not know how much is below the surface. This is precisely why we cannot say anything about the full size of the iceberg. Claims about the existence of a compliance problem in the EU necessarily remain speculation. Nor do we have any evidence that the visible parts of the iceberg are biased toward certain member states or policy sectors. What the data shows is that noncompliance with an ever more comprehensive body of EU law has been declining, affects some member states more than others, and is concentrated in a few policy sectors.

To date, infringement proceedings are the most comprehensive, valid, and reliable measurement of noncompliance in the EU. They do not cover some important areas, such as state aid, monetary policy, and the rule of law. These areas have seen some spectacular cases of noncompliance. In the case of state aid, the EU enjoys some formidable enforcement powers. The opposite is the case for monetary policy and the fundamental values, where member state governments still control monitoring and sanctioning. While excluding important areas of (re-)distributive and constituent or constitutional policy, infringements concern the rules that have constituted the EU as a regulatory state for almost seventy years. The concluding chapter will discuss the implications that arise when regulatory polities like the EU do not have the authority to adopt or enforce nonregulatory policy and use their enforcement powers on regulatory policy to deal with violations involving redistributive issues and fundamental values.

POWER, CAPACITY, AND POLITICIZATION

In 1991, the EU adopted the urban waste water treatment directive.[1] It obliges the member states to provide urban agglomerations with systems collecting and treating urban waste water until the end of 2000. In Spain, two-thirds of the treatment facilities did not comply with the requirements of the directive at the time of its enactment. To finance the building of new facilities and the upgrading of existing ones, the Spanish Water Treatment Plan of 1995 envisioned public investments of about €10.8 billion, which is five times more than Spain had invested in waste water treatment between 1985 and 1993. Why should member states comply with such costly EU laws? While Spain has made efforts to put adequate systems for collecting and treating waste water in place, Italy is facing financial penalties because after almost two decades, eighty of its urban agglomerations still fail to do so.[2]

In domestic politics, compliance is the rule rather than the exception. Students of public policy have been puzzled why "great expectations of Washington are dashed in Oakland" (Pressman and Wildavsky 1973). So-called top-down studies point to weak enforcement capacities of central authorities and insufficiently specified rules and procedures (e.g., Cerych and Sabatier 1986). The "bottom-up" literature contends that local actors and their preferences need to be accommodated in the policy process (Pressman and Wildavsky 1973; Lipsky 1980; Ingram and Schneider 1990). Both perspectives give rise to little optimism with regard to compliance with international and EU law. The international system and the EU lack a centralized enforcement authority, and member states are represented by their governments, giving local actors not much voice in the policy process. The default expectation of classical theories of IR, therefore, is noncompliance rather than compliance.

Students of IR have developed two approaches to explain why states may still comply with international and EU law. The literature has referred to them as enforcement and management (Chayes, Chayes, and Mitchell 1998; cf. Raustiala and Slaughter 2002; Simmons 1998; Tallberg 2002). The two schools are based on rationalist assumptions about state behavior and the constraining and enabling effects of international institutions. Social constructivists have added a third approach, which focuses on the role of international norms and norm-guided state behavior (Koh 1997; Hurd 1999; Checkel 2001).

The three approaches share a definition of compliance as state behavior that conforms to the requirements specified by an international norm or rule (Young 1979, 104; Chayes, Chayes, and Mitchell 1998, 39; cf. Raustiala and Slaughter 2002). States are the addressees of most international norms and rules and are formally responsible for compliance. However, they are not necessarily the main or exclusive targets (Chayes, Chayes, and Mitchell 1998, 52–53). Rules on climate change, for instance, target the production behavior of business, the driving behavior of car owners, and the energy consumption of private households. If the behavior of these non-state actors does not conform to international or EU law, states are in noncompliance because they fail to enforce the legal commitments they made. So is the Italian government, if its municipalities do not provide for the proper treatment of their waste water.

Enforcement, management, and legitimacy take compliance rather than non-compliance as the default preference of states. Enforcement expects states only to enter international agreements that correspond to their interests and shape them accordingly. This is why good news about compliance is not necessarily good news about international cooperation (Downs, Rocke, and Barsoom 1996). States are reluctant to make legal commitments that require costly domestic changes. If they do, noncompliance is likely, owing to the lack of strong enforcement at the international level, which depends on the willingness of states to exert material pressure. Such pressure can also arise, however, at the domestic level, where noncompliance may result in "audience costs" (Fearon 1994, 577) with domestic constituencies who support the international norm or rule (Dai 2007; Simmons 2009). "Electoral enforcement" (Simmons 2009, 369) can pull states toward compliance with costly international obligations.

Management assumes that noncompliance occurs because states lack the capacity rather than willingness to honor their international commitments (Chayes and Chayes 1993). This is less of an issue where international and EU law obliges states to refrain from certain actions, such as imposing tariffs or interfering with citizens' rights. Compliance with regulatory standards (e.g., for the treatment of waste water) in contrast, requires sufficient financial, technical, and human resources that states have to be able to mobilize to ensure effective implementation and enforcement (Weiss and Jacobsen 1998; Simmons 2009, chap. 8).

Legitimacy, finally, anticipates that states feel morally obliged to comply once they have internalized international norms and rules (Hurd 1999). States obey international and EU laws irrespective of their material costs because they accept them as legitimate and redefine their interests and identities accordingly (Franck 1990; Checkel 2001).

The three approaches specify different factors driving (non)compliant behavior. Enforcement focuses on material factors, which inform actors' preferences and shape their power to realize these preferences, thereby leading to (non)compliance. Social constructivist approaches stress the importance of the legitimacy of international institutions for shaping (non)compliance preferences of states. The management school assumes a general preference for compliance and sees insufficient state capacities as the major driving force for rule violations. These explanatory factors have informed many studies on compliance with international and European law. The growing body of empirical research, both quantitative and qualitative, has demonstrated that none of the three approaches alone is able to account for why states renege on their legal obligations (Tallberg 2002; Simmons 2009; Börzel et al. 2010). For enforcement, it is hard to explain why states comply with international norms and rules if these are costly. Management has to come to terms with states that refuse to abide with international and EU law despite having the capacity to comply. Legitimacy faces the challenge of noncompliance in states with a strong rule-of-law culture and public support for law beyond the nation state.

To address these puzzles, compliance studies started to work with more middle-range explanations focusing on particular issue areas, such as human rights (Simmons 2009; Risse, Ropp, and Sikkink 2013), trade (Goldstein, Rivers, and Tomz 2007; Kono 2007), security (Morrow 2007), or environment (Mitchell 2003b; DeSombre 2006). Students of compliance have explored specific causal mechanisms, including external enforcement pressures, domestic veto players, or transnational social mobilization. Quantitative methods have enabled the testing of an abundance of variables at a time. This has come with an "embarrassment of riches," though. The ambition of arriving at a coherent theoretical framework often has gotten lost in the attempt to cover a (too) broad range of possible explanatory factors.

This chapter develops a theoretical framework that combines power- and capacity-related factors with the concept of politicization in a theoretically consistent way. This will enable me to solve the three puzzles of this book: Why the member states that joined in 2004/2007 are less noncompliant than most of the older member states, why noncompliance has been declining since the mid-1990s, and why noncompliance is concentrated in policy sectors that seek to protect the rights of EU citizens.

The PCP Model

The PCP model conceptualizes the politics of noncompliance as a two-stage game played across two levels. To explain noncompliance, it is not sufficient to analyze the implementation and enforcement of international and EU law at the domestic level; we also need to consider the stage at which law is negotiated and adopted at the international or EU level. The PCP model systematically integrates the two stages of policy making by identifying factors that affect the costs of compliance and the ability of states to shape and take these costs at both the international and the domestic level.

Rooted in a rational institutionalist framework, the PCP model focuses on material costs of compliance and the power of states to shape these costs in EU decision making and to resist them in domestic implementation, as well as their capacity to cope with compliance costs at the domestic level. This reasoning follows the meta-theoretical willingness-opportunity framework (Cioffi-Revilla and Starr 1995; Starr 1978). The general claim is that every political action originates from the will or intent of states to act and their capability to do so. In other words, rule-consistent behavior of states requires both willingness and capacity.

The PCP model acknowledges that ideational factors matter. Norms have constitutive effects on actors' identities and preferences. They generate a sense of moral obligation to comply with their behavioral prescriptions. The international norm of law abidance linked to the principle of *pacta sunt servanda* sustains compliance with specific agreements (Chayes and Chayes 1993, 1995; Koh 1997). States also adapt their beliefs, standards for appropriate behavior, and even identities to international norms they have internalized (Checkel 2001). The EU is a community of law for which the supremacy of EU law is constitutive (Weiler 1999; Joerges 1996; Chalmers 1997). Membership in the EU has a constitutive effect on states and the way in which they exercise their sovereignty (Sbragia 1994; Laffan, O'Donnell, and Smith 2000; Risse 2010; Bickerton 2012). "The EC was created by law, . . . its institutions are bound by law, and in turn the EC is a source of law" (Temple Lang, quoted in Laffan, O'Donnell, and Smith 2000, 16). The general commitment of the member states to the rule of law may explain why the EU has no general compliance problem. Arguably, the default preference of member states is compliance.

However, taking for granted that EU law is the law of the land does not mean that member states always comply with all EU legal acts all the time. Rather than explaining why member states comply with EU law, the PCP model seeks to understand why at times they do not, and why some do less than others do. It does so by making the constitutive effects of the EU's fundamental values defined in Article 2 TEU and the Charter of Fundamental Rights part of the context in which noncompliance may still occur.

Preferences and Costs

The PCP model starts from the assumption that actors are rational, goal oriented, and purposeful. Guided by their strategic rationality, actors operate instrumentally in order to maximize their interests or preferences over outcomes. The PCP model is state centered. Noncompliance is a "matter of state choice" (P. Haas 1998, 19). Preferences are crucial for shaping state choices of compliance or noncompliance (Thomson et al. 2006; Thomson, Torenvield, and Arregui 2007; König and Luetgert 2009; König and Luig 2014; König and Mäder 2014b). States' power and capacity affect whether and how they can pursue their choices. The PCP model assumes that states have basic interests, such as security, prosperity, or the respect for human rights and the rule of law. These basic interests are taken as given. So are states' policy preferences, such as opening markets or protecting the environment. Exogenizing basic interests and preferences over policy outcomes, the PCP model focuses on preferences over strategies.[3] Compliance and noncompliance are strategies by which states seek to achieve their most preferred policy outcome deploying the power and capacity at their disposal.

Finally, actors create institutions in order to advance their preferences over outcomes. Institutions set the rules of the game. They embody rules and procedures, which regulate conflicts between states and help them to overcome collective-action problems (North 1990). Since the focus of the PCP model is on strategic preferences, it specifies how institutions create costs and benefits influencing states' strategic choices for (non)compliance.

Following the reasoning of enforcement approaches, states' preferences for (non)compliance are primarily shaped by the costs of compliance. States comply when international norms and rules coincide with their preferences over outcomes (Goldsmith and Posner 2005). Conversely, they will violate even technical and narrow legal acts if these require costly institutional or behavioral changes (Downs, Rocke, and Barsoom 1996). This is particularly the case if states face the risk of other states defecting. This risk makes them inclined to shirk the costs, too. The way to effectively prevent noncompliance is by increasing the costs of noncompliance (Martin 1992; Dorn and Fulton 1997). Establishing external institutionalized monitoring and sanctioning mechanisms can alter the strategic cost-benefit calculations of states (Axelrod 1984; Oye 1986). The likelihood of being detected and punished raises the anticipated costs of noncompliance in form of economic sanctions, retaliation, financial penalties, withdrawal of membership privileges, or expulsion (Chayes and Chayes 1991, 314–318; Martin 1992; Fearon 1998). Such costs may finally lead to a change of strategic behavior toward compliance.

Even highly legalized enforcement mechanisms, however, ultimately rely on the willingness of states to impose sanctions authorized by the dispute settlement panels of the World Trade Organization, the United Nations Security Council, or under the Article 7 procedure of the EU (Hafner-Burton 2005; Lebovic and Voeten 2009). Enforcement acknowledges the importance of power for state-to-state coercion to enforce costly norms and rules. States, however, may not only use their power to deter or sanction the defection of others. Power allows them to reduce compliance costs and makes them less susceptible to sanctions in the first place.

Power

Power is closely related to the ability of states to shape legal acts according to their preferences over outcomes (Giuliani 2003; Moravcsik 1997a; Fearon 1998; Keohane and Nye 1977; Thomson et al. 2006). The extent to which a state has managed to realize its preferences in the decision-making process shapes the adjustment costs, which a state has to invest in order to comply (cf. Börzel 2002a, 2003a; Giuliani 2003). States that are more powerful should be better compliers, since they are able to reduce the costs of compliance by shaping international and EU law according to their policy preferences.

If adjustment costs matter, a state's overall cost sensitivity crucially affects its strategic preference for noncompliance. Following the argument of Keohane and Nye (1977) on power and interdependence, states can be regarded as being more sensitive to sanctioning costs imposed by others if they have less power and are more dependent than other states on future goodwill and cooperation. Powerful states can afford to be more resistant to enforcement pressures, since they have more alternatives for cooperation and can more easily afford reputation or material damages. In other words, power affects the cost sensitivity of a state. Less powerful states should be more susceptible to sanctioning costs and therefore be less likely to violate international or EU law (Martin 1992). Conversely, powerful states can be recalcitrant and resist enforcement pressures (Börzel et al. 2010).

The power of a state does not only allow it to shirk compliance costs or avoid them in the first place, by shaping international decisions according to its preference. State power can also deter the enforcement authority—the institution that monitors compliance and authorizes sanctions against free riders and norm violators. Assuming a principal-agent relation, the enforcement authority (agent) ultimately depends on the states (principals) since the latter can always renounce the power of the former (Horne and Cutlip 2002, 301; Garrett, Kelemen, and Schulz 1998; Tallberg 2000a; Fjelstul and Carrubba 2018; Larsson and Naurin 2016). Powerful states should be less compliant, since enforcement authorities, as well as other states, are more reluctant to inflict noncompliance costs on them.

In sum, power matters for compliance because it affects compliance costs, although in conflicting ways. "While the strong do what they can . . . the weak suffer what they must," as classical realism would have it (Thucydides 2009, 5.89-[1]). Strong states can use their power either to reduce compliance costs, to resist them, or to deter enforcement authorities. If they choose resistance or deterrence, states are more likely to be noncompliant. If, however, they use their power to shape international and EU laws, they should be better compliers than states that are less powerful.

Power is not the only determinant of costs. Management approaches stress the importance of states having the necessary capacities to implement and enforce international and EU law. States can use their capacities (as well as their power) at the decision-making stage to reduce compliance costs by shaping legal obligations according to their interests and policy preferences. Capable shapers are also capable takers.

Capacity

States generally have been willing and able to abide by their international obligations. The PCP model draws on the three preconditions that management approaches have identified for the ability of states to comply: sufficient state capacities, clear definitions of legal obligations, and adequate timetables for achieving compliance (Chayes and Chayes 1993; Chayes, Chayes, and Mitchell 1998; Young 1992; P. Haas 1993, 1998; Jacobsen and Weiss Brown 1995).

A state's ability to act in accordance with its international legal requirements is a function of its legal authority and financial, military, and human resources (Przeworski 1990; Haas 1998; Simmons 1998). States need sufficient and adequately qualified personnel to effectively implement international and EU law. They must also have the legal knowledge of the precise behavioral requirements that result from the law and the technical expertise for the practical application of the law and the monitoring of compliance (cf. Chayes and Chayes 1993). Financial resources do not only allow for the acquisition of additional personnel, expertise, and technical equipment. They can also help pay off the delegation of implementation tasks to third actors (outsourcing) and compensate potential losers of a policy (cf. Börzel 2003a, 30–34; cf. Simmons 1998; Zürn 1997).

Yet even if a state has legal, financial, military, and human resources, its administration may still have difficulties in pooling and coordinating them, particularly if the required resources are dispersed among various public agencies (e.g., ministries) and levels of government. Compliance depends on the efficiency of a state's bureaucracy in using available resources to ensure rule-consistent behavior (Simon 1962; cf. Bouckaert, Peters, and Verhoest 2010; Rauch and Evans 2000; Fukuyama 2015). When centralization is too costly or institutionally not an option, public administrations have to rely on coordination procedures. Moreover, the efficiency of a bureaucracy hinges on its professionalism and the extent to which its organization is rational (Gajduschek 2003). Clientelism and other forms of corruption systematically undermine bureaucratic efficiency since public resources are (ab)used for rent seeking rather than delivering (international) policy outcomes (Rothstein and Teorell 2008; Rothstein 2011; Mungiu-Pippidi 2015). The less efficient the bureaucracy of a state is, the more likely noncompliance becomes.

Finally, states require the autonomy to make decisions and reach goals independently of societal interests (Nordlinger 1981, 1; cf. Katzenstein 1978; Evans 1995; Evans, Rueschemeyer, and Skocpol 1985). "Involuntary defection" (Putnam 1988) often results from powerful domestic veto players that block the ratification and implementation of international agreements because of the costs they, or their constituents, have to bear (Alesina and Rosenthal 1995; Tsebelis 2002). By definition, veto players have the ability to prevent changes of the status quo (Tsebelis 2002). States with a high number of domestic veto players are more likely to violate international and EU law because of their reduced capacity to make the changes to the status quo that are necessary for their compliance with costly rules.

The capacity to comply is primarily a function of a state's resources, its bureaucratic efficiency, and its domestic autonomy. Management approaches also identify factors that are not related to states but affect their capacity to comply. International and EU laws differ in how demanding they are on state capacities. States have greater difficulties in complying with imprecise and complex norms and rules since they are unclear about what rule-consistent behavior requires and may arrive at diverging interpretations of what they are expected to do (Chayes and Chayes 1993; Chayes, Chayes, and Mitchell 1998). Complex rules may not only give rise to diverging interpretations; they also involve a bigger workload, requiring more legal and administrative measures to enact new and amend existing national legislation. Precise and simple international norms and rules have better chances to be complied with (Kahler 2000; Abbott et al. 2000; Tallberg 2002; Helfer and Slaughter 1997).

Compliance with international and EU law, finally, requires states to introduce legal, administrative, and social changes that take time. Strict deadlines may be a disciplining factor for states to step up their compliance efforts. If deadlines are too tight, however, states may not have sufficient time to clarify their legal obligations, mobilize resources, and introduce the required institutional and behavioral changes (Chayes and Chayes 1993, 195–197). The less time international and EU laws leave states to comply, the more likely those laws are to be violated.

In sum, states that want to comply with international and EU law need the necessary resources, efficiency, and autonomy to do so. Moreover, some laws require more state capacity than others. While management approaches focus on the capacity of states to take international and EU law, resources and efficiency should also help states shape it according to their preferences. Domestic autonomy, in contrast, has an opposed effect on shaping and taking.

Politicization

International norms often cannot rely on international enforcement mechanisms that substantially raise noncompliance costs. Research has therefore increasingly focused on social mobilization at the domestic level as an alternative way to raise the costs of noncompliance. Domestic actors, in transnational alliances with NGOs, exploit international norms and institutions providing information on norm violations to generate pressure for compliance on state actors (Rogowski 1989; Brysk 1993, Keck and Sikkink 1998; Risse, Ropp, and Sikkink 1999). International enforcement activities empower them to punish state governments for noncompliance (Börzel 2000a; Dai 2007; Simmons 2009). Such "audience costs" (Fearon 1994, 577) tend to be higher in democratic states, which are the focus of this study. Governments are office seeking and vulnerable to electoral costs imposed by larger numbers of citizens who support international and EU law, and NGOs form powerful transnational alliances (Gaubatz 1996; Slaughter 1995). At the same time, "electoral enforcement" (Simmons 2009, 369) is often undermined by anti-compliance constituencies that mobilize against the costs of changing the status quo.

The PCP model focuses on domestic mobilization against, rather than in favor of, compliance, since its general assumption is that states comply with EU law. The challenge is to explain why states do not comply, which should be more likely when they run into powerful domestic resistance. The compliance literature tends to focus on advocacy coalitions, NGOs, interest groups, or companies pulling states toward compliance (e.g., Keck and Sikkink 1998; Börzel 2003a;

Slaughter 2004; Dai 2007; Simmons 2009). Yet transnational and domestic actors not only monitor compliance, pressure international institutions to take action against state violations, or mobilize and litigate against states that are reluctant to abide with international law. They can also put pressure on states to shirk their legal obligations.

Domestic mobilization against compliance is not only a function of the costs incurred on domestic actors (Siegel 2011). To mobilize, these domestic actors have to be aware of and care about the costs. Two-level-game scholars have convincingly argued that the main reason for states to pool and delegate decision-making power in international institutions is that it allows them to adopt policies they would "never get accepted at home" (Putnam 1988, 440; cf. Evans 1993). "Cutting slack" (Putnam 1988) or trading national sovereignty for problem-solving capacity has helped to "rescue the nation-state" (Milward 1992) and "strengthens the state" vis-à-vis particularistic interest in their societies (Moravcsik 1994, 1997b; Wolf 2000). State governments use international negotiations to achieve policy outcomes that their constituencies might otherwise reject. Circumventing domestic opposition works because citizens tend to be less informed about international and EU law. Since international law falls into the realm of foreign policy, which is the government's prerogative, citizens often do not hold strong opinions either.

With the expansion of their political authority after the end of the Cold War, however, international institutions have become increasingly visible and politically contested (Zürn 2012; Zürn, Binder, and Ecker-Ehrhardt 2012). Rather than being indifferent, citizens have been taking a stance on costly international and EU policies, the Transatlantic Trade and Investment Partnership being a prominent example. The literature refers to the visibility and political contestation of international institutions as politicization. Politicization has three dimensions (see, e.g., De Wilde, Leupold, and Schmidtke 2016; Hutter, Grande, and Kriesi 2016, 7–12; Risse 2015a):

- Increasing issue salience of international and EU laws in the various public domains
- Increasing levels of polarization pertaining to international and EU law (i.e., citizens strongly oppose or support EU laws rather than being neutral, ambivalent, or indifferent)
- Increasing mobilization and expansion of actors in the various public domains (i.e., domestic actors are willing to act politically on their polarized views, going to the polls or protesting in the streets)

Research has primarily dealt with politicization as an impediment for international and regional governance (Zürn 2018; Hooghe, Lenz, and Marks 2019).

It does not only affect the making of international and EU law. Politicization also undermines the chances of compliance by mobilizing domestic opposition, reducing the autonomy of states to comply. This is particularly likely in states where citizens are skeptical of global or regional governance (Norris 2000; Pichler 2012; Jung 2008) and where public support for membership in international institutions and the EU is low (Börzel 2016, 2018). Euroscepticism should increase the propensity of domestic audiences and veto players to pull states away from rather than toward compliance with EU law. Yet politicization does not necessarily have to increase the odds of noncompliance. Similar to domestic veto players, politicization constrains the number of international outcomes that a state government can get ratified at the domestic level. This domestic weakness can turn into international strength (Schelling 1960). The degree of *anticipated* opposition in a state determines the size of the domestic win-set—that is, the number of outcomes that are likely to be ratified at the domestic level. The more constrained the autonomy of the government, the smaller the size of its domestic win-set tends to be in international negotiations. The smaller its domestic win-set is, the greater a government's ability to shape policy outcomes at the international level because it can "tie its hands" to the preferences of its main constituencies (Putnam 1988; Evans, Jacobson, and Putnam 1993; Bailer and Schneider 2006). The greater the saliency a government attaches to the legislative output, the greater its shaping power (Schneider, Finke, and Bailer 2010). Governments of states where support for international and EU law is low can more credibly claim that their hands are tied by their domestic publics, since those publics are likely to mobilize against compliance with costly legislative outputs (Hug and König 2002; Finke and König 2009).

Somewhat paradoxically, the very reason why states pool and delegate authority at the regional and international level may empower their governments to obtain international policy outcomes that satisfy the domestic constituencies whose opposition they seek to circumvent. A state with autonomy vis-à-vis society is more prone to noncompliance because its government can isolate itself from domestic audience costs (see above). The government also has reduced power to achieve less costly policy outcomes at the international level.

Summing up, the PCP model takes the costs of compliance as the crucial determinant of states' preferences for or against complying with international and EU law. In a two-level game approach, power, capacity, and politicization condition these costs. They do so in partly conflicting ways, though, depending on the stage of the compliance game. The remainder of this chapter spells out how the compliance game plays out across the two levels and two stages. This will provide the model specification necessary to account for variation in noncompliance across states as well as time and policy areas.

The Politics of Noncompliance: A Two-Stage Game across Two Levels

Most theories approach European integration and EU policy making as a multilevel process (for an overview see Wiener, Börzel, and Risse 2019). Where they differ is how the domestic and the EU level interlink. Liberal intergovernmentalism emphasizes the gatekeeping role of national governments, which control access to decision making at the EU level (Moravcsik 1993, 1998). While domestic actors are important in forming the policy preferences of member states, they do not have an independent role in shaping policy outcomes at the EU level. Nor do supranational actors. The European Commission, the ECJ, or the European Central Bank (ECB) help member state governments arrive at policy outcomes that serve their national interests. Neofunctionalism and its variants contend that domestic interests (e.g., business associations, trade unions, and subnational authorities) demand further integration to promote their economic or political preferences. They form transnational alliances with like-minded groups from other states and ally with supranational actors, thereby bypassing their state governments, since the latter are reluctant to pool and delegate political authority at the regional level. The European Commission and the ECJ provide domestic actors with direct access to the EU policy arena out of institutional self-interest in increasing the power of supranational institutions over the member states (E. Haas 1958; Sandholtz and Stone Sweet 1998; Hooghe and Marks 2001).

Without denying the relevance of supra- and subnational actors, the PCP model adopts the liberal intergovernmentalist conceptualization of EU policy making as a two-level game. The focus, however, is not on domestic preference formation but on the "reciprocal relationship" (Andersen and Liefferink 1997) between politics at the domestic and the EU level, with the national governments functioning as the core mediators between the two. This is not to say that supranational actors do not matter for compliance. As enforcement authorities, the Commission and the ECJ can increase the costs of noncompliance. Moreover, through its case law, the ECJ can directly shape EU laws increasing the costs of compliance (Schmidt and Kelemen 2014; S. Schmidt 2018).

I argue that it is not sufficient to study compliance at the stage at which member states "take" EU laws by implementing and enforcing them (*policy-taking* stage). We also need to look at how member states shape EU laws in their negotiation and adoption (*policy-shaping* stage) because this is the stage that defines the size of compliance costs in the first place (Börzel 2002a, 2003c; Dai 2005, 2007).[4] At the domestic level, actors pressure their national governments to shape EU laws in a way that favors their interests. At the EU level, member state governments push for EU laws that satisfy the interests of their constituencies, while minimizing their adverse consequences at the domestic level (Putnam 1988, 434; cf. H. Wallace 1971; Héritier, Knill, and Mingers 1996; Bomberg and Peterson 2000; Börzel 2002a; Dyson and Goetz 2004). Two-level game approaches provide a link between the shaping (decision-making) and the taking (implementation) stages of the EU policy process. While research on the shaping and taking of EU policies shows significant overlap, few attempts have been made to draw the two strands of literature together (but see Keulen 2006; Börzel 2002a; Börzel and Hofmann 2010; Siegel 2011; Sprungk 2011; Knoll 2016).

Member states share a general incentive to shape EU laws according to their domestic policy arrangements. Because of their political, economic, and social diversity, they have, however, diverging policy preferences and differ significantly with regard to their ability to both shape EU laws in order to reduce compliance costs, and to take EU laws coping with compliance costs. The ability to shape and take EU laws is heavily influenced by the three principal components of the PCP model—power, capacity, and politicization.

The Shaping Game: Reducing Compliance Costs

THE EU LEVEL

The literature on state power in EU decision making focuses on the political clout (Wright 1999) or institutional weight (Hosli and Soetendorp 2001) of the member states in EU decision-making bodies. Large member states have significant voting power under qualified majority voting in the Council of the EU. Because of QMV, they cannot be ignored by others in EU decision making (cf. Thomson et al. 2006). The institutional power of the largest member states reflects the size of their populations and their economies.[5] The EU's "big four," Germany, France, the UK, and Italy, are able to block the adoption of EU laws in the Council. As the largest economies in the EU (measured by GDP), they pay more than 60 percent of the EU budget. After the UK left in 2020, Germany, France, and Italy have gained even more weight.[6]

Shaping EU policy outcomes does not merely depend on votes or budget contributions, though. Unable to push national positions through the EU negotiation process against the opposition of other member states with diverging policy preferences, small member states often rely on their capacity to efficiently coordinate and articulate their policy preferences in the EU policy-making process (Kassim et al. 2000; Zeff and Pirro 2001; Bulmer and Lequesne 2005). Denmark, Sweden, or the Netherlands, where EU-related policy-making competencies are concentrated in the central government, are able to formulate and represent a coherent bargaining position and stand a better chance to be heard than countries like Greece or Italy, where competencies are fragmented and as a result the government does not always speak with one voice (Kassim et al. 2000; cf. Kronsell 2002; Panke 2010a). Offering expertise and information to the European Commission in the drafting of policy proposals is also an effective way of injecting national preferences into the European policy process. So is the secondment of national bureaucrats to Brussels for up to three years. The Commission often asks member states to send experts with specific knowledge to help prepare European directives (Andersen and Liefferink 1997). Being present in the various networks that prepare and accompany the EU negotiation process demands considerable staff, expertise, and information, as well as a significant amount of coordination, which the member states do not have equally available. The efficient use of their resources allows smaller states to "punch above their weight" (Panke 2010a).

THE DOMESTIC LEVEL

For two-level game approaches, domestic veto players are an important domestic source of state influence in international or EU negotiations. Because they have the power to block the ratification of international and EU law, domestic veto players give governments additional leverage in negotiating outcomes that are closer to their policy preferences. This is particularly relevant for EU directives, which need to be transposed into national law and often require the involvement of national parliaments. Moreover, industry may mobilize against investments in new technologies or against changes in their production processes necessary to meet international or EU environmental, social, or safety standards. Trade unions may fear the loss of jobs. Environmental, social-rights, and consumer groups may be concerned about a lowering of existing standards or demand even stricter standards than the ones prescribed by international or EU law. The more veto players a government is likely to face at home, the greater its advantage in shaping policy outcomes that entail lower compliance costs.

In the literature, the power of domestic veto players is largely determined by domestic institutions. EU member states are liberal democracies, in which power is divided and shared, albeit to different degrees, between the three government branches (executive, legislature, judiciary) as well as between different levels of government (national, regional, local). In states with corporatist structures, veto players also arise from institutionalized forms of cooperation between state and society. Rather than the number of veto players or institutional veto points (Immergut 1990), however, the PCP model focuses on politicization as the domestic constraint that empowers member state governments to shape EU law. On the one hand, similar to domestic veto players, politicization increases the chances of noncompliance with costly EU laws. If business, interest groups, or citizens are aware and care, they are more likely to mobilize against compliance costs, threatening to withdraw their political support for the government.

On the other hand, member state governments that can credibly claim that costly EU laws will likely become politicized have an advantage in shaping EU policy outcomes. They can tie their hands against compromising in EU negotiations by arguing that costly EU laws stand little chance of compliance at home. Claims about domestic politicization are more credible when domestic support for the EU is low. Eurosceptic publics are more likely to be aware of and care about compliance costs. Politicization can thereby not only substitute for domestic veto players. It can also render domestic veto players more likely to invoke their power to block compliance with costly EU laws. Conversely, a low likelihood of domestic politicization owing to strong public support for the EU undermines hand-tying strategies of member state governments because they cannot credibly threaten that veto players will actually use their power to prevent compliance with costly EU laws. Instead of tying their hands, consistent public support for the EU allows governments to expand their domestic win-set. They can accommodate EU policy outcomes that their constituencies might otherwise reject by presenting them as take-it-or-leave-it decisions or by blaming them on the need to compromise with other member states, the Commission, and the European Parliament in order to reach an agreement at all (the very common adage "Brussels made us do it"). Conversely to tying hands, cutting slack results in higher compliance costs, which, however, are less likely to be politicized at the domestic level but still require capacity to cope with.

So far, the shaping game focuses on the ability of member states to lower compliance costs. However, power, capacity, and politicization of the member states are country-related variables. They cannot explain variation across time and across policy sectors. The PCP model therefore introduces EU institutions that mitigate the ability of member states to shape EU law. They have changed over time and differ according to the policy sector.

EU INSTITUTIONS

EU rules by which EU law is adopted define the degree to which member state governments can shape compliance costs. Since the early 1990s, the EU more than doubled in member states; it also expanded QMV in the Council and the co-decision powers of the European Parliament (EP). This subsequent widening and deepening of European integration increased the heterogeneity of member state preferences while diminishing the veto power of individual member states. Not only do member states have to compromise in the Council to reach agreement. The EP has the power to amend decisions of the Council that move policy outcomes further away from its own preferred policy outcome. The relative voting power of member states has not substantially changed. Throughout the various treaty changes, France, Germany, Italy, and the UK have remained able to resist compliance costs. However, if member state governments are outvoted in the Council of Ministers, or if they have to compromise with the European Parliament under the co-decision procedure, compliance costs are likely to be higher because policy outcomes are moved further way from their policy preferences (Moravcsik and Vachudova 2003; König and Bräuninger 2004; Kaeding 2006; Thomson, Torenvield, and Arregui 2007; Steunenberg and Kaeding 2009; Dimitrova and Toshkov 2009; Steunenberg and Rhinard 2010; Plechanovová 2011). Finally, the ECJ can increase compliance costs by adopting case law in response to domestic actors that seek to expand the scope of EU law (see chapter 1; Schmidt and Kelemen 2014; S. Schmidt 2018).

The nature of EU law adopted at the shaping stage has major implications for the costs member states have to take. Flexibility reduces compliance costs by providing member states with more time to take them. EU law grants transition periods and (temporary) exemptions. Such differentiated integration (Holzinger and Schimmelfennig 2012; Leuffen, Schimmelfennig, and Rittberger 2013) pays tribute to differences in capacity and competitiveness among the member states. The most prominent example is the euro. Member states are obliged to adopt the EU's single currency—but only if they have sufficient capacities to comply with the Maastricht convergence criteria. Likewise, participation in the Schengen Agreement, which abolishes any kind of border control among the member states, is conditional on effective external border control systems. This "preferential treatment of the weak" (Schimmelfennig 2014a) supports the integration of new members, particularly if they are newly democratizing and poor (Sedelmeier 2005, 9).

Flexibility also varies between the two main types of legal acts that member states have to comply with. Directives and regulations are adopted by the same decision-making procedures. Directives, however, leave member states more flexibility because they should only "specify the results to be achieved" but "leave to national authorities the choice of form and methods," while a regulation "shall be binding in its entirety and directly applicable in all Member States" (Article 249 TEU).

At the same time, however, directives are framework legislation, which increases their complexity. They define broad goals and have to be explicitly incorporated into national law. Unlike regulations, which are directly applicable and automatically override national laws, directives require transposition into national law involving a multitude of actors (civil servants, parliaments) to adjust domestic structures. Besides coping with the additional workload that directives entail, these actors can block or at least delay compliance.

Costs also arise from the novelty of EU law. New laws require comprehensive changes in the domestic structures of the member states in order to reach compliance with EU law. These changes should be smaller, and thus less costly, if EU law amends already existing legislation rather than issuing new regulations. Updating technical standards or tightening environmental standards requires fewer changes than adopting new legislation and setting up new administrative procedures.

Finally, delegation reduces the risk of compliance costs becoming politicized. Depending on the legislative procedure, directives are adopted by either the Council as the sole legislator (special legislative procedure) or the Council and the European Parliament as co-legislators (ordinary legislative procedure).[7] A third type of directive can be adopted by the Commission as "tertiary legislation" (Junge, König, and Luig 2015). Tertiary legislation can take the form of delegated or implementing acts. These acts involve the further elaboration or updating of standards and technical issues of an existing legislative act. Commission directives are not only less costly to comply with for public administration. They are also less likely to become politicized because they are more technical in nature and are (therefore) adopted by the Commission rather than the Council and the Parliament (cf. Héritier et al. 2013). The chances of politicization are further reduced by the lack of parliamentary involvement. Parliamentary debates raise the salience of EU policies (Rauh and De Wilde 2017; S. Schmidt 2018), also at the EU level when the European Parliament debates legislative proposals and introduces amendments (Häge 2010). Highly salient EU laws mobilize political opposition by and within national parliaments (Dimitrakopoulos 2001).

Variables related to characteristics of EU laws are time sensitive but do not necessarily differ between policy sectors. In order to explain sectoral variation, the PCP model needs to incorporate factors that are sector or policy specific. Drawing on the seminal work of Theodore Lowi (1972), public policy analysis distinguishes between different policy types and regulatory logics. (Re)distributive policy (e.g., agriculture, or regional policy) requires direct public expenditures; the member states need to deal with these costs at the stage of decision making. Once states have agreed how much money to allocate to funding regional development projects, costs are no longer an issue because those who will not benefit from them or have to pay for the costs are not involved in the implementation. For regulatory policy it is the opposite; the costs of policy formulation and decision making for environment or health and food safety regulations are relatively low at the EU level but often significant—in material and political terms—when it comes to the implementation of EU laws at the domestic level. In other words, regulatory policy produces higher compliance costs than nonregulatory policy (Majone 1993, 1996).

Costs are particularly high when regulatory policy aims at correcting market failures. Compliance with regulatory policy designed to open national markets may incur costs for some domestic actors, such as companies that are not internationally competitive. However, such market-making policy does not require member states to take action or develop and police the application of new legislation. In order to remove obstacles to market integration, member states mostly have to abstain from interfering with the free flow of market forces by not levying import tariffs and export fees and not controlling borders. Market-correcting policy, in contrast, explicitly requires states to actively interfere in market and society (Scharpf 1999; H. Wallace 2005). The implementation of common environmental, health, or labor standards is more costly than the control of mergers, price collusions, or state subsidies. Member states have to enact new legislation, invest additional administrative resources, and strengthen administrative coordination to enforce it. The costs of market-correcting policy are also more likely to become politicized. The "regulatory competition" (Héritier 1996) among the member states makes any compromise at the EU level prone to domestic opposition, by, for instance, business sectors that face higher production costs because they have to invest in new abatement technology or pay higher wages.

In sum, EU law is often costly at least for some member states. How high the costs are and who ultimately has to bear them depend on the degree to which member states are able to shape EU law according to their policy preferences. This is a matter of power and capacity, as well as the politicization that states are likely to face when taking EU law.

Costly EU law does not automatically result in noncompliance, though. The PCP model assumes that the default strategic preference of states still is compliance. Member states generally accept the supremacy of EU law and have a common interest in making the EU work. Whether member states violate costly EU laws ultimately depends on how they cope with the compliance costs. The PCP model argues that power, capacity, and politicization are as important in the taking game as they are in the shaping game.

The Taking Game: Coping with Compliance Costs

Once an EU law is adopted, member states have to implement it. For directives, this entails the transposition into national law. Regulations, in contrast, are directly applicable. Member states have to practically apply and enforce both types of EU law. They can cope with the ensuing compliance costs either by resisting the necessary changes at the EU level or by bearing the costs at the domestic level.

THE EU LEVEL

Power should not only allow member states to shape EU policy outcomes according to their policy preferences. Power also matters for the extent to which they are able to resist compliance costs by simply noncomplying. Institutional mechanisms for monitoring compliance and coordinating sanctions are intended to mitigate the risks of such free-riding behavior (Keohane 1984; Boyle 1991). Institutions increase the likelihood of noncompliance being detected and punished, thereby raising the (anticipated) costs of noncompliance. As the guardian of the treaties, the European Commission has ample monitoring and sanctioning powers. Besides carrying out its own investigations, it can rely on information provided by business, interest groups, and citizens. Infringement proceedings allow the European Commission to prosecute offenders. Legal action may not only result in financial penalties. The loss of credibility as a reliable cooperation partner may also lower the political leverage of governments in future negotiations (Morrow 1999).

Powerful states are less vulnerable to sanctioning costs. Financial penalties imposed by the ECJ are calculated on the basis of a member state's GDP. Still, rich member states are better able to pay than poor member states, which are heavily dependent on EU funding and thus the financial and political support of other member states. Large member states can also more readily afford to lose reputation since the European Commission and smaller member states are not in the position to ignore them; their consent is needed for the adoption of EU law.

Rather than resisting noncompliance despite additional sanctioning costs, states could also use their power to deter international institutions or other states from enforcing compliance in the first place. The first member state to violate the Maastricht convergence criteria was Germany. Unlike Portugal, Greece, or Ireland, Europe's largest economy was never officially reprimanded under the Stability and Growth Pact, which the euro-group countries adopted, pressured by Germany, to enforce fiscal discipline (Heipertz and Verdun 2004). The European Commission could be more reluctant to enforce compliance against big and rich member states because of their political and economic power.

THE DOMESTIC LEVEL

Member states may not only be unable to dodge compliance costs at the EU level; they may also lack the capacity to cope with them at the domestic level. Effectively taking EU laws by paying off the costs they incur requires resources as does shaping EU laws to reduce the costs in the first place. States substantially differ in their resource endowment. Industrial countries, in principle, should have the resources necessary to comply with their obligations under international and EU law. The challenge they face is to mobilize and pool available resources or coordinate those parts of the administration whose legal competence or technical expertise is required to introduce legal and administrative changes and apply the new policy.

Next to resources and efficiency, state governments need to have the autonomy to implement and enforce their legal obligations. In the shaping game, domestic veto players should increase the ability of governments to reduce costs, decreasing the chances of noncompliance. Once an EU law is passed, however, these veto players have the opposite effect, making noncompliance more likely because they have the power to block the changes necessary for compliance (Tallberg 2002; Börzel et al. 2010; Zhelyazkova, Kaya, and Schrama 2016). Yet simply counting the number of domestic actors that are able to veto compliance to shirk costs ignores that these actors have to be aware and care about the costs. The question then is what makes international agreements publicly visible and politically relevant to domestic actors, particularly in the EU, which has for the longest time evolved through "integration by stealth" (Majone 2005).

Domestic politicization is more likely in member states where public support for the EU is low. Moreover, research has shown that EU laws are particularly likely to become politicized when parliaments get involved. Parliamentary debates raise the salience of EU laws (Rauh and De Wilde 2017). This is also the case at the EU level when the European Parliament debates legislative proposals and introduces amendments (Häge 2010). Highly salient EU laws mobilize political opposition by and within national parliaments (Dimitrakopoulos 2001). As important veto players, parliaments are a direct source of noncompliance. At the same time, parliamentary involvement has a more indirect effect by making the politicization of compliance costs more likely so that national governments will prefer to shirk them.

EU INSTITUTIONS

EU institutions do not only influence the ability of member states to shape compliance costs, introducing temporal and sectoral variation. They also affect the taking of these costs by rendering noncompliance more costly or by helping member states to cope with the costs.

Institutional monitoring and sanctioning mechanisms shall "raise the costs of violation or . . . lower its profit" (Audretsch 1986, 410). The more monitoring information the European Commission obtains through complaints and petitions from business, interest groups, and citizens, or its own investigations, the greater the risk for member states to get caught in noncompliance. The EU has developed new monitoring tools, such as SOLVIT and EU Pilot, which are intended to assist citizens and business complaining about the improper application of directives (Hobolth and Sindbjerg Martinsen 2013; Koops 2011). In 1992, the Maastricht Treaty introduced the possibility for the ECJ to impose financial penalties to sanction persistent noncompliance (see chapters 1 and 4). The Internal Market Scoreboard, which was established in 1997, is designed to increase reputational costs by naming and shaming member states. The worst performers are put on the spot, not only among fellow governments but also in the public media (Tallberg 2002, 63).

Next to strengthening its enforcement capacity, the EU has developed different instruments to manage compliance by helping member states to take EU laws. To weed out cases caused by legal uncertainty and misunderstandings, such as those due to poor drafting, the Commission installed a series of contracting mechanisms. These include informal information and consultation during the preliminary stages of the infringement proceedings, and the bilateral meetings the legal services of the Directorate-Generals hold with their colleagues in the corresponding national ministries of the member states. The Commission also issues recommendations, resolutions, guidelines, action plans, and other forms of soft law to provide the member states with guidelines on how to interpret EU directives and regulations (Scholten 2017; Maggetti and Gilardi 2014; Falkner et al. 2005). To help build the necessary capacity for member states to take EU law, the EU offers financial and technical assistance under various EU funds and funding programs, such as the European Regional and Development Fund or the Cohesion Fund. It also orchestrates transgovernmental networks that bring together national administrators in charge of implementing EU law to foster the development of a common understanding of what compliance entails and facilitate processes of mutual learning from best practices on how to achieve compliance (Hobolth and Sindbjerg Martinsen 2013; Yesilkagit 2011; Scholten 2017).

The ways in which power, capacity, and politicization affect noncompliance at the two levels and stages of the compliance game are summarized in table 2.1.

Expectations

Conceptualizing compliance as a two-stage game played by rational actors across two levels implies that the more successful member states are in shaping EU policies, the fewer problems they are likely to face in taking these policies. The question is whether the shaping ability and the taking ability of states depend on the same factors. The PCP model suggests that good shapers are also good takers. Effective shapers face lower compliance costs. If they have the capacity to shape the costs, they can also use their capacity to take costs. Even if states are powerful, they do not need to invoke their power to resist compliance and deter enforcement authorities. Politicization, finally, enhances the ability of a state to shape EU law, thereby reducing the importance of the capacity to take it as well as the power to defy compliance.

TABLE 2.1 PCP in a two-level compliance game played across two stages

	SHAPING			TAKING		
	States	*Time*	*Sector*	*States*	*Time*	*Sector*
POWER	*EU:* reducing compliance costs through assertive bargaining *Domestic:* reducing compliance costs through *tying hand* to domestic veto players	*EU:* increasing compliance costs due to more supranationalization		*EU:* resisting compliance costs due to insensitivity to enforcement costs *Deterring enforcement authorities*	*EU:* less resistance against compliance costs due to better enforcement	*EU:* more resistance against regulatory, *market-correcting policy* due to higher costs
CAPACITY	*EU:* reducing compliance costs through efficient bargaining	*EU:* decreasing compliance costs due to less complex, more flexible, and amending legislation	*EU:* regulatory policy that shifts costs to the taking stage	*Domestic:* coping with compliance costs through bureaucratic quality and few veto players	*EU:* better coping with compliance costs through better management	*Domestic:* more capacity required for coping with regulatory, *market-correcting policy*
POLITICIZATION	*Domestic:* reducing compliance costs through *tying hands* to *Eurosceptic publics*	*EU:* decreasing compliance costs due to *delegated legislation*		*EU/domestic:* resisting compliance costs due to domestic mobilization triggered by parliamentary involvements	*Domestic:* stronger resistance against compliance costs due to *higher salience*	*Domestic:* stronger resistance against compliance costs of regulatory, market-correcting policies due to *higher salience*

EU-level factors, such as the decision-making rules, the nature of EU laws, and the enforcement and management capacity of EU institutions, should reduce compliance costs for all member states, help them cope with the costs, or influence their propensity of becoming politicized. Rather than explaining country variation, EU institutions help account for changes in noncompliance across time and policy sectors.

Based on these considerations, the PCP model allows us to formulate fairly clear expectations for empirical research regarding the variation in noncompliance across countries, time, and policy sectors. While capacity should have a negative effect on noncompliance at both the shaping and the taking stages, power and politicization pull in opposite directions. Strong power and the propensity of politicization strengthen the ability of states to reduce compliance costs at the shaping stage, making noncompliance less likely. At the same time, however, power allows states to resist compliance costs, while politicization decreases the autonomy of states to take them. Taking into account all the possible combinations would make for a very complex model. Existing research, including my own, has found that power matters more for taking than for shaping, while for politicization it is the other way round (Mbaye 2001; Giuliani 2003; Sverdrup 2004; Perkins and Neumayer 2007; Jensen 2007; Börzel et al. 2010). I will therefore consider politicization only at the shaping stage and power only at the taking stage. Power and politicization are expected to have adverse effects on noncompliance at the shaping and the taking stages. This will allow me to empirically test whether my intuition is correct.

(1) *Powerful states with weak capacity and low levels of politicization show more noncompliance than less powerful member states with strong capacity and a high propensity of politicization.*

Powerful states with weak capacity and low levels of politicization may be able to push through their preferred policy outcomes at the EU level. At the same time, even their power is mitigated by QMV, and their bureaucracies are not efficient enough to shape EU laws otherwise. Nor can they tie their hands to domestic opposition against costly EU laws. Their low capacity, as well as their power to resist compliance costs and to deter enforcement authorities, turns them into poor takers of EU law. Less powerful states, in contrast, are not able to force their preferences on other member states. With their capacity, however, they can still be effective shapers of EU law, particularly if EU law is likely to become politicized. Their strong capacity, on the one hand, and their lack of power to defy compliance and deter enforcement authorities, on the other, make them effective takers of costly EU laws.

In sum, a decline in power and a growth in capacity decrease the chances of noncompliance. At a given level of power and capacity, politicization brings noncompliance down, since it lowers the relevance of power to resist compliance and deter enforcement authorities, as well as the need for capacity to ensure effective implementation. Put differently, politicization reduces the positive effect of power and enhances the negative effect of capacity on noncompliance. Once the empirical analysis of chapter 3 shows whether my intuition is correct, I will model the eight different outcomes of the combination of power, capacity, and politicization, placing them on a continuum between high and low noncompliance.

The PCP model conceptualizes power, capacity, and politicization as country-related factors, which are rather time and policy invariant. EU institutions mitigate the effect of these three factors on noncompliance and thereby allow us to account for variation across time and policy.

(2) *The more institutions constrain the shaping power of states, make resistance to compliance more costly for them, spare or strengthen their capacity to cope with compliance costs, and lower the chances of compliance costs becoming politicized, the less likely noncompliance becomes.*

Supranational decision-making rules deprive member states of their power to veto costly EU laws. EU institutions thereby make noncompliance more likely by increasing costs. Their more effective monitoring and sanctioning render noncompliance more costly. At the same time, EU capacity building helps member states to cope with compliance costs. Differentiated integration eases compliance costs by allowing member states to opt out of legal obligations (temporarily). EU laws that introduce new and complex regulations are more demanding on member state capacities and more prone to noncompliance. Delegated legislation entails not only less costs because of its technicality. Owing to the lack of parliamentary involvement, these costs are less likely to become politicized at the domestic level.

(3) *Policy sectors that impose higher costs, being more likely to be politicized, attract more noncompliance than policy sectors that are less demanding on state capacity and are politically less sensitive.*

Policies systematically differ with regard to the compliance costs they incur on states. Regulatory policy entails higher compliance costs than nonregulatory policy, particularly if the aim is to harmonize social, political, or environmental standards of the member states to protect EU citizens against market failure. Replacing national regulation by new EU regulation requires not only capacity to cope with the costs. These costs are also more likely to be politicized.

The empirical analyses in chapters 3–5 evaluate these theoretical expectations. They also control for social constructivist factors that may influence how governments shape and take EU law, affecting their chances of noncompliance. Socialization and legitimacy give rise to expectations that conflict with the PCP.

(4) *The more states are socialized into EU law, the less noncompliant they are.*

Member states are socialized into EU law, internalize its supremacy, and take it for granted. This should privilege the "upgrading of the common interest" (E. Haas 1958, 287) over the pursuit of purely national self-interest in the shaping of EU law, which is likely to result in EU laws that are costly for all member states. Member states should also have a default preference for compliance, irrespective of the compliance costs incurred.

(5) *The less legitimacy the EU and EU law enjoy, the more likely is noncompliance.*

A rule is legitimate because it is embedded in an underlying institution or a legal system that is generally characterized by a high level of social acceptance (Hurd 1999; Kohler-Koch 2000). Voluntary compliance is generated by the diffuse support for and the general acceptance of the rule-setting institution. Rules are not only complied with because laws ought to be obeyed, but because the rules are set by institutions that enjoy a high degree of support and general acceptance (Dworkin 1986; Hurrell 1995; Gibson and Caldeira 1995; Hurd 1999; Franck 1990; Finnemore and Toope 2001; Checkel 2001). The social constructivist expectation is the opposite of what the PCP model suggests. Low public support for the EU means a higher propensity of politicization, resulting in less rather than more noncompliance at a given level of power and capacity.

Beside institutional legitimacy, actors comply even with costly rules because they believe that these rules have been adopted "in accordance with right process" (Franck 1990, 706). This procedural legitimacy can be generated by involving the same actors in the shaping of EU law at the EU level who are in charge of taking EU law at the domestic level. They will then effectively implement decision outcomes and comply with them, regardless of the costs and benefits involved, because they perceive the decision-making process as right and fair (Dworkin 1986; Hurrell 1995).

The PCP model developed in this chapter lends itself to more than three propositions. Likewise, social constructivist research on compliance offers more than two alternative or competing hypotheses. However, the five hypotheses speak directly to the three puzzles the remainder of the book explores: why old member states comply less than new member states, why noncompliance has declined since the 1990s, and why noncompliance is most prevalent in areas of EU law that protect citizen rights.

The PCP model focuses on variation in noncompliance of states. Since the governments of the member states dominate both stages of the compliance game, linking the two, their ability to shape and take compliance costs of EU law plays a prominent role. Powerful member states with strong capacity and a high propensity of politicization should be both effective shapers and takers and hence show lower levels of noncompliance. Conversely, member states with limited power, capacity, and politicization are unlikely to effectively shape or take EU law and should be among the top noncompliers.

EU institutions affect power, capacity, and politicization. As systemic factors, EU institutions allow us to account for variation in noncompliance across time and policy sectors. The extension of supranational rules and procedures mitigates the power of member states to reduce compliance costs. The strengthening of EU monitoring and sanctioning mechanisms renders resistance against compliance more costly, while increased EU capacity building helps member states cope with compliance costs. Certain types of EU law, finally, require less capacity and have a lower propensity to become politicized at the domestic level.

Chapters 3–5 apply the PCP model to each of the three puzzles the book seeks to tackle. To explain why long-standing member states are less compliant than new member states, why overall noncompliance has declined since the 1990s, and why noncompliance is more pronounced in sectors of EU law that protects citizen rights, I proceed in three steps. First, I review the existing literature for conceptualizations and operationalizations of power, capacity, and politicization and analyze their empirical relevance. In the second step, I employ my findings to specify the PCP model. This will prevent inflating the model with too many variables. Finally, I evaluate the empirical implications of the PCP model by using descriptive data, statistical data, and narrative evidence. The concluding chapter of this book reassembles the model in light of the empirical findings of chapters 3–5, presenting a comprehensive theoretical account of noncompliance in the EU and beyond.

WHY SOME STATES COMPLY LESS THAN OTHERS

This chapter tackles the first puzzle of the book: Why do long-standing member states comply less than states that joined the EU more recently? Enforcement, management, and legitimacy approaches address member state noncompliance. Yet the question is not only—and increasingly less so—why states (do not) comply but why some comply less than others. Enforcement has to come to terms with France and Italy wielding power in the EU similar to that of Germany and the UK but being much less compliant. The UK and Germany are equally resourceful but differ in their compliance performance, which is hard to explain for management. Neither enforcement nor management can account for why twelve of the thirteen countries that joined the EU in the 2000s and whose power and capacity are equally limited comply on average better than the old member states of the EU-15. This is also a problem for legitimacy, since the new member states have had less time to internalize EU norms and rules. Nor can legitimacy explain why member states, such as the UK and Sweden, where public support for the EU is low, are among the top compliers.

The PCP model solves these puzzles by combining power, capacity, and politicization. Member states like Italy and France, which have the power to resist compliance with costly EU laws and limited capacity to cope with the costs, are the worst compliers. Germany and the UK have similar power but more capacity, as a result of which they are better compliers. Unlike France and Italy, Greece and Portugal have no power to resist compliance, but their capacity is equally limited. Politicization helps explain why Belgium, Ireland, and Luxembourg comply less than other small countries, such as Sweden, Finland, and Denmark, with similarly high capacity. Their Europhile publics render politicization less likely, so governments cannot claim their hands are tied and negotiate for less costly EU laws in the Council. This also accounts for the different noncompliance behavior of Germany and the UK, which do not differ in their power and capacity either. The UK was the member state with by far the highest level of Euroscepticism, allowing it to either opt out of costly EU law or to reduce the costs by bringing EU law closer to its policy preferences. Politicization is the answer to why Eurosceptic member states comply better than member states with strong public support for the EU.

Noncompliance is not a problem of the EU's southern member states. Nor is it an eastern problem. On the contrary, the ten CEE countries that joined the EU in the first decade of the twenty-first century have performed better than most of the long-standing member states. The PCP model explains this puzzle by the limited power of the newcomers to resist costly EU laws and the specific capacity they built up during the accession process for coping with compliance costs. To evaluate this argument empirically, the second part of the chapter reviews the state of the art on member state noncompliance with EU law for conceptualizations and operationalizations to identify power, capacity, and politicization. A statistical model, which tests the observable implications of power, capacity, and politicization for their causal relevance, reduces the number to five specifications of those three concepts: voting power, bureaucratic quality, public opposition to the EU, political constraints, and parliamentary scrutiny. The second part draws on these findings to refine the PCP model with regard to variation in member state noncompliance. I use descriptive data and narrative evidence to show how power, capacity, and politicization work together in affecting the noncompliance behavior of the member states.

From a Southern to an Eastern Problem?

At first sight, member state noncompliance in the EU may suggest a North-South divide (figure 3.1; see also figure 1.4).

The variation revealed by the distribution of infringement data largely conforms to findings in the broader literature. There is an uncontested group of compliance leaders, which include the three Nordic countries, the UK, and the Netherlands.[1] There is equal agreement on the laggards comprising Greece, Portugal, Italy, Belgium, and France. This leaves Germany, Austria, Spain, Luxembourg, and Ireland for the inconspicuous, the latter two of which are sometimes placed in the laggards group (Bergman 2000; Falkner, Treib, and Holzleitner 2008). The contrast between the exemplary performance of the Nordic countries, on the one hand, and the poor record of Italy, Greece, and Portugal, on the other,

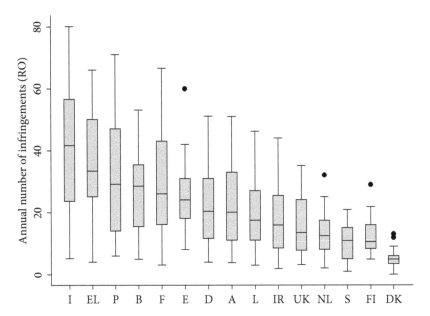

FIGURE 3.1. Annual average of reasoned opinions by member states, EU-15, 1978–2017

Source: Own compilation, with data from the Berlin Infringement Database. The graph shows the statistical distribution of the annual number of infringements (1978–2017) per member state. For acceding member states, the first year of membership was omitted.

gave rise to arguments that noncompliance in the EU was a "southern problem" (La Spina and Sciortino 1993; Pridham and Cini 1994; Falkner et al. 2005). Southern European member states allegedly share some features of their political and administrative systems that render them unable to effectively implement EU law. First, these countries appear to lack the capacity to effectively implement European policies. Southern administrations often do not possess sufficient technical expertise, staff, and infrastructure to effectively apply and enforce EU legislation (Pridham 1994, 89–90; La Spina and Sciortino 1993, 224). Moreover, policy making in these countries is reactive in style, which often contradicts the proactive approach embodied in EU policies (Aguilar Fernandez 1994; Pridham 1996, 53). Second, horizontal and vertical fragmentation of administrative structures tends to be high. As a result, resources required for effective implementation are scarce and widely dispersed among a multitude of public authorities and bureaucracies, which are too inefficient to pool them in the implementation process. Third, societal actors are found to be weak as a result of late modernization and democratization. Authoritarian legacies have undermined the organizational capacities of civil society. Lower levels of socioeconomic development have prevented the emergence of post-material values, a precondition for strong social movements, which could generate domestic compliance costs (Eder and Kousis 2001). Finally, some authors have implied that the problems of the southern member states in complying with EU law can be understood as the result of a fundamental clash of political cultures. Southern European countries have political systems traditionally dominated by party patronage and bureaucratic clientelism (Sotiropoulos 2004). Political parties offer voters jobs in the public sector, sidestepping regular recruitment procedures. Likewise, after each government turnover, top administrators in the civil service are replaced by appointees of the new governing party. Patronage and clientelism undermine bureaucratic efficiency. They result in an overproduction of laws and decrees that frequently lack implementation and enforcement, further undermining the respect for public authority. This Mediterranean political culture contradicts the Northern European political culture, which is built on corporate forms of social organization and which also forms the base of many EU laws (La Spina and Sciortino 1993; Aguilar Fernandez 1994; Pridham and Cini 1994; Falkner et al. 2005).

There can be no doubt that the Southern European member states have considerable problems in complying with EU law. But it is doubtful whether these problems are part of a homogeneous phenomenon or a "disease" dubbed the "Mediterranean syndrome" (La Spina and Sciortino 1993). First, the Southern European countries are quite diverse with respect to their political and administrative institutions (cf. Börzel 2003a). Second, if there exists such a thing as a "southern problem" or a "Mediterranean syndrome," why do we find considerable variation in noncompliance among and within the Southern European and Northern European member states? France may still be considered a Southern European country; Belgium is certainly not. At the same time, Spain performs closer to Luxembourg, Ireland, Austria, and Germany, which are firmly based in the Northern European camp. Interestingly, no study assigns Spain to the laggards group led by Italy and Greece (Haverland, Steunenberg, and van Waarden 2011; Haverland and Romeijn 2007; Hartlapp and Leiber 2010; König and Luetgert 2009; Falkner, Hartlapp, and Treib 2007; Kaeding 2006; Börzel 2000b). Italy, finally, violates EU law significantly more than Greece and Portugal. In short, the South of Europe has a problem with noncompliance, but noncompliance is not a southern problem.

Eastern enlargement has fueled arguments about a geographic patterning of noncompliance in the EU. Similar to the Southern European laggards, the Central and Eastern European (CEE) countries were suspected of showing symptoms of the "Mediterranean syndrome": inefficient administrations ridden by patronage and corruption, legacies of authoritarianism, weakly organized societal interests, and low levels of socioeconomic development. The problems of weak states and weak societies were inherent to state socialism (Sissenich 2005; Börzel 2009b; Crawford and Lijphart 1997; Cirtautas and Schimmelfennig 2010). They met in Central and Eastern Europe with the formidable challenges of mastering a triple transition toward democracy, market economy, and (new) nations (Offe 1991; Elster, Offe, and Preuss 1998; Kuzio 2001), on the one hand, and the accession to the EU, on the other (Mungiu-Pippidi 2014; Bruszt and Vukov 2018). EU membership was to support and lock in the political, economic, and social transition processes (Linden 2002; Jacoby 2004; Vachudova 2005; Grabbe 2006; Epstein 2008). At the same time, the implementation of the *acquis communautaire* with its thousands of laws put further strains on the scarce administrative and political capacities of the candidate countries (Börzel 2009a). EU accession conditionality and assistance was to tackle the problem of high costs and low capacities (Schimmelfennig, Engert, and Knobel 2003; Schimmelfennig and Sedelmeier 2004; Vachudova 2005; Börzel 2009a; Bruszt and McDermott 2009; Börzel and Sedelmeier 2017; Bruszt and Langbein 2017). With membership, however, the powerful leverage of accession conditionality was gone (Schimmelfennig and Sedelmeier 2005, 226; Steunenberg and Dimitrova 2007, 1; Sedelmeier 2008, 809–810; Börzel and Schimmelfennig 2017). Moreover, despite profound political and economic reforms, clientelism and corruption largely survived the collapse of state socialism. Where one party used to capture the state, several political parties compete now for the extraction of state resources (Houghton 2014). "Competitive particularism" (Mungiu-Pippidi 2006) and state capture reigns in post-communist countries, though in different forms and to different degrees (Gryzmala-Busse 2007; Kopecky and Scherlis 2008; Batory 2012; Innes 2014). Similar to the situation in the Southern European member states, the combination of high costs, weak incentives, and limited capacity of both state and society have raised concerns about (sustained) compliance with EU law (Falkner, Treib, and Holzleitner 2008; Dimitrova 2010).

It is still difficult to assess the compliance performance of the new member states (cf. Epstein and Sedelmeier 2009; Schimmelfennig and Trauner 2010). As in the case of Southern European member states, the Commission granted the CEE countries a period of grace before it started to systematically open infringement proceedings (Tosun 2011). Quantitative studies do not find a particular compliance problem in the East of Europe (Sedelmeier 2006, 2008, 2012; Toshkov 2008; Dimitrova and Toshkov 2007; Steunenberg and Toshkov 2009; Zhelyazkova et al. 2014; Zhelyazkova and Yordanova 2015; Zhelyazkova, Kaya, and Schrama 2016, 2017; Börzel and Sedelmeier 2017). While the number of infringement proceedings briefly peaked in 2004, it kept declining ever since. As chapter 4 will show in more detail, eastern enlargement has had no discernible effect on the reported infringements of EU law. This is also the case for preliminary rulings. The annual average number of preliminary rulings for the new member states is among the lowest.

The Commission has been full of praise for the newcomers, stating that "the new Member States . . . perform better in transposing Internal Market directives on time than the EU-15 Member States despite having had to absorb the whole acquis in a short time frame" (European Commission 2005, 5). It calls the new member states "the champions in reducing transposition deficits" (ibid., 12). They transpose directives as fast, some even faster, than the old member states. They also tend to settle their infringement procedures more swiftly, too (Dimitrova and Toshkov 2007; Sedelmeier 2008; Toshkov 2007a, 2008; Steunenberg and Toshkov 2009).

Case study research on the new member states, however, has revealed serious violations of EU norms and rules in their practical application and enforcement. Some have taken this as an indication that the EU's southern problem has turned into an eastern problem based on the same symptoms of captured states and weak civil societies (Falkner, Treib, and Holzleitner 2008; Spendzharova and Vachudova 2012; Trauner 2009; Kriszan 2009; Buzogány 2009). The diverging findings are not necessarily contradictory or produced by different data and methods. Rather, they may point to a decoupling between reasonable legal compliance, on the one hand, and poor practical application and enforcement on the ground, on the other (Falkner, Treib, and Holzleitner 2008; Batory 2012; Cirtautas and Schimmelfennig 2010; Sedelmeier 2012; Avdeyeva 2010; Dimitrova 2010; Dimitrova and Steunenberg 2013; Trauner 2009; Slapin 2015; Zhelyazkova, Kaya, and Schrama 2016). In the "world of dead letters" (Falkner, Treib, and Holzleitner 2008), EU law gets swiftly incorporated into national law but is not put into action. Such decoupling was already observed during the accession process of the CEE countries, where "many rules have been only formally transposed into national legislation but are not fully or reliably implemented" (Schimmelfennig and Sedelmeier 2005, 226; Hughes, Sasse, and Gordon 2004; Jacoby 2004; Sissenich 2005; Goetz 2005; Leiber 2007). Post-accession studies have even found some evidence for reversing compliance with EU law. Such backtracking, however, significantly varies both across countries and policy sectors and appears to be limited by the extent to which the new member states are dependent on EU aid and trade, as well as by the mobilization of societal interests (Pridham 2008; Blauberger 2009a; Levitz and Pop-Eleches 2009, 2010; Hollyer 2010; Sedelmeier 2012; Dimitrova and Buzogány 2014).

Even if the new member states face problems in practically applying and enforcing EU law, their compliance behavior cannot be simply reduced to being transposition leaders but application laggards, which would put them ultimately into the same camp as Greece, Italy, Portugal, Belgium, or France. First, the formal compliance records of the new members vary too much for decoupling to be a uniform phenomenon (figure 3.2).[2]

More substantively, case studies have so far failed to establish "dead letters" as a pervasive problem for all CEE members. Evidence for this claim relies primarily on the study of social policy directives in the new members by Falkner, Treib, and Holzleitner (2008). Yet the social policy directives examined, and gender equality at the workplace in particular, are generally highly prone to decoupling in old and new members alike. To some extent, decoupling might be characteristic of issue-area-specific difficulties of enforcement, even if the relevant domestic enforcement bodies for workplace regulation are particularly weak in post-communist new members (Falkner 2010). Other case studies have found hardly any evidence of an "eastern world of dead letters." Toshkov's detailed analyses of three policy areas—electronic communications, consumer protection, and animal welfare—suggest that shortcomings with practical implementation and application of EU law in the eastern member states are not "of a greater scale and different nature in CEE, and there is no evidence that the EU rules have been mindlessly copied and forgotten" (Toshkov 2012, 108). The comparative analysis by Zhelyazkova, Kaya, and Schrama (2017) that draws on in-depth conformity

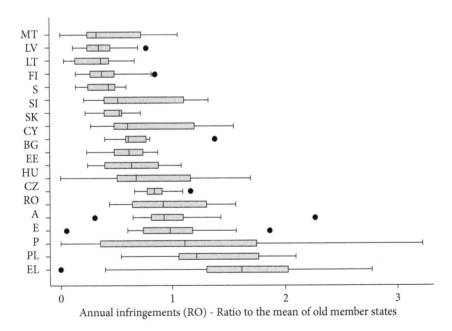

FIGURE 3.2. Annual reasoned opinions of new members compared to old member states
Source: Own compilation, with data from the Berlin Infringement Database.

studies of practical application of twenty-four directives across four policy areas (Internal Market, Environment, Social Policy, and Justice and Home Affairs) also suggests that decoupling is not more prominent in the new members than in the EU-15—with the exception of Social Policy (Zhelyazkova, Kaya, and Schrama 2016, 2017). Of course, such counterevidence may be prone to criticism, too, for instance for relying too much on evaluation reports prepared by consultancies contracted in many cases by the Commission, as a result of which their quality may be contested (see Mastenbroek, van Voorst, and Meuwese 2015). Moreover, many studies draw conclusions from a limited number of policy areas (Falkner, Treib, and Holzleitner 2008). Clearly, there is evidence for some serious compliance problems regarding the practical application of EU law in post-communist member states, which merit further investigation. It might be too early to dismiss decoupling completely as a possible explanation for the good record of eastern new members. However, it appears equally questionable that decoupling is a pervasive phenomenon that explains away their performance.

Second, similar to the Southern Europeans, the CEE newcomers do not form a homogeneous group. While thirteen years (ten years for Romania and Bulgaria) of infringement data may not allow for a systematic comparison yet, existing research has identified Bulgaria and Romania as notorious compliance laggards. They do not only fail to fight corruption and transborder crime, for which the EU installed some post-accession conditionality (Gateva 2010; Pridham 2007; Spendzharova and Vachudova 2012). They do not abide with EU law in the other areas, either (Noutcheva and Bechev 2008; Trauner 2009; Hille and Knill 2006; Knill and Tosun 2009). The three Baltic countries, Slovenia, and Slovakia perform considerably and consistently better, whereas Hungary, Poland, the Czech Republic, Malta, and Cyprus range in the middle (Hille and Knill 2006; Knill and Tosun 2009; Steunenberg and Toshkov 2009). Infringement data confirms variation but finds different patterns (Börzel and Sedelmeier 2017). Lithuania is as good a complier as Denmark, while Bulgaria and Romania are close to Hungary, Latvia, Slovenia, Slovakia, Sweden, and Finland. The Czech Republic and Poland are closing in with Germany and Spain (see figure 1.3 in chapter 1).

The lack of support for an East-West divide does not come as a surprise for the PCP model. While not necessarily denying the effect of socialist legacies on noncompliance in Central and Eastern Europe, "these legacies do not carry equal weight across the region" (Cirtautas and Schimmelfennig 2010, 428; cf. Seleny 2007; cf. Toshkov 2007b, 2008; Sedelmeier 2009; Schwellnus 2009; Börzel and Sedelmeier 2017).

The following sections review research on noncompliance with EU law for conceptualizations and operationalizations of power, capacity, and politicization.

The aim is to limit the number of variables included in the PCP model to those the literature has found to be empirically relevant.

Explaining Member State Noncompliance

Shaping Compliance Costs

The PCP model expects noncompliance to be the more likely the more limited the ability of member states is to shape EU law according to their policy preferences and thus reduce compliance costs in the taking of EU law.

POLITICAL AND ECONOMIC POWER

The power of member states to shape policy outcomes at the EU level plays an important role in the compliance literature. The focus has been on the number of votes that member states hold in the Council of the EU, as well as their budget contributions and trade shares. Many studies find that more voting, budgetary, and economic power leads to more rather than less noncompliance (Mbaye 2001; Giuliani 2003; Sverdrup 2004; Perkins and Neumayer 2007; Jensen 2007; Börzel et al. 2010). This indicates that power may be relevant to resist compliance costs or deter enforcement authorities at the taking stage rather than to reduce costs at the shaping stage.

The PCP model assumes that EU institutions mitigate the power of member states (see also Panke 2010b). Findings on whether QMV increases the probability of noncompliance because majority rule deprives individual member states of their power to veto proposals that go against their preferences are inconclusive (Mbaye 2001; Haverland and Romeijn 2007; König and Luetgert 2009). This may be at least partly due to voting rules being policy or issue specific. QMV does not systematically vary across countries (Börzel and Knoll 2013). Whether member states that voted against an EU law or abstained are less likely to comply is not clear either. Studies have found that negative votes or abstentions in the Council yield positive, negative, or no significant effect on noncompliance (Linos 2007; Toshkov 2010, 34; Angelova, Dannwolf, and König 2012, 1278).

CAPACITY AND POLITICIZATION

Compliance studies show that capacity-related factors are relevant in the taking rather than shaping of EU law and its costs. The same is true for politicization (see below). Research has so far neglected whether and to what extent the resource endowment of member states, their bureaucratic efficiency, and their domestic autonomy enable them to obtain more favorable policy outcomes *thereby* affecting their noncompliance behavior.

POLICY MISFIT AND EU BENEFITS (CONTROLS)

Several studies have developed concepts and indicators to capture the costs of noncompliance directly rather than as the effect of the shaping power of states. Costs are the result of the degree of misfit between EU and domestic law. The higher the policy misfit, the higher the compliance costs, and the more likely is noncompliance (Duina 1997; Duina and Blythe 1999; Knill 1998; Thomson 2007; Thomson, Torenvield, and Arregui 2007; König and Mäder 2013; König and Luetgert 2009). Policy misfit is hard to quantify. It is also difficult to see why it should vary systematically among member states, unless their ability to shape EU law according to their preferences is brought in. Moreover, empirical research has shown that governments comply with even costly EU laws if these laws correspond to their policy preferences and vice versa (Ademmer and Börzel 2013; Börzel and Pamuk 2012; Sprungk 2011, 2013; König and Mäder 2014b). Finally, member states weigh the costs of compliance against the benefits. Scholars have argued that member states should be less likely to violate costly EU laws if compliance yields general benefits because a large share of their trade goes into the Internal Market or they are net recipients of EU funds (Mbaye 2001; Perkins and Neumayer 2007; König and Luetgert 2009; Knill and Tosun 2009). Not being directly part of the PCP model, the empirical analysis will include policy misfit and EU benefits as control variables to the extent that data is available.

Taking Compliance Costs

According to the PCP model, member states are the more likely to violate EU law the less able they are to resist compliance costs, to deter enforcement authorities, and to cope with compliance costs domestically.

POWER: RECALCITRANCE AND DETERRENCE

The robust support in the literature for a *positive* relationship between the voting power of member states and the size of their economy and population, on the one hand, and their violations of EU law, on the other (see above), corroborates the expectation of the PCP model that power primarily enables member states to be recalcitrant and resist compliance (see Börzel et al. 2010; Börzel, Hofmann, and Panke 2012). They could also use their votes, budget contributions, or trade shares to deter the Commission and the ECJ from enforcing EU law. In this case, we would expect their noncompliance performance to be lower, because they should face fewer infringements. I have argued in chapter 1 that there is no deterrence effect. The empirical analysis should lend further support for my argument that member state power does not bias infringement data.

CAPACITY: RESOURCES AND EFFICIENCY

When it comes to the capacity to cope with compliance costs, EU scholars have found that economic wealth, fiscal revenue, and government expenditure are not associated with noncompliance (Mbaye 2001; Hille and Knill 2006; Börzel et al. 2010). Rather than state resources, they emphasize bureaucratic efficiency—the ability of a government to apply its resources to the effective implementation of EU law (Siedentopf and Ziller 1988; Falkner et al. 2005; but see Ciavarini Azzi 1988; Pridham and Cini 1994; Dimitrakopoulos 2001). Both quantitative and qualitative research have generated strong evidence that bureaucratic inefficiency is a crucial problem for noncompliance. Even if a state has sufficient resources and the autonomy to deploy them, its administration may still have difficulties in pooling and coordinating them, particularly if the required resources are dispersed among various public agencies (e.g., ministries) and levels of government (Mbaye 2001; Linos 2007; Egeberg 1999; Mastenbroek 2003; Börzel 2003a; Haverland and Romeijn 2007; Steunenberg 2006; Steunenberg and Toshkov 2009; Zhelyazkova, Kaya, and Schrama 2016). Member states with Weberian-type bureaucracies are found to be better compliers because of the competence and independence of civil servants (Mbaye 2001; Bursens 2002; Berglund, Grange, and van Waarden 2006; Börzel et al. 2010; Hille and Knill 2006; Toshkov 2008). In a similar vein, a high level of corruption undermines a member state's capacity to comply with EU law, since the enforcement of (costly) EU legislation is likely to be determined by political favoritism (Mbaye 2001; Linos 2007; Kaeding 2006).

Eastern enlargement has corroborated the importance of bureaucratic efficiency for compliance with EU law. Coordination problems undermine a state's capacity, superseding any other factor in accounting for noncompliance in the CEE countries, before (Zubek 2005; Hille and Knill 2006; Dimitrova and Toshkov 2007) as well as after their accession to the EU (Knill and Tosun 2009; Dimitrova and Toshkov 2009; Falkner 2010; Zubek 2011; Zubek and Goetz 2010).

Italy and France are two cases where the two components of capacity diverge. They are among the largest economies of Europe and command more resources than Greece, which belongs to the poorest member states. Yet these three member states are equally plagued by relatively inefficient bureaucracies, although France still fares better than Italy (Nachmias and Rosenbloom 1978, 181; Auer, Demmke, and Polet 1996; Charron, Dijkstra, and Lapuente 2010).

POLITICIZATION: VETO PLAYERS AND EUROSCEPTICISM

Compliance studies find that veto players are a major source of noncompliance. Next to the number of institutional veto players, the degree of territorial decentralization (regionalism/federalism) has a positive effect on noncompliance

(Dimitrova and Steunenberg 2000; Mbaye 2001; Linos 2007; Thomson 2007; Haverland and Romeijn 2007; Jensen 2007; Kaeding 2008; König and Luetgert 2009; Borghetto and Franchino 2010; Thomann 2015). So do the number of national ministries involved (Mastenbroek 2003; Steunenberg 2006; Haverland and Romeijn 2007; Steunenberg and Toshkov 2009), the number of parties in government (Toshkov 2007b, 2008; König and Luetgert 2009; Luetgert and Dannwolf 2009), and interest-group pluralism (Giuliani 2003; König and Luetgert 2009; Jensen 2007).

Findings on corporatism, by contrast, are inconclusive, which might be related to its theoretically ambivalent effect of social partners constituting (in some sectors) powerful veto players, on the one hand (König and Luetgert 2009; Kaeding 2006), and helping to neutralize veto players through negotiations, on the other (Héritier 2001; Lampinen and Uusikylä 1998; Mbaye 2001; Börzel and Risse 2003; Hille and Knill 2006; Thomson 2007). The involvement of national parliaments and their scrutiny of EU laws in decision making have not produced robust results either. While some treat parliaments as veto players (Steunenberg 2006; König and Luetgert 2009), others argue their involvement fosters political acceptance (Krislov, Ehlermann, and Weiler 1986; Bergman 2000) or find that the effect of parliamentary involvement varies depending on the outcome variable (Linos 2007).

Euroscepticism features at best indirectly in compliance research. It is the opposite of EU support. Legitimacy approaches argue that member states are less likely to violate EU law the more it is accepted as part of the law of the land either by the national government or by the broader public. The first may depend on the affinity of political elites or government parties to the EU as the rule-setting institution (Linos 2007; Hille and Knill 2006; König and Luetgert 2009); the latter is shaped by citizens' support for European integration and their respect for the rule of law, and the length of membership (Gibson and Caldeira 1995; Lampinen and Uusikylä 1998; Mbaye 2001; Toshkov 2007b; Slapin 2015).

The literature has found little support for the effect of ideological positions of ruling parties and their EU affinity on noncompliance (Jensen 2007; Linos 2007; Toshkov 2007a, 2007b; Hille and Knill 2006; but see Toshkov 2008; Sedelmeier 2009). Length of membership, support for the EU, and respect for rule of law have yielded no consistent results (see above). Public acceptance of EU membership is either irrelevant or leads to more, not less, noncompliance. It has been argued that support is picked up by capacity because citizens hope that the EU will compensate for the incapacity of their state to provide public goods and services (Sánchez-Cuenca 2000; Toshkov 2007a). The poor results for rule of law, finally, have been at least partly attributed to measurement problems (Börzel et al. 2010; Berglund, Grange, and van Waarden 2006). Next to the lack of good data, culture is an institutional variable that shows very little longitudinal and no sectoral or policy variation. Moreover, the Nordic countries, whose populations show high levels of respect for the rule of law (Sverdrup 2004; Beach 2005; Falkner et al. 2005), also feature high levels of capacity (Lampinen and Uusikylä 1998; Bergman 2000; Toshkov 2007a). Indicators for bureaucratic efficiency, such as bureaucratic quality or corruption, highly correlate with rule of law.

The PCP model accounts for the mixed findings of the effects of politicization on noncompliance. Veto players and Euroscepticism reduce the autonomy of a state vis-à-vis its society. At the taking stage, domestic actors that are aware of and care about compliance costs increase the likelihood of noncompliance because they are likely to block or delay the implementation of EU law. At the shaping stage, veto players and opposition to the EU increase the ability of member states to limit compliance costs because they can tie their government's hands, which should reduce the chances of noncompliance. The next section puts these conflicting expectations to an empirical test.

Evaluating Power, Capacity, and Politicization

To limit the possibilities of model specification, I confine myself to those variables that have found at least some support in the literature in explaining country variation in noncompliance. Moreover, the variables need to yield empirically observable implications that can be measured by meaningful time series data. Some, such as policy misfit or salience, are rule or policy specific and will be considered in chapters 4 and 5. For others, such as the respect for the rule of law, there is simply no data available that covers all EU member states over a period of thirty years.[3] This may explain why these factors do not fare well in quantitative studies. In other cases, including EU affinity of the ruling party or party ideology, neither case studies nor statistical analyses of more limited scope offer sufficient support to merit efforts to compile new and better data. Finally, veto players, and the professionalism of the public administration, do not show much variation across time. I have, therefore, opted for alternative variables as proxies for capacity and politicization that have not figured prominently in the literature so far.

Data and Method

For evaluating the effects of power, capacity, and politicization variables on member state noncompliance, I can use the absolute numbers of reasoned opinions sent, because the amount of EU legislation in a given year that member states in that year have to comply with is the same. Since data on some independent variables is only available till 2012, the initial analysis focuses on the EU-15 (see chapter 1). Data on two of the independent variables is only available for directives, which lie at the heart of EU noncompliance (see chapter 4). Nevertheless, I decided to include all infringements in the analysis. The results of my analyses remain the same irrespective of whether I take the official infringements of regulations and directives or directives only.

The dependent variable is the annual number of reasoned opinions based on noncompliance with EU legal acts that a member state receives. A closer look at the distribution of this count variable reveals that the variance is greater than the mean. This overdispersion in the data violates a central assumption of the Poisson regression. A negative binomial regression is used in the first model to avoid inefficient estimates. Summary statistics are listed in table A1.1. The Hausman test is highly significant regarding the unit-specific differences between years. The level of noncompliance varies systematically between years. To control for the time effects, I calculate a negative binomial count model with year fixed effects. Country fixed effects are not included, since the Hausman test is insignificant for them. Moreover, country fixed effects would eliminate precisely the between-country variation in which I am interested.

The operationalization of the independent variables is more challenging, particularly when it comes to the factors that are relevant at the shaping stage (for a summary see table A3.1). The power to shape compliance costs or resist them can be operationalized with two measures. They account for the two different aspects of power—*voting power* and *economic power*. Member states that have both cannot be ignored by others in EU decision making, even if they may have lost credibility by not abiding with previously agreed-upon rules (Perkins and Neumayer 2007; Jensen 2007; Börzel et al. 2010). In addition, their economic power renders them less sensitive to sanctioning costs in the form of financial penalties or the withholding of EU subsidies. *Voting power* can be captured by the proportion of times when a member state is pivotal (and can thus turn a losing into a winning coalition) under QMV in the Council of Ministers (Shapley Shubik Index [SSI], Shapley and Shubik 1954; Rodden 2002). GDP is a proxy for *economic power* (Keohane 1989; Martin 1992; Moravcsik 1998; Steinberg 2002). Population is relevant but heavily influences both power indicators, GDP and the SSI. The number of votes a member state has in the Council of Ministers is based on the size of its population, even though the conversion factor for population to relative voting power has changed over time owing to the successive enlargements of the EU. The Lisbon Treaty introduced the double majority, requiring 55 percent of member states to be in favor of a proposal representing 65 percent of the total EU population. This new rule has applied since 2014, which is outside the time covered by this analysis. Not surprisingly, GDP and SSI voting power significantly correlate. There is also a high, negative correlation between GDP and net recipient, which reflects the design of EU redistributive policies (see chapter 5). My previous research has shown that the size of the economy does not matter when it comes to infringements on EU law (Börzel et al. 2010). Accordingly, GDP is dropped from the model.

Capacity is equally relevant to the shaping and taking of EU law and its costs. Unlike power and politicization, its effect on noncompliance does not differ depending on the stage of the compliance game. To test for the influence of *capacity* on the distribution of noncompliance, I include two indicators that are prominent in the literature. *GDP per capita* is a general measure for the *resources* on which a state can draw to ensure compliance (Brautigam 1996). The data comes from the World Development Indicators of the World Bank. Some studies use fiscal revenue (Mbaye 2001; Hille and Knill 2006), yet it highly correlates with GDP, SSI, and net recipient (see table A2.2).

Whether a state has the capacity to mobilize its resources is captured by bureaucratic efficiency. The operationalization is not easy, mostly because of the lack of time series data. For instance, Auer and her colleagues developed a bureaucratic quality index consisting of three components: performance-related pay for civil servants, lack of permanent tenure, and public advertising of open positions (Auer, Demmke, and Polet 1996; Mbaye 2001; Berglund, Grange, and van Waarden 2006; Hille and Knill 2006; Toshkov 2008). However, they cover only the year of 1993. The World Development Indicators of the World Bank, such as government effectiveness or regulatory quality, are not available for the entire time period analyzed either. The International Country Risk Guide (ICRG) provides some rare time series data for *bureaucratic quality*. It measures the ability and expertise of states to govern without drastic changes in policy or interruptions in government services, the extent to which their bureaucracy is autonomous from political pressure and has an established mechanism for recruitment and training, and also evaluates policy formulation and day-to-day administrative functions. The advantage of *ICRG bureaucratic quality* over alternative measurements is not only its availability but also its validity. It highly correlates with the World Development Indicators of the World Bank for government efficiency and regulatory quality, as well as with different corruption indicators, which are frequently used as an indicator for bureaucratic quality (Mbaye 2001; Linos 2007; Zhelyazkova, Kaya, and Schrama 2016).

Politicization is a function of domestic veto players that have the institutional power to block domestic change required to comply with EU law and the likelihood that they actually invoke their power to oppose compliance costs. At the shaping stage, politicization makes noncompliance less likely, since it enhances the ability of governments to negotiate for less costly EU laws. At the taking stage, in contrast, domestic opposition increases the risks of noncompliance. The most prominent indicator used in the literature is the number of veto players in the political system of a member state (Tsebelis 2002; Immergut 1998). However, even if the number of the institutional and partisan veto players remains constant over time, the interests of these actors regarding (non)compliance may change. This is also the case for corporatism and interest pluralism, which may explain why they do not show any consistent results. Therefore, I use two alternative indicators. First, the *political constraints* index (POLCON) provides an alternative veto player index that accounts for the interests of veto players in such a way that interdependences between veto players and the respective political system are taken into consideration (Henisz 2002). It is based on a simple spatial model of political interaction among government branches (horizontal separation of power), measuring the number of independent branches with veto power and the distribution of political preferences across these branches. They can be interpreted as a measure of political constraints that either preclude arbitrary changes of existing policies or produce gridlock and so undermine the ability of the government to change policies when such change is needed. Second, next to the horizontal separation of power, I also cover the vertical dimension in terms of the degree of territorial decentralization using the *regional authority* index (Marks, Hooghe, and Schakel 2010; Hooghe et al. 2016). In federal states, subnational authorities are true institutional veto players in the legal implementation process through their representation in the second chamber of the national legislature. They are also in charge of practical application and enforcement. So are provinces, counties, and municipalities in regionalized and decentralized states (Mbaye 2001; Linos 2007; Thomson 2007; König and Luetgert 2009; Jensen 2007; Kaeding 2008; Borghetto and Franchino 2010; Thomann 2015; Tatham 2018).

Two alternative indicators of political constraints are discussed in the literature: the executive control of the parliamentary agenda measured by the extent to which the government can successfully initiate drafts and rely on stable majorities in the legislative branch (Döring 1995; Tsebelis 2002), and the parliamentary oversight of government measured by the material (e.g., number of committees) and ideational resources (e.g., information-processing capacity) relevant for the oversight of the government (Harfst and Schnapp 2003). I do not include these two variables, because of multicollinearity concerns. Moreover, in my previous work, I controlled for both and found robust evidence that they were not significantly correlated with noncompliance (Börzel and Knoll 2013; cf. Knoll 2016). I measure *parliamentary scrutiny*, though, with the help of data compiled by Thomas König and his collaborators on the average proportion of national transposition measures requiring parliamentary involvement per member state and year (König and Luig 2014; König and Luetgert 2009).

Data on Euroscepticism or *public opposition to the EU* are obtained from Euro-barometer surveys. The nonacceptance of European institutions can be quantified by the question that refers to the opposition to the membership of one's own country in the EU. The literature uses the percentage of respondents who think that the membership of their country in the EU is a "good thing" (Gibson and Caldeira 1996; Mbaye 2001; Bergmann 2000; Börzel et al. 2010). Accordingly, I use the percentage of respondents considering European integration a "bad thing" (public opposition).

As for the control variables, two country-specific factors influence the benefits of compliance, which should render violations of EU law less likely. *Intra-EU trade* is the sum of exports and imports of goods within the EU-15 as share of the GDP in US$ (Mbaye 2001; Perkins and Neumayer 2007; König and Luetgert 2009; Knill and Tosun 2009). The data is obtained from the OECD International Trade by Commodity. *Net recipients* receiving more money from the EU than they pay in membership contributions are identified on the basis of the operational budget balance provided by the annual EU budget financial reports and marked by positive values.

Misfit is rule-specific and very hard to quantify for hundreds of legal acts in up to fifteen member states and over a period of more than thirty years. Moreover, studies on member state noncompliance have hardly found any support for its causal relevance. However, there is data on the distance of the outcome of a directive and the party preferences of the ministers in charge of transposition at the time of notified transposition or the transposition deadline (König and Luig 2014). The country-directive specific variable *ministerial approval* was aggregated by the mean on the country level for each year. While being a rather crude simplification, the data shows some systematic country variation. Lower values represent party preferences in line with the EU legislation in a given year.

To facilitate the interpretation of the results, the independent variables have been rescaled into a two-digit range. All independent variables have been lagged by one year to allow them to take effect. Together with the limits of available data, this leaves us with some missing observations for several independent variables (see table A1.2). Dropping the last two years and the first four years from the analysis does not change the results. I therefore use the 1979–2012 period and fill the missing observations with the values of the previous and, respectively, following year(s). Ministerial approval and national parliamentary scrutiny are available only for directives. For the latter, this is not an issue, since parliamentary scrutiny applies only to the transposition of directives. Ministerial approval can relate to regulations as well. Since the results of the analysis are robust when using infringements of directives only, I decided to include both variables.

Results and Discussion

The results show that power, capacity, and politicization have a significant effect on member state noncompliance with EU directives (table 3.1). Some specifications of the three principal components of the PCP model are more relevant than others, though.

POWER

As expected, power matters at the taking rather than at the shaping stage. The voting power in the Council of Ministers (SSI) has a significant positive effect on noncompliance. France, Italy, and Germany have more Council votes and violate EU law more frequently than member states with low voting power, such as Denmark, Finland, Sweden, or the Netherlands. Recalcitrance, however, has difficulty in accounting for the compliance performance of the UK, on the one hand, and

TABLE 3.1   Power, capacity, and politicization (EU-15, 1979–2012)

Power	
Voting power (SSI)	**0.0718****
	(0.00724)
Capacity	
GDP per capita	−0.00395
	(0.00267)
Bureaucratic quality (ICRG)	**−0.0401****
	(0.00464)
Politicization	
Political constraints	0.00310
	(0.00189)
Regional authority	**−0.00755****
	(0.00234)
Parliamentary scrutiny	**0.00646***
	(0.00258)
EU opposition	**−0.0201****
	(0.00288)
Controls	
Intra-EU trade	**0.00762****
	(0.00137)
Net recipient	5.77e-06
	(7.84e-05)
Ministerial approval	0.000898
	(0.00542)
Constant	3.135****
	(0.200)
Observations	440
Number of years	34

Standard errors in parentheses
*** $p < 0.01$, ** $p < 0.05$, * $p < 0.1$

Greece, Belgium, and Portugal, on the other. The latter three have considerably less voting power than the UK but are among the worst compliers. Since voting power makes noncompliance more likely, it does not seem to be relevant at the shaping stage, where it should reduce the likelihood of noncompliance. Likewise, power is about resistance rather than deterrence at the taking stage. If powerful member states deterred the European Commission from opening infringement proceedings, they should face fewer infringement proceedings. My previous work corroborates these findings. It has shown that power enables member states to resist compliance against increasing pressure by EU enforcement authorities rather than deterring them (Börzel, Hofmann, and Panke 2012). Powerful states are able to sit out long and escalating infringement proceedings. Portugal and Denmark tend to cave in to the EU's compliance pressure quickly and at an early stage. Italy, France, and Germany drag their feet and frequently carry their cases to the ECJ. In some instances, they have even defied rulings of the ECJ after being convicted twice—first for violating EU law and then for not acting on the court's original judgment. Should powerful states try to use their power for deterrence, this effect is more than offset by their recalcitrance.

CAPACITY

Capacity bears similar relevance for noncompliance as voting power. Resource endowment measured by *GDP per capita* has the expected negative effect on noncompliance, which, however, is not significant. Greater bureaucratic efficiency brings about fewer violations of EU law. The coefficient for *bureaucratic quality* is negative and significant. This is in line with other studies, which find that the command of resources is less of an issue in the EU, while their efficient use does make a difference (Mbaye 2001; Hille and Knill 2006; Steunenberg 2006; Börzel et al. 2010). Compliance depends on the capacity to mobilize existing resources. This explains why France and Italy, which are among the richest member states of the EU, comply as badly as relatively poor countries like Greece and Portugal.

POLITICIZATION

The findings on politicization are mixed. The *political constraints* coefficient is positive but not significant. If at all, their number increases the chances of noncompliance. So does parliamentary scrutiny (see below). Similar to power, political constraints appear to matter at the taking rather than shaping stage of the compliance game. *Regional authority*, by contrast, is significant but does not have the expected positive sign. The contradicting results could be related to the effect the PCP model would expect regional actors to have at the shaping stage by helping member state governments to reduce compliance costs.

My previous findings on the role of (quasi-) federal states in the implementation of EU law imply that subnational authorities differ from other political constraints, such as coalition parties or supreme courts (Börzel 2001a, 2002b). Federal states, regions, and provinces are invested with executive power, also in unitary and decentralized states where subnational authorities are administrative units (of the central state). Even if they are not formal veto players, their role in the implementation of (EU) legal acts gives them significant potential to distort at least the practical application of EU directives and regulations. In 2016, for instance, several French *régions* and *départements* reintroduced the so-called *clause Molière*, which requires people employed on public transport or building sites where construction is being carried out using public money to speak French. Justified as a security measure, the impositions of the use of French as the working language violates the free movement of workers as one of the four fundamental freedoms enshrined in Article 45 TFEU. Language-based restrictions on access to the labor market for EU citizens are also in noncompliance with the Posted Workers Directive of 1996, whose implementation the French regional actors had no legal power to block.[4]

Member states with subnational authorities that have a strong role in the implementation of EU law have developed institutionalized mechanisms to coordinate their legislative and administrative action. The *conferencias sectoriales* in Spain, the Italian *conferenza stato-regioni*, or the various committees the Belgian regions and German and Austrian *Länder* set up to cooperate on domestic affairs have greatly facilitated the implementation of EU law. At the same time, the vertical coordination mechanisms give subnational authorities an inlet in the shaping of EU law. Federal states even have the right to sit directly at the negotiation table when an EU law affects their exclusive competencies. Where they share authority with the central government, they have a say in the formulation of the national bargaining position. Since they can legally block the transposition of directives in the upper house of the national legislature and undermine their practical application and enforcement, their preferences are likely to be taken into account by the national governments when negotiating the directive at the EU level (Börzel 2002b; Callanan and Tatham 2014; Panara 2015). Member states may also use their regions to tie their hands, which is at least as credible as in the case of the national parliament, where governments usually control the majority (see below). Finally, regional authorities can facilitate the taking of EU law if their preferences have been accommodated at the shaping stage.

The result on the lower house of the national legislatures is in line with the expectations of the PCP model on political constraints. *Parliamentary scrutiny* significantly increases the chances of noncompliance. If national parliaments get a say in the transposition of directives, noncompliance becomes significantly more likely (Haverland, Steunenberg, and van Waarden 2011; Kaeding 2006; Mastenbroek 2003; Steunenberg and Rhinard 2010). As we will see in more detail in chapter 4, parliaments are more likely to get involved at the taking stage when directives are politicized at the EU level.

The negative and significant effect of *public opposition to the EU* on noncompliance corroborates the PCP expectation about governments tying their hands to Eurosceptic publics. British, Swedes, Fins, and Danes are most opposed to the EU but are the least inclined to violate EU law. In the worst compliance laggard, Italy, the EU faces little opposition; in Portugal and Greece the public is still only half as Eurosceptic as in Sweden or the UK.

CONTROLS

Benefits from *intra-EU trade* (Perkins and Neumayer 2007) are statistically significant. However, contrary to theoretical expectations, higher benefits correlate with more rather than less noncompliance (Mbaye 2001; Bergman 2000; Sverdrup 2004; Huelshoff, Sperling, and Hess 2005; Börzel et al. 2010). Trade with the EU may be a crude proxy for the benefits of compliance. Being an EU *net recipient*, however, does not show the expected sign either, nor is it significant. This is not too surprising, as the four so-called cohesion countries of the EU-15, Spain, Greece, Portugal, and Ireland, have benefited the most from EU funds compared to their membership contribution but are among the weaker compliers.[5] The net contributors, by contrast, are top compliers (Denmark, Finland, Netherlands, Sweden, and UK), with the exception of Germany, which ranges in the middle. The misfit between the party preferences of the minister in charge of implementation and the EU legal act has neither the expected sign, nor is it significant. This finding is corroborated by a recent study that assessed member state compliance with regard to the correct application of directives and regulations in four policy sectors (Zhelyazkova, Kaya, and Schrama 2016). *Misfit* is measured at the level of individual legal acts, which are then aggregated at the member state level. *Ministerial approval* reflects party positions that may therefore vary across sectors rather than across member states. This could also explain why *misfit* has explanatory power when it comes to changes in noncompliance over time (see chapter 4).

The findings of the EU-15 model are robust when including five additional years (2013–2017), even though some of the explanatory variables had to be imputed through extrapolation from the latest available value (table A4.1). *Political constraints* and *net recipient* are still positive and now significant. As expected by the PCP model, domestic veto players appear to matter at the taking rather than the shaping stage. Receiving more money from the EU than paying in membership contributions may be an indicator of low capacity to ensure compliance rather than of the benefits of compliance.

Power and capacity together account for a substantial part of the observed variation in member state noncompliance. Politicization needs to be brought in to fully understand why some member states comply less with EU law than others.

The PCP Model at Work: Powerful, Inefficient, and Supportive of the EU

I start with a rather simple specification of the PCP model that works with the one power and the one capacity variable that proved significant in the statistical analysis: voting power and bureaucratic quality.

Voting Power and Bureaucratic Quality

Figure 3.3 places the member states with regard to voting power and bureaucratic quality. I then compare their placement with their noncompliance behavior in relative terms.

The PCP model expects big states, such as France and Italy, whose greater share of votes in the Council makes them less sensitive to enforcement pressure and sanctioning costs, to be in more noncompliance than member states with less voting power (figure 3.3, top versus bottom). Countries with highly efficient bureaucracies, such as Denmark, Finland, the Netherlands, and the United

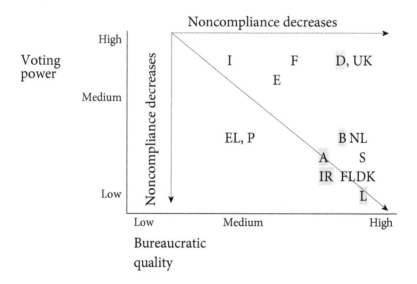

FIGURE 3.3. Power, capacity, and noncompliance in the EU-15

Kingdom, should have a better compliance record than states with lower bureaucratic quality, such as Greece, Portugal, or Spain (figure 3.3, right versus left). The combination of limited capacity and significant power brings together the incapacity to comply and the power to be recalcitrant in the face of looming sanctions. The compliance record of member states should improve as we move from the top left to the bottom right corner of figure 3.3.

Indeed, we see considerable overlap with the actual noncompliance ranking of the EU member states (figure 3.1). Denmark and Italy mark the extremes of the infringement spectrum. Most of the other countries also perform according to where the combined effect of voting power and bureaucratic quality would place them in the noncompliance matrix (figure 3.3). Spain, Greece, and Portugal should infringe more frequently on EU law than Ireland, Luxembourg, Austria, the Netherlands, and the Nordic member states—an expectation supported by the data.

The overall predictive accuracy of power and capacity is remarkable. Combining voting power and bureaucratic quality also accounts for the noncompliance behavior of states that appear to be outliers from the perspective of enforcement and management. While the UK is as powerful as France and Italy, it complies better with EU law thanks to its higher bureaucratic efficiency. Conversely, Greece is one of the least powerful countries in the EU, but almost as bad a complier as powerful Italy. What the two member states share is the lower quality of their bureaucracies compared to Denmark and the United Kingdom.

At the same time, five member states deviate from the expectations of combined power and capacity. They are shaded in gray. Germany's level of noncompliance should be closer to the UK's, given its similar power and capacity. Austria, Belgium, Ireland, and Luxembourg, in contrast, should be in the compliance leader group with the Netherlands and the Nordic countries. They are more noncompliant than their levels of power and capacity would predict. Politicization makes sense of these deviations.

Opposition to the EU and Political Constraints

Germany has voting power and bureaucratic quality similar to those of the UK. In noncompliance, however, it is closer to Spain and France, which are equally powerful (Spain a bit less) but have less efficient bureaucracies. Germany's underperformance compared to the UK is explained by its lower propensity of domestic politicization. Despite the higher number of domestic veto players, the consistent public support for EU membership does not allow the federal government to tie its hands the way the British government was able to do with its Eurosceptic public to reduce compliance costs at the shaping stage. The English, who still control political majorities in the UK, have never joined the "community of Europeans" (cf. Risse 2010), which made the UK the most likely candidate for leaving the EU. The British government usually holds the majority in parliament; it faces neither federal states nor a constitutional court that could veto the incorporation of EU law into domestic structures. Despite the absence of political constraints, it could credibly tie its hand in EU negotiations to a Eurosceptic public that was easily mobilized by Europhobic media and which empowered Eurosceptic members in the House of Commons. In instances where the other member states were not willing to accommodate its policy preferences, such as the euro or Schengen, the UK opted out and ultimately left the Union for good in 2020.

Germany is politically more constrained than the UK. While low opposition to the EU mitigates the effect of political constraints on Germany's ability to shape EU law, domestic veto players undermine Germany's capacity to take EU law. The lower house (Bundestag) and the upper house (Bundesrat), as well as the powerful Federal Constitutional Court (Bundesverfassungsgericht), have resisted or at least delayed compliance with politically controversial EU laws, such as the data retention directive.[6] Because of fierce political opposition in the Bundestag, Germany did not transpose the directive in time. Moreover, the Bundesverfassungsgericht declared parts of the German law transposing the directive as unconstitutional.[7]

Instead of pleading tied hands in order to lower compliance costs, the German government has drawn on the general public support for the EU to cut it slack getting at times costly EU laws passed that later run into opposition of powerful veto players. Germany's persistent noncompliance with the access to information directive is a case in point. The Council adopted the access to information directive by qualified majority in 1990, with Germany being the only member state that voted against. German environmental authorities at the regional and local level have fiercely opposed the directive, fearing administrative overload owing to numerous citizen requests to access documents relevant to the licensing of public and private projects, such as roads, waste dumps, or industrial plants. By contrast, the federal ministry of the environment, headed by Angela Merkel at the time, supported the new policy despite being outvoted in the Council (Börzel 2003a, 124, 128). She went home, washed her hands of responsibility, and hoped to use the general support for the EU to overcome domestic resistance by both houses of the German parliament. Germany's power has allowed it to resist the timely and later the correct transposition of the directive for almost ten years (Börzel 2003a, 123–131). To this day, German citizens do not have the access to environmental information that EU law provides for (De Ville and Siles-Brügge 2016).[8]

The directive on environmental impact assessment (EIA)[9] is another example of Germany resisting compliance with a costly EU law rather than seeking to reduce the costs at the shaping stage. The procedural approach of the directive to assess the potential impact of certain public and private projects on the environment in a cross-sectoral way has strongly contradicted the regulatory structures in Germany, whose media-specific (water, air, soil, etc.) environmental legislation lacked any comparable arrangements. The UK, in contrast, had practiced environmental impact assessments, albeit on a voluntary basis, since the 1970s. Even though the EIA directive was largely in line with its regulatory tradition, the British government raised objections against the original Commission proposal because of concerns that the EIA procedure could empower the courts vis-à-vis public authorities. In over forty meetings of the Council working group on environmental affairs, it successfully negotiated a series of amendments, which, among other issues, reduced the list of projects subject to mandatory environmental impact assessment. The German government, in contrast, did not obtain any concessions that would reduce the need for substantial modifications of its environmental legislation and administrative practice. Instead, the German parliament delayed the transposition of the directive for more than two years. Then transposition was still incomplete. After the Commission had taken the issue to the ECJ twice, Germany finally enacted the required legal changes in 2001— fourteen years after the directive had entered into force (Börzel 2003a, 123–131, 107–115, cf. Knill 2001).

The other four outliers lack Germany's power to resist compliance. Belgium combines high bureaucratic quality with limited voting power. It should be less noncompliant than France and Spain and be closer to the Netherlands and Sweden. What distinguishes Belgium from the two smaller states is its high degree of territorial decentralization, which constrains its autonomy. Belgium is the most decentralized member state in the EU. The federal and the regional level are each responsible for implementing EU laws that fall within their respective jurisdictions, and the regions jealously guard their competencies against any interference by the federal government (Bursens 2002, 188), as the case of the Comprehensive Economic and Trade Agreement (CETA) with Canada forcefully demonstrated. In 2016, the small Belgian region of Wallonia almost blocked the signing of the agreement, which the EU and Canada had negotiated for more than seven years. Regional veto power notwithstanding, the findings of my analysis indicate that strong regional authority leads, if it leads at all, to *less* noncompliance. The veto power of regional authorities may allow the Belgian government to tie its hands at the shaping stage, at least for issues of high domestic salience (see below). However, subnational authorities have become involved in the shaping of EU law to facilitate the implementation at the taking stage (Hartlapp 2009; Jensen 2007; Bursens and Geeraerts 2006; Falkner et al. 2005; Bursens 2002; Börzel 2002b, 224–226).

What constrains Belgium politically in complying with EU law are its coalition governments. Belgium has numerous political parties, which are strictly organized along community lines—there are no national parties. Linguistic divisions between Flemish-speaking Flanders in the north and francophone Wallonia in the south have been exacerbated by the political and economic polarization between these two regions. Regionalist parties must always work together to form a federal government. In 2014 and 2019, coalition negotiations left Belgium for months without a government. With next to the highest political constraints among all member states, the country is plagued by political instability and weak central government. The literature blames Belgium's poor compliance performance on the prioritization of domestic concerns over EU obligations (Falkner, Hartlapp, and Treib 2007, 405) or "a lack of European awareness" (Bursens 2002, 189). Belgian politicians, civil servants, and public opinion, more broadly speaking, highly support the EU but simply take no interest in EU policies, making compliance with EU law "at best one goal among many" (Hartlapp 2009, 484). Similar to the situation in Germany, the low salience of EU law limits the ability of the Belgian government to reduce compliance costs at the shaping stage. At the same time, low salience reduces the chances of compliance costs to be coped with at the taking stage. Once an EU directive incurs high costs that are publicly visible and concern politically sensitive issues, Belgium's political constraints provide domestic opposition the opportunity to block or delay compliance (Falkner, Hartlapp, and Treib 2007, 409).

Ireland, Luxembourg, and Austria have still less power than Belgium to resist compliance. Compliance research on these three member states is even scarcer than on Belgium. The three countries are as small as Sweden, Finland, or Denmark but comply worse. While Austria and Luxembourg score high on bureaucratic quality, Ireland, some argue, suffers from problems similar to those of the Southern European member states, including clientelism and corruption (Siedentopf and Hauschild 1988; Laffan 1989; Coyle 1994). Together with Greece, Portugal, and Spain, Ireland once belonged to the EU's so-called cohesion countries, with a gross national income per inhabitant lower than 90 percent of the EU average. Yet Ireland experienced a period of rapid real economic growth since the first half of the 1990s, before it was hit by the banking crisis in 2008. During that time, the bureaucratic quality of the Irish administration increased significantly, reaching the levels of Germany, Denmark, and Finland (Charron, Dijkstra, and Lapuente 2010). More recent work has therefore attributed noncompliance problems to politicization rather than lacking bureaucratic quality (Laffan and O'Mahony 2008; Falkner et al. 2005). For instance, Irish farmers and landowners fiercely opposed the implementation of the so-called habitat directive, "push[ing] the issue up the political agenda and ensur[ing] that it would receive considerable attention in parliament, the media and from senior political figures" (Laffan and O'Mahony 2008, 184). The transposition of the directive was severely delayed and has been incomplete and incorrect. Its practical application is at best selective. The implementation of the access to environmental information directive, in contrast, has been rather smooth in the absence of domestic politicization (Bugdahn 2005). Yet, like Belgium, Ireland is a member state where domestic opposition to the EU is low. Rather than focusing on sporadic cases of highly politicized directives, the PCP model attributes Ireland's mediocre compliance record to the lack of shaping power, along with "a culture of neglect" (Falkner et al. 2005, 339). Being a poor shaper of EU law, it does not dedicate the resources necessary to ensure compliance with EU law, either.

No shaping power and low salience may also explain Luxembourg's underperformance. Luxembourg is by far the smallest member state, with the highest public support for the EU and equally high bureaucratic quality. Noncompliance therefore appears to be a question of neglect to mobilize existing resources rather than the incapacity to do so (Falkner et al. 2005, 302; Falkner, Hartlapp, and Treib 2007, 407).

Austria, finally, shares with Belgium, Luxembourg, and Ireland the capacity to implement EU law and the limited power to resist compliance pressures. Yet Austrian citizens are almost as nonsupportive of the EU as are the British. This has frequently resulted in domestic conflicts over EU laws, leading to serious compliance problems (Falkner et al. 2005, 271, 333). The negative effect of politicization on Austria's noncompliance is amplified by the highest level of parliamentary involvement in the transposition of directives among all member states (König and Luetgert 2009). Parliamentary debates on how to transpose an EU directive into national law raise public awareness and provide an arena for domestic interests to voice their opposition to anticipated compliance costs. The question remains, however, why the Austrian government has apparently not used the high propensity of politicization to tie its hands and shape EU law to make it less costly. It seems to be the only member state in which EU opposition (and Euroscepticism more broadly) increase domestic awareness and public visibility of EU law, making domestic conflict likelier, as expected—but without increasing the government's shaping power, as a result of which we see more rather than less noncompliance.

All other Eurosceptic member states are among the top compliers. In the UK, Sweden, Finland, and Denmark,[10] EU opposition is significantly above EU average, and noncompliance is the lowest. Luxembourg, Belgium, and Ireland are in the opposite group, belonging to the least Eurosceptic member states, which display significantly worse noncompliance records. Given the similar bureaucratic quality and voting power of Austria, Luxembourg, Belgium, Ireland, Sweden,

Finland, Denmark, and the Netherlands, and no systematic differences in political constraints, Euroscepticism appears to be the driver for their diverging noncompliance patterns.

The PCP model is able to account for the finding of Eurosceptic member states being less noncompliant. Legitimacy expects the opposite: lower support for the rule-setting institutions should result in more noncompliance, not less. The literature may be able to explain why Europhile Luxembourg, Belgium, and Ireland comply worse than more Eurosceptic Finland and Sweden. Compliance laggards could show greater support than compliance leaders for the EU because citizens give the EU credit for compensating the weak capacities of their state in providing public goods and services (cf. Sánchez-Cuenca 2000). This does not explain, however, why compliance leaders oppose the EU whose laws they so diligently obey. The Eurosceptic member states have sufficient capacity to comply with EU law. Rather than being a side-product of capacity, the negative correlation between EU opposition and noncompliance suggests an indirect effect of the former on the latter, which works through the power to shape EU policies as proposed by the PCP model. Member state governments with a Eurosceptic home constituency are in a better position to bargain for EU laws that entail lower compliance costs. Instead of a permissive consensus, they face a "constraining dissensus" (Hooghe and Marks 2009), which limits the range of EU policy outcomes acceptable back home. Whether governments use the possibility to tie their hands to a Eurosceptic public is a different matter, which may explain why Eurosceptic Austria complies worse than Finland or Sweden. Likewise, tying hands is not the only bargaining strategy of small states to shape EU policies (Panke 2010a; Börzel 2002a). EU-supportive Netherlands is very effective in writing policy drafts for the European Commission and brokering compromises among the member states, often punching above its weight (Liefferink and Andersen 1998; Kronsell 2002). It might therefore comply equally well with EU law as more Eurosceptic Finland and Sweden. Finally, member state governments that have to deal with Eurosceptic publics among their electorates are less likely to cut slack in achieving policies at the EU level that would not get adopted domestically.

In sum, the outliers of the combination of voting power and bureaucratic quality are best captured by politicization. Eurosceptic publics enhance the ability of small states to shape EU law according to their preferences, reducing compliance costs. This explains why Europhile Belgium, Ireland, and Luxembourg comply worse than more Eurosceptic Sweden or Finland, although they have similar capacities to comply with EU law and equally limited power to resist compliance costs. The more effective shaping of EU law can also account for the different compliance behavior of two member states with equal voting power and bureaucratic quality. Germany and the UK both have the capacity to take compliance costs, as well as the power to resist them. The UK was a much more effective shaper of EU law than Germany (Börzel 2002a), even though it is less politically constrained. Rather than veto players, the higher risk of politicization gave the UK greater bargaining leverage. Costly and publicly visible EU laws are more likely to mobilize domestic opposition. The UK faced lower compliance costs and had less cause to be recalcitrant. At the same time, Germany has more opportunities for cutting slack, which, however, may backfire if the implementation of an EU legal acts becomes politicized and mobilizes various institutional veto players.

Politicization can make noncompliance both more and less likely. The paradox is resolved by an interlinked but differential effect of politicization on the two stages of EU policy making. At the taking stage, politicization increases the likelihood that governments prefer noncompliance, particularly if they face powerful domestic veto players in the implementation process. At the shaping stage, member state governments facing greater risks of domestic opposition in implementation have the power to shape EU legal acts so that they incur lower compliance costs.

Traveling East

While the analysis so far has been confined to the fifteen long-standing member states, the PCP model also accounts for the rather good performance of the ten CEE countries that joined in 2004 and 2007. A comparison of the annual reasoned opinions of new member states relative to the mean of old member states during the first ten years of membership confirms once again that the CEE newcomers outperform most of the old member states (figure 3.2; cf. Börzel and Sedelmeier 2017; Börzel and Buzogány 2019). The newcomers transpose EU directives even before the deadline. Moreover, efficient transposition does not come at the price of weak practical implementation (Zhelyazkova, Kaya, and Schrama 2017). While the new member states lose their edge further down the implementation chain, they do not lag behind the older member states when it comes to practical application. The new member states do not generally constitute a "world of dead letters," except for the area of social policy that Falkner and colleagues examined (Falkner, Treib, and Holzleitner 2008).

At the same time, there is significant variation. Poland and, to a lesser extent, the Czech Republic are on their way to joining the compliance laggards. The other new member states are firmly in the leaders' camp. Top CEE laggard Poland resembles Spain, having considerable voting power, while its bureaucratic quality is weak. The Czech Republic has less voting power and accordingly is not as noncompliant as Poland. The eastern compliance leaders, in contrast, appear to perform much better than the combination of power and capacity would expect (figure 3.4, shaded in gray). Their power is small, but their capacity is as low or, in the case of Romania and Bulgaria, even lower than Greece's. Nevertheless, their noncompliance rates match those of the Netherlands, Finland, or Sweden (figure 1.3 in chapter 1). The reason for the counterintuitive performance of most of the eastern new member states lies in the specific capacity that they built for implementing EU law during the accession process.

According to the so-called *acquis conditionality*, the candidate countries had to incorporate large parts of the existing EU legislation into their domestic laws and put administrative procedures in place that would ensure effective application and enforcement. This was accomplished through administrative coordination mechanisms established during the accession process, which centralized the adoption of the *acquis* in the hands of the core executive and gave parliaments little voice. Moreover, the accession process helped build the bureaucratic quality of candidate countries to get EU laws on the books, which was a priority of the Commission (Hille and Knill 2006; Dimitrova and Toshkov 2009; Steunenberg and Dimitrova 2007; Sedelmeier 2008; Toshkov 2008; Zubek 2005; Zubek 2011; Börzel and Sedelmeier 2017). The EU provided candidate countries with substantive financial and technical assistance. Moreover, the inefficiency of postcommunist bureaucracies led the executives to centralize the policy process for

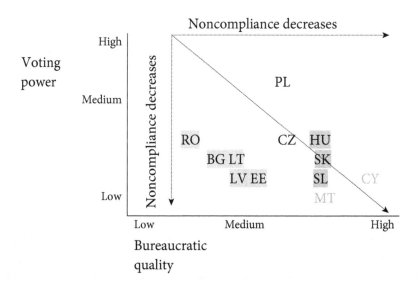

FIGURE 3.4. Power, capacity, and noncompliance in the new member states (EU-10+2)*

* Malta and Cyprus are not part of the Central and Eastern European newcomers.

the implementation of EU law and to use fast-track procedures to bypass parliament and shield themselves against other political constraints (Sadurski 2006). The new centralized procedures allowed the tracking of EU-related legislative commitments, to monitor progress and to review the quality of transposition (Zubek 2011). They entailed "sophisticated EU co-ordination mechanisms which often included levels of co-ordination and political attention unseen in the 'older' member states" (Dimitrova and Toshkov 2009, 2; cf. Dimitrova and Toshkov 2007). These "islands of excellence" (Goetz 2001) are as efficient in coordinating the taking of EU policies as the more general administrative coordination mechanisms in old member states with overall high bureaucratic quality (Verheijen 2007).

The use of pre-accession conditionality and pre-accession assistance toward the new members to improve their bureaucratic quality explains why they perform better than the Southern Europeans despite the generally low capacity in these countries. In other words, the capacity of the newcomers to comply with EU law is higher than their generally low bureaucratic quality suggests (Goetz 2001; Verheijen 2007, 25–27; Sedelmeier 2008, 20–21). The establishment of narrower and specific capacities for the implementation of EU law is not captured by general capacity indicators. At the same time, similar bureaucratic quality and voting power explain why the performance of most of the CEE is closer to the compliance leaders of the EU-15, and why Poland's performance as the only middle power among the newcomers deviates from the overall good compliance record of the others, closing in with Spain, with its similar voting power and bureaucratic quality (figure 1.3 in chapter 1).

Finally, pre-accession conditionality may also explain why support for European integration appears to be negatively related to noncompliance. Unlike in the EU-15, Europhile new members comply better, not worse, with EU law. First, pre-accession conditionality made them exclusive takers of the vast majority of EU law. When they joined, the newcomers had to have on the books the entire body of EU law that was in force at the time of their accession. Afterward, they continued to be takers, given the EU's tendency to amended existing legislation rather than adopt new laws (see chapter 4). Second, greater public support for EU membership propelled pro-EU governments into power, which were willing and empowered to pool resources and centralize procedures as to ensure the swift implementation of EU law to prove themselves as trustworthy members (Perkins and Neumayer 2007; Toshkov 2008; Sedelmeier 2008; Börzel and Sedelmeier 2017). The eagerness to improve bureaucratic quality in areas related to EU law shows above all in transposition, where centralized mechanisms are particularly effective in ensuring that legal implementation of EU law is timely. The effect begins to wear off in practical implementation, which is more decentralized. Yet public support for the EU makes politicization of compliance costs less likely. This explains why the new member states lose their cutting edge in practical implementation, without, however, performing worse than the old member states (Zhelyazkova, Kaya, and Schrama 2016, 2017).

After accession, many pro-EU governments were swept out of power and replaced by right-wing populist forces with Eurosceptic leaders, such as Viktor Orbán in Hungary and the Kaszyński brothers in Poland (Taggart and Szczerbiak 2004; Houghton 2014). Yet public support for the EU has remained stable, even in Hungary and Poland. This may suggest that people did not necessarily vote for right-wing populist parties primarily because they are Eurosceptic.

Evaluating the relevance of the PCP model for the enlarged EU is still tricky. The period of membership is rather short, particularly for Romania and Bulgaria, which only joined in 2007. They are therefore excluded. Moreover, a number of independent variables lack data, including EU intra-trade, ministerial approval, and parliamentary scrutiny, which had to be dropped. The results for the remaining variables, however, are still interesting.

The principal components of the PCP model are robust (table 3.2). Voting power, bureaucratic quality, and opposition to the EU show the same effect on noncompliance as in the EU-15. Political constraints have the same positive effect, which is significant now. Regional authority changes the sign but is not significant. The results for net recipient and GDP per capita also differ between the EU-25 and the EU-15. Both are now statistically significant. GDP per capita turns positive, while net recipient has no substantial impact. These changes may be explained by the homogeneity of the EU-15 with regard to the three variables. Once we control for old versus new members by introducing a highly significant EU-15 dummy, the results of the EU-15 and EU-25 model converge. Net recipient and GDP per capita lose significance, and the latter turns negative. Regional authority returns to be negative but remains insignificant. Only four of the ten CEE newcomers have substantial levels of regional authority, of which two, the Czech Republic and Poland, comply below average. These two member states are the only ones with democratically elected regional governments (Loughlin, Hendriks, and Lidström 2012). Moreover, the level of involvement of subnational authorities in EU policy making still has to catch up with the old member states (Panara 2015; Baun and Marek 2008; Bruszt 2008; Scherpereel 2007). Political constraints, finally, has a positive effect on noncompliance, which is highly significant. This is unlikely to be related to the accession of ten new member states, which do not systematically differ from the EU-15 by exhibiting stronger political constraints. I suspect it is a spurious correlation. For lack of data, I could not include intra-EU trade—which is highly significant in the EU-15 model—in the EU-25 model. If I take intra-EU trade out of the EU-15 model,

TABLE 3.2 Power, capacity, and politicization (EU-25, 1979–2012)

	(1)	(2)
Power		
Voting power (SSI)	0.0613***	0.0560***
	(0.00628)	(0.00609)
Capacity		
GDP per capita	0.0105***	−0.000448
	(0.00201)	(0.00268)
Bureaucratic quality (ICRG)	−0.0347***	−0.0296***
	(0.00461)	(0.00440)
Politicization		
Political constraints	0.00444**	0.00541***
	(0.00177)	(0.00172)
Regional authority	0.00239	−0.00325
	(0.00219)	(0.00222)
EU opposition	−0.0172***	−0.0214***
	(0.00290)	(0.00283)
Controls		
Net recipient	0.000192**	0.0000871
	(7.48e-05)	(7.43e-05)
EU-15		0.645***
		(0.101)
Constant	2.324***	2.170***
	(0.185)	(0.183)
Observations	520	520
Number of years	34	34

Standard errors in parentheses
*** $p < 0.01$, ** $p < 0.05$, * $p < 0.1$

political constraints turn significant. The observation that the effect of political constraints turns strongly significant only when controlling for intra-EU trade may suggest that political constraints pick up some of the variation left unexplained by not including intra-EU trade. The two variables correlate significantly (table A2.1).

In sum, the core variables of the PCP model show robust results. Voting power, bureaucratic quality, and EU opposition have the expected effect on noncompliance in both the EU-15 and the enlarged EU-25. They also stand the robustness check with updated models, which include five more years (2017) but have to rely on imputed values for certain variables for the lack of data (tables A4.1 and A4.2). The positive effect of political constraints appears to depend on whether we control for intra-EU trade. In the most recent model for the EU-27, political constraints are highly significant, even though intra-EU trade could not be included (table A4.2). While I can only speculate at this point, the PCP model would expect domestic veto players to gain in importance owing to the growing politicization of the EU, particularly in the EU-15.

Noncompliance research has focused on explaining why states do not comply with legal acts they have agreed on in the first place. The findings of this chapter confirm that power and capacity matter but need to be combined with politicization to account for why some states comply less than others. Moreover, we have to disentangle specific variants of the three principal components of the PCP model whose relevance differs depending on the stage of the compliance game. Thanks to their voting power in the Council, member states are able to resist compliance costs at the taking stage rather than to reduce costs at the shaping stage. At the shaping stage, in turn, politicization matters, as Euroscepticism allows governments to tie their hands and negotiate for EU laws closer to their policy preferences. Veto players, in contrast, impair the ability of governments to take EU law and its costs, making noncompliance more likely. Capacity, finally, matters for both stages. However, it is efficiency in mobilizing existing resources, and not resource endowment, that increases the ability of member states to shape and take EU law.

By bringing politicization into the equation, the PCP model explains why countries with rather high bureaucratic quality and similar voting power vary in their noncompliance with EU law, depending on how much their publics support or oppose the EU. Belgian, Irish, or Luxembourgian citizens, who are generally supportive of the EU, tend to take little or at best selective interest in EU law. Low salience results in noncompliance, because existing capacity is not used in the implementation of EU law. Eurosceptic publics, in contrast, are likely to be more aware of and mobilize against the EU and its policies, giving their governments greater leverage in negotiating less costly laws. Politicization as driven by Euroscepticism allows us to account for the consistent but counterintuitive finding that higher EU support increases the chances of member state noncompliance.

Overall, Euroscepticism has not increased in the member states over the past forty-five years. But politicization is not only driven by Eurosceptic publics. With the expansion of the EU's political authority, the media has become more receptive of EU affairs, and Eurosceptic parties have used the various crises the EU has faced since 2005 to mobilize EU opposition in national elections and referenda (De Wilde and Zürn 2012; Risse 2015b; De Wilde, Leupold, and Schmidtke 2016; Hutter, Grande, and Kriesi 2016). Interestingly though, the growing awareness of, mobilization around, and polarization of the EU and its policies in the member states have neither undermined public support for the EU as such nor resulted in more noncompliance with EU law, as we will see in the next chapter. The exceptions are EU budgetary rules and asylum and migration laws. EU budgetary rules are not subject to infringement proceedings but rely on their own monitoring and enforcement regime in the euro zone. So do violations of the fundamental values of the EU codified in treaty articles, which so far have been confined to

Hungary and Poland. Asylum and migration, however, are part of JAIN, which subsequently moved from intergovernmental coordination under the third pillar of the Maastricht Treaty to supranational decision making applying to most areas of the Internal Market (the former first pillar; cf. Börzel 2005, 2010). As we will see in chapter 5, JAIN is the policy sector where noncompliance is most pronounced.

WHY THERE IS NO GROWING NONCOMPLIANCE

This chapter solves the puzzle of why noncompliance has decreased rather than increased ever since the EU deepened and broadened its political authority and widened its membership. The PCP model argues that conditions for noncompliance today are different from what they were forty years ago because the nature of EU law has changed. EU institutions have made noncompliance less costly. The first part presents a dynamic analysis of the extent to which the PCP factors that reduce compliance costs and their politicization have changed over time and whether these changes correspond to the decline in noncompliance we observe since the 1990s. Because of the limited number of years covered by the analysis, I mostly rely on descriptive data to show that the increasing adoption of amending and delegated legislation since the completion of the Internal Market is inversely related to the decreasing numbers of infringements. In the second part, I use a static statistical analysis to test whether time-sensitive PCP variables have a significant effect on noncompliance. The results confirm that amending and delegated legislation, which is less prone to politicization since it reduces parliamentary involvement, renders noncompliance less likely. The third part zooms in on the ten most infringed directives to corroborate that issue- or legal-act-specific PCP variables have a major influence on the chances of noncompliance. The chapter concludes by discussing the broader implications of these findings. Depoliticization through delegation has helped reduce noncompliance. However, this has come at a price—the marginalization of parliaments results in "policy without politics" (V. Schmidt 2006). To put it differently, the depoliticization of EU policies exacerbates the democratic deficit of the EU and contributes to the politicization of the EU as a polity by nationalist populist forces.

The Iceberg Is Melting

EU scholars and policy makers alike have claimed that the EU suffers from a growing compliance problem, which they believe to be systemic or pathological to the EU (Krislov, Ehlermann, and Weiler 1986; Weiler 1988; Snyder 1993; Mendrinou 1996; Tallberg 2003; Cremona 2012; Commission of the European Communities 2011). They base their assessment on the increasing number of infringement proceedings the European Commission has been opening against member states for violating EU law (figure 4.1). The year 2004 saw a record high of more than nineteen hundred letters of formal notice sent to the member

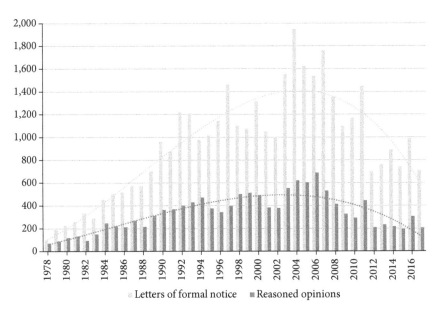

FIGURE 4.1. Letters of formal notice and reasoned opinions, absolute numbers, 1978–2017

Source: Own compilation, with data from the Berlin Infringement Database. The annual number of reasoned opinions was aggregated from the data set by year of the infringement proceeding (YearIN). The number of letters of formal notice sent per year can be directly retrieved from the European Commission's Annual Reports on Monitoring the Application of EU Law (for years 1978–2010) or from the online database on the Commission's infringement decisions (for years 2011–2017).

states. This was four times more than what they had received twenty years before. Yet these numbers have to be put into context. Strictly speaking, infringement proceedings do not allow us to draw any valid conclusion about whether the EU has a compliance problem (see chapter 1). At the same time, the evidence we have gives us no reason to be pessimistic. The European community of law appears to be working quite well. Overall, less than 20 percent of the 14,132 laws that entered into force in the EU until 2012 have received at least one reasoned opinion. The vast majority of these infringements refer to around eighteen hundred directives. The more than twelve thousand regulations that make up for the bulk of EU law that member states have to comply with are hardly violated (less than 2 percent). This is not to deny that infringements depict only "the tip of the iceberg" (Hartlapp and Falkner 2009). Rather, we have no means to measure how large the iceberg really is. We should be careful to make any statements about its absolute size.

What the data allows us to do is to assess whether the visible part of the iceberg has changed its size over time. Simply comparing the number of infringement proceedings across time does not say much about changes in the level of noncompliance in the EU. Infringement numbers have to be measured against the number of legal acts that can be potentially infringed on, as well as the number of member states that can potentially infringe on them. The amount of legal acts in force has increased almost four times since 1978. Nineteen more member states have joined the EU that can potentially violate them. If we control for violative opportunities (see chapter 1), noncompliance in the EU had steadily increased before it started to decline in the early 1990s (figure 1.4 in chapter 1). Since 2005, the decline is even visible without controlling for the multiplication of violative opportunities. Moreover, the time trend does not depend on the measurement. It also shows with letters of formal notice (figure 4.1).

The trend of increasing noncompliance with EU law reversed in the early 1990s—despite an exponential increase in EU laws to be complied with and the accession of three more states that could violate them (Austria, Finland, and Sweden). After 1994, the number of infringements is inversely related to the violative opportunities—despite the "big bang" enlargement of 2004/2007, which almost doubled the number of member states.

Research on noncompliance in the EU has been quite insensitive to time. Researchers have been predominantly interested in why member states do not comply with EU law or why some are less compliant than others. They tend to start from the assumption that the EU is facing a compliance problem and seek to explain why that is. The member states are considered as the main source of non-compliance. Eastern enlargement triggered a debate as to whether the accession of twelve new member states, with their limited capacity to cope with costs, has exacerbated the EU's noncompliance problems (Sedelmeier 2008, 2012; Falkner, Treib, and Holzleitner 2008)—which chapter 3 finds no evidence for. Whether there is a time effect independent of changes in membership has not been systematically explored.

Explaining Noncompliance over Time

Member state variation in noncompliance is rather stable over time. So are key factors that affect states' ability to shape and take compliance costs (see chapter 3). Accordingly, the PCP model would expect noncompliance to decline over time when compliance costs are decreasing and are less likely to become politicized at the shaping stage because of changes in EU decision-making rules or in the nature of EU law. At the taking stage, more effective EU enforcement and management, respectively, should make member states less likely to violate EU law because they face higher noncompliance costs and receive assistance in coping with the costs.

Shaping Compliance Costs: EU Decision-Making Rules and the Nature of EU Law

MORE SUPRANATIONAL DECISION MAKING: QUALIFIED MAJORITY AND CO-DECISION

Supranational decision making mitigates the ability of member states to shape compliance costs by depriving them of their individual veto power. The Single European Act of 1986 systematically introduced QMV in the Council and started to elevate the European Parliament (EP) from a consultative to a real decision-making body. Subsequent treaty reforms extended supranational decision making in the EU. Since 2010, QMV is the default decision rule under the ordinary legislative procedure. Moreover, the introduction of the co-decision procedure has made the EP an equal co-legislator with the Council, which has absolute veto over any legislative proposal. Member states increasingly have to accept EU laws that do not correspond to their preferred outcome because they have to compromise twice—once in the Council, and then with the EP. The literature has found that directives adopted under co-decision are indeed more frequently violated than directives adopted by the Council or the Commission only (König and Luetgert 2009; Luetgert and Dannwolf 2009; Börzel and Knoll 2013). Finally, the case law of the ECJ can increase compliance costs even after the Council and the EP passed an EU law (Schmidt and Kelemen 2014; S. Schmidt 2018). Through the preliminary ruling procedure, societal and economic actors seek to extend their rights under EU law, to which the ECJ has often responded positively in its ruling. As we will see in chapter 5, some of the most infringed directives have been shaped by ECJ case law.

Yet, overall, noncompliance has decreased despite the extension of QMV in the Council, co-decision with the EP, and case law of the ECJ. In fact, the supra-nationalization of EU decision making, which rendered member states less able to shape compliance costs, on the one hand, and the declining noncompliance with EU law, on the other hand, appear to be opposite trends.

MORE FLEXIBILITY: DIFFERENTIATED INTEGRATION

In a community of law, members are subject to uniform legal obligations. By widening its membership, however, the EU has become increasingly more diverse. Differentiated integration is a major instrument to achieve the flexibility to make "unity in diversity"[1] work (Kölliker 2005; Leuffen, Schimmelfennig, and Rittberger 2013).

Differentiated integration has been used since 1958, when the Treaty of Rome came into force. It took off with the Maastricht Treaty in 1993. Some member states started to become more reluctant to deepen and broaden European integration by extending majority voting in the area of the Internal Market, centralizing monetary policy, and extending EU competencies into internal and external security. The most prominent form of differentiated integration is the so-called opt-outs. They allow member states that oppose EU law by blocking its adoption at the shaping stage, or by not complying with it at the taking stage, to stay behind when others move toward deeper (vertical) and broader (horizontal) integration. The loosening of integration for member states objecting to costly or politically controversial EU law could have helped bring down noncompliance.

EU institutions have indeed responded to the progressive deepening, broadening, and widening of the EU. Differentiated integration became a major tool to mitigate the conflict between the majority of member states supporting further integration and the more reluctant Europeans. The overall share of treaty articles with provisions on differentiated integration has steadily increased after it had jumped up with the Maastricht Treaty establishing the euro as the common currency and the Schengen Agreement on free travel entering into force (figure 4.2). Differentiation of primary or treaty law was pushed again by eastern enlargement and climbed to an all-time high of 43 percent with the Lisbon Treaty and the euro crisis (cf. Schimmelfennig and Winzen 2014, 2017).

At the level of secondary law, rules that exempt member states from their obligations to comply with EU legal acts (almost exclusively directives) also increased over the years and peaked in the early 2000s. Their share in the legislation in force, however, has been decreasing over time, from 17 percent in 1958 to only

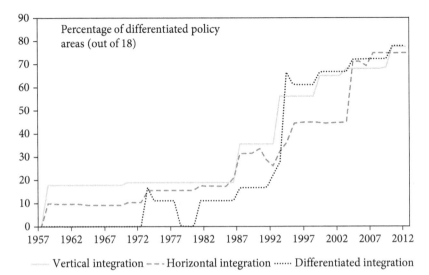

FIGURE 4.2. Deepening, widening, and loosening
Source: Graph provided by Katharina Holzinger and Frank Schimmelfennig from their project "Differentiated Integration in the European Union" (2012), https://www.research-collection.ethz.ch/handle/20.500.11850/47890, last accessed 2 May 2020.

1 percent in 2012. Less than 10 percent of all legal acts in force, mostly directives, contain opt-out clauses that have been used by at least one member state. There are four peaks, in the early 1970s, early 1990s, the late 1990s, and the mid-2000s (figure 4.2). They are the result of temporary exemptions granted to new member states that joined in these periods—the UK, Denmark, and Ireland in 1973 (northern enlargement); Eastern Germany in 1990 (German unification); Austria, Finland, and Sweden in 1995 (EFTA enlargement); and the ten post-communist countries in 2004 and 2007 (eastern enlargement), respectively (cf. Schimmelfennig and Winzen 2014, 2017).

Only the use of differentiated integration in the EU's primary law has increased over the years. Opt-outs from EU treaty changes took off after the Maastricht Treaty when noncompliance started to decline. Yet the member states have not made use of more than 12 percent of the opt-out opportunities granted by the EU treaties in any given year (Schimmelfennig and Winzen 2014). Most of these opt-outs are temporary—that is, are terminated by member states opting in (Sion-Tzidkiyahu 2012). This is particularly the case for differentiation originating from enlargement. New member states want to end discrimination, which old member states managed to impose on them. As part of the accession negotiations, differentiated integration was introduced to delay economic and financial losses the newcomers might incur on the old member states when they have to open up their labor markets or redistribute EU funds. Old member states have an interest in terminating those temporary exemptions, which the EU granted to newcomers to help them adapt to market pressures and further build up their capacities to comply with EU regulatory standards (Schimmelfennig and Winzen 2014). Each enlargement round resulted in a rise of differentiated integration. Most of the opt-outs, however, phased out ten to fifteen years after accession, with the number of exemptions for the newcomers converging with those of the old member states. Only the UK, Denmark, and Ireland have continued to obtain opt-outs. For the CEE countries, it is still too early to tell, but the number of exceptions granted to the newcomers is only slightly above for the old member states (Schimmelfennig and Winzen 2017), with the exception of the UK, Denmark, and Ireland, of course. Differentiated integration obtained in the revisions of the EU treaties, by contrast, tends to be long-term or even permanent, since it is to buy out member states that object to a deepening or broadening of integration. While the majority of the member states move forward—for example with the euro as the common currency, the Schengen border-free zone, or the fiscal compact—opponents can stay behind.

In sum, differentiated integration is likely to have contributed to the fact that noncompliance has not increased after enlargements of the EU. Exemptions for newcomers helped ease their compliance costs. Such easing is only temporary, though. The exceptions are Denmark, the UK, and Ireland, which, however, obtained most of their current opt-outs as part of treaty revisions that introduced the euro and the Schengen zone. Moreover, fiscal policy is not subject to infringement proceedings; the euro zone has its own monitoring and sanctioning regime. Finally, Denmark, the UK, and Ireland opted in on a fair amount of JAIN legislation. Opt-outs, therefore, hardly account for the overall trend in declining noncompliance. Nor do they explain the exemplary compliance record of the UK and Denmark as they outperform the other member states in policy sectors of which they have not opted out.

LESS COMPLEXITY: REGULATIONS

Complexity is a major cost factor. The more complex EU law is, the more compliance requires legal and administrative measures to enact new and adopt existing national legislation at the domestic level and the more actors need to be involved to bring about the necessary institutional and behavioral changes (Mastenbroek 2003; Kaeding 2006; Thomson 2007; Haverland and Romeijn 2007; Steunenberg and Kaeding 2009; Steunenberg and Rhinard 2010).

Complexity substantially varies between regulations and directives as the two main forms of secondary EU law. As framework legislation, directives require legal adoption at the domestic level. Incorporating a directive into national law may involve between forty and three hundred legislative measures at the national level, ranging from statutory law, government decrees, to ministerial orders.[2] Depending on the legal system of the member states, governments need the approval of their national parliaments (Steunenberg 2006). This offers national parliaments the opportunity to block or delay compliance that does not exist for regulations making noncompliance with directives considerably more likely (Dimitrova and Steunenberg 2000; Steunenberg 2006; Kaeding 2006; Jensen 2007; König 2007; König and Luetgert 2009; Haverland, Steunenberg, and van Waarden 2011; Angelova, Dannwolf, and König 2012).

Directives are more complex and more prone to noncompliance than regulations. The EU has always used more regulations than directives. In 1992, the ratio between the two was still 4:1, lower than what it used to be in 1982. In 2012, however, regulations outnumbered directives already by 5:1; three years later, it was almost 7:1. The number of legal acts in force has increased almost four times since 1978, spanning virtually all policy sectors in which member states have been legislating. After the turn of the millennium, this expansion of EU law appears to be largely driven by the growing adoption of regulations, which account for more than 87 percent of the legislation in force (figure 4.3).

The increasing adoption of regulations relative to directives is linked to the completion of the Internal Market (Ciavarini Azzi 2000). In 1985, the Delors Commission published a white paper identifying three hundred measures to

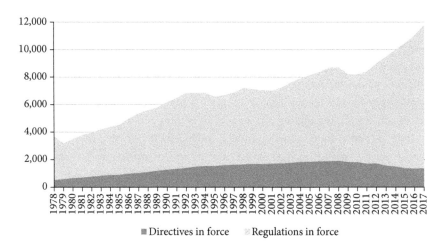

FIGURE 4.3. Legislation in force, 1978–2017; regulations and directives compared
Source: Statistics on directives and regulations in force as provided by the EUR-Lex Helpdesk.
Note: Because of continuous inconsistencies in the online database EUR-Lex with regard to "legislation in force" per year, data on "incoming" and "outgoing" directives and regulations was retrieved directly from the EUR-Lex Helpdesk on request on 11 April 2019.

complete the Internal Market by 31 December 1992. The Single European Act (Article 100a EEC Treaty) provided the legal basis for the adoption of these measures by qualified majority. The prohibitions of discriminatory behavior and other restrictive practices by the member states and the approximation of their laws and standards were issued as directives. The use of such framework legislation corresponded to the approach of the Delors Commission to avoid exhaustive harmonization (cf. Pelkmans and Winters 1988). After the Internal Market had been official launched on 1 January 1993, the EU continued to increase its use of regulations to put the Internal Market into practice. While their numbers more than doubled since 1993, the growth of directives in force has been more modest and even started to recede in 2008.

The rising numbers of less complex regulations after the completion of the Internal Market correspond to the decline in noncompliance, which started in the mid-1990s. Regulations account for only around 18 percent of the infringement proceedings reaching the official stage (reasoned opinions). More than 60 percent of directives have been infringed at least once. For regulations, it is less than 2 percent. The relative share of regulations and directives in the legislation in force is inversely related to their relative share in the infringements (compare figures 4.3 and 4.4).

Yet, a closer look at the data reveals that the declining trend of noncompliance has been largely driven by decreasing infringements of directives (figure 4.4). Noncompliance with regulations has always been substantially lower in comparison to directives. Violations of directives (tov_1, tov_2 + 3) had reached their highest peak in 1994, before their numbers plummeted quite substantially, shortly peaked again at a lower level in 2001 and then 2006, before they returned to a steady decline (figures 4.4 and 4.5). Distinguishing between different types of violations also reveals that infringement dynamics are largely driven by one particular type of violation of directives, namely delayed and incomplete transposition into national law (figure 4.5). Delayed or incomplete transpositions (tov_1) account for more than half of all official infringements of EU law. The higher noncompliance with directives should not be too surprising, as transposition provides domestic veto players with a formidable opportunity to block or at least substantially delay the coming into force of costly EU law and to water down costly provisions by not fully or not correctly transposing them into national law.

A final factor related to complexity that according to the PCP model renders directives more prone to noncompliance is time. Member states often have difficulty in meeting implementation deadlines because of strong domestic opposition or the lack of necessary resources to adapt their legislation to complex EU laws (Ciavarini Azzi 2000; Mastenbroek 2003; Thomson 2007; Haverland, Steunenberg, and van Waarden 2011; Kaeding 2008; König and Luetgert 2009;

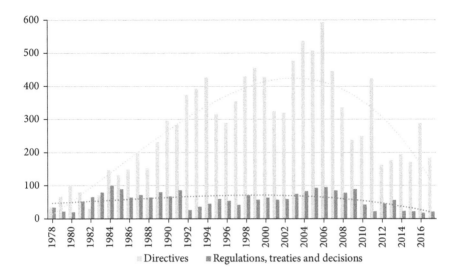

FIGURE 4.4.   Reasoned opinions by directives and regulations, 1978–2017
Source: Own compilation, with data from the Berlin Infringement Database. The number
of reasoned opinions per year was counted according to the year when the infringement
proceeding was launched (YearIN).
Note: Figure 4.4 combines data on regulations, treaty articles, and decisions. While
the aggregate data in the Annual Reports does not permit a breakdown of infringement
proceedings according to type of legal act, the Berlin Infringement Database distinguishes
between violations of directives, on the one hand, and regulations, treaty articles, and
decisions, on the other. Given that the current Treaty of the European Union contains
less than 350 articles, and the number of decisions is equally limited, their number is
negligible at this point.

Luetgert and Dannwolf 2009; Steunenberg and Kaeding 2009; Steunenberg and
Rhinard 2010).

In sum, if the EU has had a noncompliance problem, it has been with the
transposition of directives into national law. Their need for transposition renders
directives more complex than regulations. What explains the decline in noncompliance with directives is a change in their nature.

LESS NOVELTY: AMENDING LEGISLATION

The PCP model would expect the more effective transposition of directives to
be related to decreasing compliance costs. One major cost-reducing factor at
the shaping stage is that the EU has increasingly amended existing directives
rather than setting new ones. This is indeed what we can observe (figure 4.6).
The completion of the Internal Market reduced the need for new legislation
(see above). Moreover, the rise of subsidiarity (Nugent 2016) and the shift of

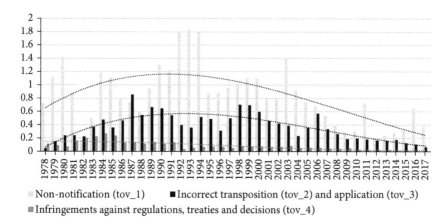

Non-notification (tov_1)   ■ Incorrect transposition (tov_2) and application (tov_3)
■ Infringements against regulations, treaties and decisions (tov_4)

FIGURE 4.5. Reasoned opinions according to types of violation and relative to violative opportunities, 1978–2017
Source: Own compilation, with data from the Berlin Infringement Database. The number of reasoned opinions per year was counted according to the year when the infringement proceeding was launched.

the policy agenda toward more politicized issues related to the extent to which the completed Internal Market should be regulated (Hix 2008) made it increasingly difficult for the Commission to table proposals for entirely new legislation. Amendments fill regulatory voids left in the original directive, specify general regulations, or update regulatory standards. They are rather technical in nature and incur lower costs on the member states because of the lower misfit. Member states have to adjust already existing legislation rather than create new laws (Knill 1998; Haverland, Steunenberg, and van Waarden 2011). The causal relevance of misfit is contested in the compliance literature (see, e.g., Duina 1997; Börzel and Risse 2003; critical: Falkner et al. 2004; Haverland 2000). Amending directives, however, are less likely to give rise to delayed transposition than are directives that enact new stipulations (Mastenbroek 2003; Kaeding 2006; Haverland and Romeijn 2007; Haverland, Steunenberg, and van Waarden 2011; Steunenberg and Rhinard 2010; König and Luetgert 2009; Luetgert and Dannwolf 2009).

MORE DELEGATION: COMMISSION DIRECTIVES

While amending directives reduce compliance costs according to the PCP model, delegation makes their politicization less likely. Politically sensitive and visible EU legal acts carry a higher probability of noncompliance, as domestic actors are more likely to mobilize against compliance costs (Kaeding 2006; Falkner, Hartlapp, and Treib 2007; Versluis 2007; Steunenberg and Kaeding 2009; Dimitrova and Toshkov 2009). A means for the Council and the Commission to avoid

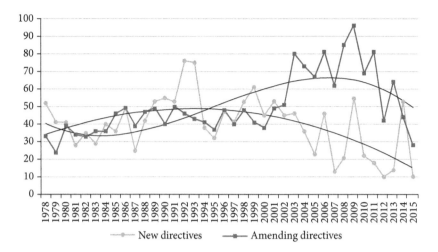

FIGURE 4.6. Adoption of amending directives versus new directives, 1978–2015
Source: Own compilation, using data obtained from the data set compiled by Dimiter
Toshkov, "Legislative Production in the EU, 1967–2012," http://www.dimiter.eu/Data.html,
last accessed 23 March 2014 and updated with EUR-Lex.

politicization is to delegate the adoption of directives to the Commission (Bergström, Farrell, and Héritier 2007).

Delegated acts involve the further elaboration or updating of standards and
technical issues of an existing legislative act (Héritier et al. 2013). The legal act
must delegate to the Commission the power to "supplement or amend certain
non-essential elements of the legislative act" (Article 290 TFEU). It has to specify
the objective, content, scope, and duration of delegation (Kaeding and Hardacre
2013). Before the entering into force of the Lisbon Treaty in 2009, delegated acts
used to be passed through the so-called comitology procedure, which involved
committees consisting of member state representatives with voting power and
the Commission, which set the agenda and chaired the committee meetings
(Blom-Hansen 2011). The Commission drafted an act and sent it to the com-
petent comitology committee for review. If approved by a qualified majority,
the act was adopted as a Commission directive. If the Commission's proposal
was rejected, the Commission could amend its original proposal or submit it
to an appeals committee to negotiate a compromise. Decision making in these
trans-governmental networks took place behind closed doors and was in stark
contrast to the adoption of directives by the Council and the EP or by the Council
only, where the EP is still involved. The EP was informed since it had the right
to comment on whether a draft exceeded the implementing powers of the Commission. Unlike with the ordinary legislative procedure, however, the EP had no

power to amend or reject the directive. The Lisbon Treaty abolished the comitology procedure for delegated acts, reducing the power of the member states to revoking the delegation or canceling the legal act altogether. The option has to be explicitly laid down in the legal act that authorizes delegation. The Lisbon Treaty also elevated the role of the EP, since it now shares these powers with the Council. Both can either revoke or cancel. Overall, however, the autonomy of the Commission in adopting delegated acts has been strengthened "to the greatest extent" (Héritier, Moury, and Granat 2016, 117), since the rights of objection or revocation of the two co-legislators are only ex post—that is, after the Commission adopted the delegated legal act.

Implementing acts include measures to ensure the uniform application of EU legal acts. Their adoption by the Commission is based on the implementing powers that legal acts delegate to the Commission (Article 291 TFEU). Unlike with delegated acts, the member states remain involved in decision making through the comitology (see above). As with executive acts, the EP only has to be informed. Not surprisingly, since 2010, the vast majority of Commission directives have taken the form of implementing acts, which are preferred by both the Commission and the member states, since they minimize the role of the EP (Héritier, Moury, and Granat 2016).

The literature finds that member states violate directives delegated to the Commission far less frequently than Council directives or directives jointly adopted by Council and EP under co-decision (Mastenbroek 2003; Kaeding 2006; Borghetto, Franchino, and Giannetti 2006; Steunenberg and Rhinard 2010; König and Luetgert 2009; Luetgert and Dannwolf 2009; Haverland, Steunenberg, and van Waarden 2011). Until the Treaty of Maastricht introduced the co-decision procedure, which established the EP as a co-legislator, we can observe a steady growth of Commission and Council directives (figure 4.7). After the Maastricht Treaty entered into force in 1993, Council directives were rapidly replaced by co-decision directives, whose relative share started to decline, though, while the relative share of Commission directives continued to rise. The increasing adoption of Commission directives since 1994 is related to the completion of the Internal Market. Once the legal framework had been put in place, its technical specification was done by regulations (see above) and more detailed directives, whose adoption was delegated to the Commission. This also explains why almost 50 percent of Commission directives are amending legislation.

To conclude, both EU decision-making rules and the nature of EU law have changed substantially since the completion of the Internal Market in the mid-1990s. The expansion of QMV in the Council and of the co-decision powers of the European Parliament should have resulted in more, not less noncompliance, though. The growing use of differentiated integration has provided member

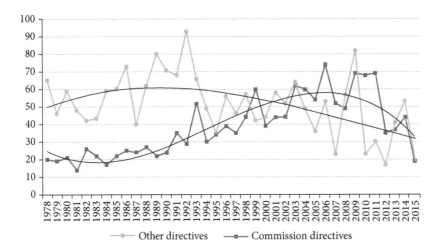

FIGURE 4.7. Adoption of Commission directives compared to other directives, 1978–2015

Source: Own compilation, using data obtained from the data set compiled by Dimiter Toshkov, "Legislative Production in the EU, 1967–2012," http://www.dimiter.eu/Data.html, last accessed 23 March 2014 and updated using EUR-Lex.

states with more flexibility, but only temporally. Changes in the nature of EU law, in contrast, closely correspond to the decline of noncompliance. While noncompliance remains confined to directives, these have become less costly over time by being less novel and less complex. Moreover, the adoption of amending directives has been increasingly delegated to the Commission, which has made compliance costs less prone to be politicized.

Taking Compliance Costs: EU Enforcement and Management

EU ENFORCEMENT: BETTER MONITORING AND TOUGHER SANCTIONING

According to the PCP model, the declining trend in noncompliance could be (also) driven by higher *non*compliance costs due to more-effective monitoring and sanctioning by EU institutions.[3]

In order to detect violations of EU law, the Commission follows a "two-track approach" (Tallberg 2002, 616). With regard to the transposition of directives, Commission officials systematically collect and assess data through in-house monitoring (centralized "police patrol supervision," Tallberg 2002, 610; cf. Jensen 2007). Monitoring whether EU law is properly applied and enforced within the member states is more difficult. The Commission carries out its own investigations (Steunenberg 2010). Since it has no central investigation unit, it is up to the DGs to set up such units, and many DGs have done so. Their investigation units maintain numerous contacts with national implementation authorities, NGOs, consultancies, researchers, and corporations in the member states. Cases of noncompliance that Commission officials have found on their own initiative are reported to the legal service of the Commission's Secretariat General. Occasionally, they send out inspectors to visit a member state. However, such on-the-spot checks are labor intensive, tend to be time consuming, politically fraught, and can be blocked by member states. Therefore, the Commission heavily relies on monitoring by external actors (decentralized "fire-alarm supervision," Tallberg 2002, 610; Hobolth and Sindbjerg Martinsen 2013).

The most important sources of information are complaints lodged by citizens, firms, and public interest groups. The threshold for lodging a complaint is extremely low, since the complainant does not have to prove a personal interest in the case and simply has to download a form from the Commission's website. *Petitions* may also be sent to the European Parliament and the European ombudsperson. Similar to national parliaments questioning their executives, the EP has the right to send parliamentary questions to the Commission regarding member state violations of EU law. The Maastricht Treaty established an ombudsperson who holds the power to investigate an EU institution on the grounds of maladministration.

Complaints, petitions, and parliamentary questions are complemented by decentralized surveillance instruments, such as SOLVIT and EU Pilot, which rely on national authorities. They are to help detect and redress compliance problems in the member states as an alternative to resorting to infringement proceedings. Finally, the obligation of the member states to notify the Commission about the transposition of directives into national law provides the Commission with an indirect monitoring mechanism. Noncommunication of transposition after the deadline expires results automatically in the sending of a letter of formal notice, the preliminary stage of the infringement proceedings (see chapter 1).

The Commission publishes data on the different sources of monitoring information in the Annual Infringement Reports as "suspected infringements."[4] The consistency and availability of information on suspected infringements vary significantly, though.[5] Between 1988 and 2010, the Commission launched two hundred to three hundred own investigations per year—with the exception of the late 1980s, where the numbers were three times as high, probably due to the intensified effort of the Commission to enforce EU law to complete the Internal Market. The numbers increased again after eastern enlargement but quickly returned to previous levels and have been dropping to an overall low in 2010. This may be related to the introduction of SOLVIT and EU Pilot, which provide the Commission with information on potential cases of noncompliance, reducing the need for launching own investigations (see below).

Complaints steadily increased until the early 1990s, then started to drop but rose again in the mid-1990s to an overall high in 2004. Afterward, numbers have continuously declined, particularly after 2004. This, again, may be due to SOLVIT and EU Pilot (Koops 2011, 180–181). Both offer alternative venues for business, societal organizations, and citizens to articulate their grievances about noncompliance.

Parliamentary questions and petitions have been more limited overall, but also peaked around the completion of the Internal Market and the Maastricht Treaty in the first half of the 1990s. Parliamentary questions and petitions briefly flared up in 1991, probably related to the completion of the Internal Market, and again around eastern enlargement (2002–2004). Ever since, they have declined.

SOLVIT and EU Pilot are designed to assist the Commission in detecting noncompliance (Heidbreder 2014). At the same time, they help redress compliance problems without resorting to infringement proceedings. SOLVIT and EU Pilot provide informal, low-cost dispute settlement mechanisms for the improper application of directives that are intended to prevent serious violations in the first place. As management tools, they will be analyzed in more detail below. SOLVIT was established in 2002 as a network of national help desks (SOLVIT centers) located at the national authority in charge of the application of EU law. It is to assist citizens and business complaining about the improper application of Internal Market directives.[6] Complaints are lodged online and handled by the member state authorities through the Internal Market Information System (IMI). IMI is an IT-based network launched in 2008 that links public bodies and allows public administrations at the national, regional, and local level to identify their counterparts in other countries and exchange information with them.[7] The basic idea of SOLVIT is that the member state responsible for the grievances shall try to work out a redress within ten weeks. If it fails to do so, the Commission considers opening an infringement proceeding (Hobolth and Sindbjerg Martinsen 2013; Koops 2011). EU Pilot, created in 2008, complements SOLVIT by applying to directives outside the Internal Market.[8] Unlike SOLVIT, however, the Commission directly interacts with the member state and the complainant. The Commission enters a complaint or inquiry into an interactive database (EU pilot database). The EU pilot contact point of the member state concerned, which is tasked to ensure coordination between the various domestic authorities and Commission services, has ten weeks to report back on how it intends to remedy the issue. The Commission notifies the complainant of the proposed solution, and if it does not hear back within four weeks, it considers the case as settled.

Noncommunication patterns are more diverse and appear to be driven by enlargement effects. Numbers were high in 1996, after Austria, Finland, and Sweden had joined, skyrocketed in 2004 after the EU had admitted ten new members, and peaked once more in 2007 when Bulgaria and Romania joined.

In sum, monitoring information fluctuates considerably over time. There is no linear upward or downward trend in own investigations, complaints, petitions, parliamentary questions, and noncommunication, which would match the overall decline in infringements.

What we are likely to observe instead is an information effect, similar to what has been discussed in the human rights literature: when monitors look harder and in more places, they tend to find more human rights abuses, which, however, is not necessarily an indication of a worsened human rights situation (Clark and Sikkink 2013; Fariss 2014). Thus, the more information the Commission obtains and the more efficient it is in processing this information, the more likely it is that it opens a higher number of infringement proceedings. These information effects, however, are only temporary. The numbers of opened infringement proceedings shot up for the first time in 1984, after the Commission published its First Annual Report. With the very first systematic compilation of data on member state noncompliance, the numbers almost doubled in this year. They peaked again in 1992–93, 2004, and 2007, years around which complaints and own investigations were high. The numbers in 1997 were propelled by a reform the Commission had implemented in 1996 to speed up the opening of infringement proceedings. The "intended meaning" of the formal letters was restated as the mere "requests for observations" rather than warnings of the Commission.[9] Avoiding any accusations, letters of formal notice were to be issued more rapidly than before. In a similar vein, the Commission changed its reporting methods in April 2004, arguably to make them more efficient.[10] Since then, it reports the noncommunication not only of "Directives applicable on the reference date (not repealed)," but of all "Directives whose deadline for implementation has passed by the reference date," irrespective of whether they are still in force. This change temporally inflated the numbers of noncommunication, which had already gone up because of ten new member states joining.

Information effects coincide with a growth of infringement numbers until the first half of the 1990s. They cannot account for the downward trend we observe when we control for violative opportunities, however (figure 1.4). This clearly indicates that the rise in absolute numbers (figure 4.1) has been driven by the growing body of EU laws and the rising numbers of member states that can violate them. If there was still a systematic information effect, the relative numbers of infringement proceedings should be even smaller.

When it comes to sanctioning, the Commission started to pursue a more aggressive enforcement strategy in the late 1980s, in order to ensure the effective implementation of the Internal Market program (Tallberg 2002). At the same time, it focused its efforts on the three Southern European countries that had joined in the first half of the 1980s once the period of grace, which the Commission grants new member states, had expired (Börzel 2001b). In the case of Greece, the Commission started to initiate proceedings two years after accession; for Spain and Portugal, the Commission waited up to four years. Because of these combined effects, both absolute and relative infringement numbers went up. As we saw in chapter 3, Spain, Portugal, and Greece are the only newcomers that have continuously violated more EU laws than older member states.

The Maastricht Treaty introduced the possibility of imposing financial sanctions on member states that failed to comply with judgments of the ECJ (see chapter 1).[11] The financial penalty does not only incur monetary noncompliance costs. Sanctioning rulings of the ECJ receive broader coverage in the public media. Such naming and shaming involves reputational costs, particularly for member states whose publics are supportive of European integration. Article 260 became effective in 1993, just when infringement numbers relative to violative opportunities had started to decline. The ECJ invoked Article 260 for the first time in 2000,[12] in a procedure the Commission had started against Greece in 1997 for not taking measures against the disposal of toxic and dangerous waste into the Kouroupitos, a river in Crete. It is questionable whether the mere anticipation of financial sanctions started to bring infringements down seven years before the member states learned that the ECJ was prepared to impose them.[13]

In 2009, the Lisbon Treaty abolished the three pillars of the EU, which the Maastricht Treaty had introduced to fence off the newly created JAIN and Common Foreign & Security Policy from the reach of supranational institutions. As a result, JAIN became fully subject to infringement proceedings. Yet this has had no effect on the declining trend—even though JAIN has become one of the most noncompliant sectors (see chapter 5). The Lisbon Treaty also simplified and accelerated the procedure for imposing financial penalties. Article 260 (2) of the Lisbon Treaty removed the necessity for the Commission to send a reasoned opinion before asking the ECJ to impose a financial penalty for noncompliance with its ruling to redress a violation of EU law. This may speed up the sanctioning procedure by between eight to eighteen months.[14] Article 260 (3) also introduced a fast-track procedure allowing the Commission to ask the ECJ to impose financial sanctions without initiating another procedure under Article 258 if a member state has not notified the transposition of a directive. It is too early to tell whether this will further propel the decline in noncompliance.

The Internal Market Scoreboard, established in 1997,[15] provides another naming and shaming mechanism. Twice a year, it reports on the performance and progress of member states in implementing Internal Market directives. The statistics convey information on all types of infringements: delayed, incomplete, and incorrect transposition, as well as improper application. The scoreboard allows for a direct comparison of member state performance. It is to "promote peer pressure between the member states by creating a forum of mutual monitoring of efforts to apply European legislation" (Commission of the European Communities 2002, 5). The worst performers are put on the spot, not only among fellow governments but also in the public media (Tallberg 2002, 63). However, the Internal Market Scoreboard, at best, reinforced the downward trend of noncompliance, particularly since it applies only to infringements related to Internal Market directives. Cases of delayed or incomplete transposition in this sector had already dropped before 1997 and started to rise in 1998 until they reached overall highs in 2004 and 2007 (figure 4.8). Cases of incorrect transposition (tov_2) are harder to trace because of changes in the reporting method. Since the annual report of 2004, the proceedings no longer allow differentiation between incomplete and incorrect transposition (tov_2) and incorrect application (tov_3). I therefore aggregated the tov_2 and tov_3 cases for the years from 1988, the first year for which complete data is available on all three types of violation, until

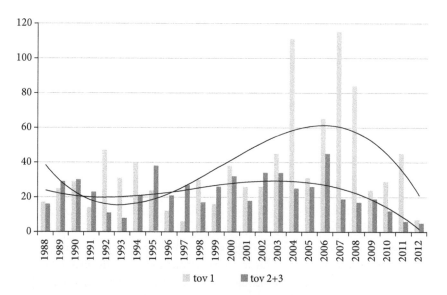

FIGURE 4.8.   Official infringements for non-notification, nonconformity, and improper application of Internal Market directives, 1988–2012
Source: Own compilation, with data from the Berlin Infringement Database.

2005, the year after the change in reporting methods (for reasoned opinions, the effect shows only after two years). From 2006 on, I took the aggregate numbers reported in the annual reports.[16] Cases of incomplete and incorrect transposition and incorrect application of directives reached a high in 1995. Then they dropped but climbed up again until they reached their overall high in 2006 before they entered into a steady decline. These roller-coaster dynamics are unlikely to have been driven by the introduction of the Internal Market Scoreboard.

Finally, the literature has argued that the preliminary ruling procedure provides the EU with a decentralized enforcement mechanism that relies on "fire alarm" rather than "police patrol." Instead of the European Commission, national courts enforce the rights citizens and companies enjoy under EU law (Tallberg 2002; Conant 2002; S. Schmidt 2018; Hofmann 2019). This includes the possibility to award damages to individuals who suffered from member state noncompliance under the principle of state liability the ECJ introduced in 1991 (Tallberg 2000b; cf. Craig 1993, 1997). The decline in infringement proceedings could be the result of the Commission increasingly relying on decentralized enforcement through courts (Hofmann 2018, 2019). The total number of preliminary rulings has indeed risen continuously. However, once we control for the number of member states in a given year, preliminary rulings started to grow substantially only in 2010, the year in which the Lisbon Treaty came into force and made JAIN subject to the jurisdiction of the ECJ (figure 4.9). Citizen rights have become

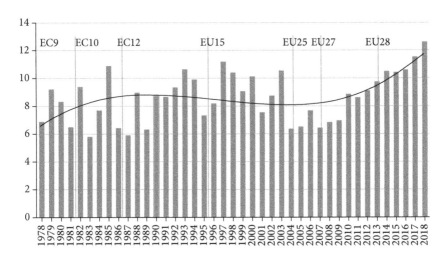

FIGURE 4.9. Annual average number of preliminary rulings per member state, 1978–2018

Source: Own compilation, with data from the online database EUR-Lex, https://eur-lex.europa.eu/legal-content/EN/TXT/?uri=LEGISSUM%3Al14552; last accessed 2 May 2020.

a key target for litigation and judicial lawmaking (Schenk and Schmidt 2018; S. Schmidt 2018). As argued in chapter 1, preliminary ruling procedures appear to be driven by judicial activism rather than enforcement.

In sum, the EU has responded to the growing body of EU law and the increasing number of member states through a series of reforms meant to strengthen its ability to monitor compliance and sanction noncompliance. If these efforts had been effective, infringement numbers should have remained stable or dropped when controlling for the growth in EU law and in membership, because member states are more likely to face noncompliance costs. Both letters of formal notice and reasoned opinions in relation to the violative opportunities in a given year have clearly declined over the years (figure 4.1). Yet the downward trend does not follow the oscillating flow of monitoring information available to the Commission. Nor does it correspond to the timing of the strengthening of the EU's sanctioning mechanisms through legal and administrative reforms or a possible shift from centralized to decentralized monitoring and enforcement.

EU MANAGEMENT: CONTRACTING
AND CAPACITY BUILDING

Besides increasing noncompliance costs, the PCP model expects EU institutions to help member states cope with compliance costs at the taking stage through contracting and capacity building.

Poor drafting of EU law can result in imprecision, open texture, and ambiguous objectives, granting the member states considerable leeway in interpreting and applying European legislation. This may lead to diverging understandings between the Commission and the member states of what constitutes (non)compliance with European law. The Commission installed a series of mechanisms of consultation and negotiation (contracting) to weed out cases caused by legal uncertainty and misunderstandings.

The Commission frequently adopts communications and other measures to provide the member states with guidelines on how to interpret EU directives and regulations. They are soft law, as they are not legally binding. Recommendations, resolutions, guidelines, action plans, or white and green papers substitute for hard law if the EU lacks the competence to adopt hard law and the member states are unable to agree on adopting a directive or regulation. Such "steering" soft law aims at realizing the same objectives as EU hard law but entails no legal obligations (Senden 2004), so noncompliance is not an issue. Or soft law complements hard law by fostering its effective and uniform implementation, for instance through guidelines on how to implement and enforce hard law (Scholten 2017; Maggetti and Gilardi 2014; Falkner et al. 2005). Guidelines, informational notices, and compliance templates help member states avoid noncompliance arising from problems of legal uncertainty and misinterpretations. Either way, the increasing use of soft law should reduce noncompliance.

The share of soft law rose from 9 percent in 2000 to 40 percent in 2007. The vast majority of these measures are Commission communications and information notices that inform the European Parliament about the progress of member states in the application of EU law and provide the member states with guidelines on implementing EU law, particularly in the field of state aid policy (Zhelyazkova et al. 2015; cf. Blauberger 2009b). Overall, the use of soft law has increased since 2000 but has been too selective, too concentrated in a few policy areas, to explain the trend of declining noncompliance. More importantly, the downturn in violations of EU hard law had set in already in the second half of the 1990s.

The SOLVIT network and the EU Pilot centers do not only work as decentralized monitoring instruments. They also provide an informal, low-cost dispute settlement mechanism for the improper application of directives. Since the inception of SOLVIT in 2002, the caseload has increased from 285 in that first year to 2,228 in 2015.[17] Over the past years, SOLVIT has managed to solve more than 80 percent of the cases submitted (Hobolth and Sindbjerg Martinsen 2013, 1417).[18] It is hard to tell whether the successful resolution of compliance problems through SOLVIT has resulted in a decline of infringement proceedings. The Commission does not provide data on letters of formal notice by sector, year, and type of violation. Moreover, as already mentioned, in 2003, the Commission collapsed cases of incorrect transposition (tov_2) and incorrect application (tov_3). The overall number of letters sent based on complaints went down after SOLVIT had been introduced. SOLVIT is intended to provide an alternative venue for citizens and companies to seek redress for violations of EU law that affect their rights and interests (Koops 2011, 180). However, the aggregate number of reasoned opinions for both types of violations of Internal Market directives has not declined since the introduction of SOLVIT in 2002 (figure 4.8). They oscillate around 150 per year.

EU Pilot, though similar to SOLVIT, has worked for cases outside Internal Market law. The Commission has processed more than two-thirds of the files submitted for these cases (Commission of the European Communities 2014, 10). Since EU Pilot was introduced only in 2008, it is too early to tell whether it has helped reduce problems of improper application of directives outside the Internal Market. Moreover, only fifteen of the twenty-seven member states initially participated; the others joined a year later. Like SOLVIT, EU Pilot initially saw its workload increase over the years; in 2013, about 1,500 new files were opened. Two years later, however, the numbers went down to 881.[19] Complaint-based infringement proceedings dropped sharply after 2008 (Koops 2011, 30). Yet it is unclear whether this is related to the introduction of EU Pilot

(Koops 2011, 181–184). The Commission ceased publishing data on the source of infringements in 2010.

In sum, EU institutions have developed a series of what management approaches refer to as contracting instruments. Yet, these instruments were introduced and took effect after noncompliance had started to decline in the mid-1990s.

Capacity building through EU funds, funding programs, and trans-governmental networks has increased over time. The volume of EU Structural Funds and the Cohesion Fund has subsequently expanded. The funds still account for the largest part of the EU budget. Likewise, sector-specific funding programs have multiplied.[20] For example, the Action for the Protection of the Environment in the Mediterranean Region (MEDSPA), the Regional Action Programme on the Initiative of the Commission Concerning the Environment (ENVIREG), or the Financial Instrument for the Environment (LIFE), provide funding to assist member states in complying with EU environmental legislation (cf. Börzel 2003b). Finally, the EU established pre-accession funding schemes in the eastern enlargement process. The tailor-made capacity-building programs of PHARE (Poland and Hungary: Aid for Restructuring of the Economies), ISPA (Instrument for Structural Policies for Pre-Accession), and SAPARD (Special Accession Program for Agricultural and Rural Development) supplied the CEE candidate countries with significant financial and technical assistance (cf. Sissenich 2007, 54–57). Technical assistance was also channeled through twinning programs and TAIEX, the EU's Technical Assistance Information Exchange Office. Member state experts assist candidate states in developing the legal and administrative structures required to effectively implement selected parts of EU legislation. Civil servants who have specific knowledge in implementing certain EU policies are delegated to work inside the ministries and government agencies of the accession countries, usually for one or two years (Dimitrova 2005).

Trans-governmental networks and EU agencies have expanded, too. In the European administrative space, administrators from the EU, national, and local levels exchange best practices and negotiate guidelines for the application of EU law (Heidbreder 2011; Trondal 2010; Egeberg 2008; Hobolth and Sindbjerg Martinsen 2013). In 1992, the Sutherland Report recommended that the EU develop a more cooperative approach to the enforcement of Internal Market legislation.[21] Ten years later, *European Governance: A White Paper* restated the importance of networks for more effective and inclusive governance of the Internal Market (Commission of the European Communities 2001). The Commission has encouraged the formation of trans-governmental networks to help solve noncompliance problems at the "decentral" level and to promote the uniform application of EU law throughout the member states. Prominent examples include the European Competition Network (ECN), the European Regulators Group (ERG), the Consumer Safety Network (CSN), the Consumer Protection Cooperation Network (CPC), the Product Safety Enforcement Forum of Europe (Prosafe), the European Union Network for the Implementation and Enforcement of Environmental Law (IMPEL), and the European Safety Assessment of Foreign Aircraft Steering Group (ESSG) (cf. Dehousse 1997; Coen and Thatcher 2008; Yesilkagit 2011; Hobolth and Sindbjerg Martinsen 2013; Scholten 2017). Such networks are part of the "New Strategy for the Single Market,"[22] which Mario Monti proposed in 2010 to make the implementation of existing regulations more effective. Acknowledging the importance of administrative capacity, the Commission has made horizontal administration coordination almost a policy goal in its own right (Heidbreder 2014, 7). Besides SOLVIT and EU Pilot, the IMI, an IT-based information network that links up national, regional, and local authorities across borders, fosters transborder communication and cooperation, strengthening the capacities of member state administrations to execute EU law.

Finally, the Commission has pushed the creation of EU agencies carrying out technical, scientific, and managerial tasks in the implementation of EU law in different policy sectors, to "improve the way rules are applied and enforced across the Union" (Commission of the European Communities 2001, 24; cf. Kaeding and Versluis 2014; Scholten 2017). Their number has more than tripled since 2002 (Scholten 2017; Kaeding and Versluis 2014). Similar to trans-governmental networks, EU agencies formulate implementation guidelines, monitor implementation activities of national authorities, and provide training for them (Gehring and Krapohl 2007; Egeberg and Trondal 2009; Groenleer, Kaeding, and Versluis 2010; Versluis and Tarr 2013). For instance, the European Chemicals Agency is in charge of the technical, scientific, and administrative aspects of the implementation of the EU's Regulation on Registration, Evaluation, Authorisation and Restriction of Chemicals (REACH). Its Forum of Exchange of Information on Enforcement (FEIE) coordinates a trans-governmental network of member state authorities responsible for developing enforcement strategies and identifying best practices.[23] Other examples include the European Medicines Agency, the European Fisheries Control Agency, the European Markets and Securities Authority, and the Anti-Fraud Office (OLAF), all of which assist the Commission and the member states in the implementation of EU law and also have direct enforcement powers.

The effects of increased EU financial and technical assistance are hard to quantify. Correlating euros and administrators with reasoned opinions not only fails to produce significant results; it does not make much sense either, since funds, networks, and agencies are sector specific or even issue specific and rarely serve merely the purpose of helping member states cope with compliance costs. Country studies provide ample evidence of how EU capacity building and the

EU's insistence on good governance, particularly the fight against corruption, have helped accession countries and (new) member states improve their compliance with EU law. Pre- and post-accession financial instruments and twinning programs have played a major role in improving bureaucratic quality in the new member states and may explain why eastern enlargement has not exacerbated the EU's compliance problems (Dimitrova 2002; Grabbe 2003; Schimmelfennig and Sedelmeier 2004; Leiber 2007; Börzel 2009a). It is less obvious how funds, networks, and agencies that were established since the turn of the millennium should have brought down infringements of directives in the old member states. The more effective transposition of directives drives the downward trend that started before the enlargement rounds of 1995, 2004, and 2007.

In sum, improvements in the ability of EU institutions to impose noncompliance costs on the member states, on the one hand, and help them cope with compliance costs, on the other, cannot explain the overall secular trend of declining noncompliance in the EU. Descriptive data and narrative evidence suggest that changes in the nature of EU law account for the decline in noncompliance. The trend is driven by a more effective transposition of directives, which have become less complex, less novel, and less likely to be politicized. Since complexity, novelty, and politicization, or lack thereof, are properties of legal acts, we can test their significance for noncompliance in a statistical analysis that correlates these properties with infringements. First, however, I will briefly discuss social constructivist factors that could have helped bring down noncompliance.

EU Legitimacy: Socialization and EU Support

The social constructivist compliance literature has focused on two sources of legitimacy, which could explain a decline in noncompliance in the EU: First, through processes of *socialization*, EU law is increasingly internalized into the domestic legal systems of the member states, and compliance becomes habitual for and taken for granted by domestic actors. Second, domestic actors are pulled into compliance by the increasing *parliamentary involvement* in EU policy making or their growing *support* for EU law and the EU as the law-making institution.

SOCIALIZATION

Socialization into EU law takes time, which could explain why noncompliance only started to decline later in the European integration process. Duration of membership should matter, then. The longer a state has been a member of the EU, the more its policy makers and administrators should have internalized the EU legal system and learned how to deal with it (Checkel 2001; Berglund, Grange, and van Waarden 2006; Dimitrakopoulos 2001). As a country-specific variable, socialization over time does not seem to affect noncompliance. The most recent newcomers comply on average better than the founding members (see chapter 3). A systemic effect, however, could emerge from a substantial widening of European integration by accepting groups of new members. Joining the EU transforms states into member states (Sbragia 1994; Bickerton 2012), which comply as a habit of obedience once they have internalized EU law. Compliance with EU law is taken for granted and constitutes a value in itself (Hurrell 1995, 59). Particularly the acceptance of twelve new member states in 2004/2007 should have resulted in a temporary increase of noncompliance because of the need to socialize them into EU law. The opposite is the case, though. Southern enlargement is the only enlargement round that systematically increased noncompliance in the EU (Börzel and Sedelmeier 2017; cf. chapter 3).

PARLIAMENTARY INVOLVEMENT AND EU SUPPORT

Procedural and institutional legitimacy promote voluntary compliance. Right and fair decision-making processes depend on the inclusion of those affected by the decision. The taking of EU law involves a variety of domestic actors, which cannot possibly all be involved at the shaping stage. The member states' executive authorities are represented by their national governments and at least partly involved through administrative networks that help prepare and negotiate EU proposals at the supranational and the national level (Kassim et al. 2000, 2001). The issue is parliamentary involvement. More democratic accountability should result in higher acceptance of EU laws (Schimmelfennig 2010) and therefore less noncompliance.

Parliaments have been increasingly empowered in the shaping and taking of EU law, both at the EU and the national level. Until 1987, the Council was free to consult the EP on the passing of EU legislation. In 1980, the ECJ ruled that the EP had to be heard on EU legislation.[24] While its opinion was not binding, the EP could use its power to delay giving a formal opinion (Kardasheva 2009). By this, it obtained some leverage over proposals it disliked, stalling the legislative process. The EP's right to be consulted also gave lobbyists an indirect channel of access to the European Commission (Bergström, Farrell, and Héritier 2007, 357). The Single European Act (1987) introduced the cooperation procedure under which the EP could make amendments, which the Council could overrule only by unanimity. The Maastricht Treaty (1992) started to put the EP on equal footing with the Council as a "genuine co-legislator" (Crombez 1997, 115) when it established the co-decision procedure. The EP thereby received the power in selected areas to veto the adoption of EU laws. The Amsterdam Treaty (1999) extended the co-decision procedure from fifteen to thirty-eight treaty articles. The Treaty of Lisbon (2010), finally, made co-decision the ordinary legislative procedure of the

EU (Article 294 of TFEU). It also extended it to policy sectors previously subject to other legislative procedures, for example Agriculture and JAIN, as well as to newly conferred competencies, such as Energy.

Unlike the EP, national parliaments have been considered "the losers" (Maurer and Wessels 2001) or "the victims" (Raunio and O'Brennan 2007) of European integration because their role was reduced to taking EU law. Yet they started to fight back in the 1990s, demanding to be formally involved in the shaping of EU law at the domestic level. By now, all member state legislatures have obtained the right to scrutinize EU legislation before it gets adopted at the EU level by receiving information on the goals and contents of legislative proposals and on the position of their national government; on the latter, they may issue statements that their governments have to take into consideration in the Council negotiations (Raunio and O'Brennan 2007; Sprungk 2010; Winzen 2013). The Lisbon Treaty for the first time formally acknowledged the role of national parliaments in EU law making (Article 5.3, 102, 12 TEU).[25] It seeks to facilitate national parliamentary scrutiny at the domestic level. National parliaments must now receive all legislative and budgetary proposals eight weeks in advance of Council deliberation on the matter to give them time to examine proposals and shape their governments' bargaining position according to national procedures. At the EU level, Protocol 2 in conjunction with Article 5.3 TEU establishes an early warning mechanism, which member state parliaments can invoke to have the Commission review a draft proposal, if one-third of them consider it a violation of the principle of subsidiarity ("yellow card"),[26] as happened in the cases of the law on strikes (Cooper 2015), the European Public Prosecutor's Office,[27] or the tobacco directive (Héritier, Moury, and Granat 2016, 120–126). If the majority of national parliaments do so, the Council or the European Parliament can vote the proposal immediately down.

Overall, parliamentary involvement in the shaping of EU law at the EU and the domestic level has significantly increased over the past thirty years. As expected, infringements in general, and problems of delayed transposition in particular, have substantially decreased since 1994. Is this correspondence indicative of a causal effect?

The EP is a crucial shaper of EU law but not involved at all in its taking by the member states. This is the responsibility of the national parliaments when directives are concerned. The participation of the EP could, of course, affect the acceptance of EU law by the national parliaments. So could their own involvement in EU decision making. The empowerment of national parliaments in EU policy making was meant not only to counter the EU's democratic deficit but also to improve the implementation of EU directives (Sprungk 2011). However, even if members of national parliaments are more prepared to swiftly transpose directives because of their increased possibilities to participate in the decision-making process or because of the co-decision powers of the EP, this is unlikely to have made a big difference. First, research has found that directives adopted under co-decision—that is, with strong participation of the EP—result in more, not less noncompliance (König and Luetgert 2009; Börzel and Knoll 2013). Second, scrutiny of EU law making by national parliaments has at best a weak effect on the effective transposition of directives (König 2007; Luetgert and Dannwolf 2009; Sprungk 2011). This is related to the limited involvement of national parliaments in the implementation of EU law. Most directives are implemented by non-parliamentary measures. Only the Nordic countries, Austria, and Germany substantially involve their parliaments in the transposition of directives (cf. König 2007; Steunenberg 2006; Raunio and O'Brennan 2007; Sprungk 2013). Third, in those cases where national parliaments participate in the taking of EU law, they tend to delay transposition (Haverland, Steunenberg, and van Waarden 2011; Kaeding 2006; Mastenbroek 2003; Steunenberg and Rhinard 2010). Chapter 3 has shown that parliamentary scrutiny is positively related to noncompliance because it increases the propensity of politicization of costly EU law.

Institutional legitimacy provides no compelling explanation of the decline in noncompliance either. Support for the EU as the rule-setting institution has remained rather stable over time (figure 4.10). During the first

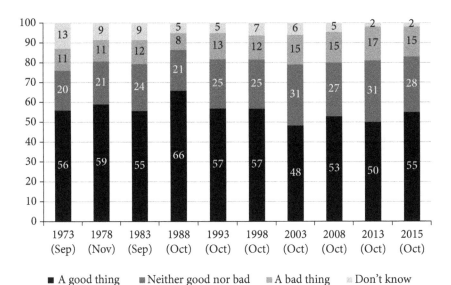

FIGURE 4.10. Assessment of one's country's membership in the EU (EU population), 1973–2015
Source: Eurobarometer 1973–2015 (own compilation, based on data provided by http://ec.europa.eu/public_opinion/index_en.htm, last accessed 1 September 2020).

twenty-five years, European integration progressed essentially by stealth and left Europeans largely detached from the EU. Their "permissive consensus" (Lindberg and Scheingold 1970) was sufficient for European and national elites to move forward with integration. This started to change with the completion of the Internal Market in the early 1990s. When European citizens became aware of how much "Europe hits home" (Börzel and Risse 2000), their support for European integration started to decline. In 1988, an all-time high of 66 percent of EU citizens considered EU membership a good thing. After the Internal Market had been completed and the Economic and Monetary Union (EMU) launched, public approval rates returned to previous levels and experienced an all-time low of 48 percent in 2003, compared to 93 percent of national elites who still thought that their country's EU membership was on balance a good thing (Hooghe 2003, 283).

Somewhat ironically, the series of crises the EU has experienced ever since the French and the Dutch rejected the Constitutional Treaty in 2005 appears to have bolstered rather than undermined public support for the EU—in 2015, almost as many EU citizens approved of EU membership as had done more than forty years before. The gulf between the publics and elites of Europe has always been wide, but it has not permanently widened. What has changed is that the EU has become increasingly politicized. Eurosceptic populist parties and movements have been more and more able to mobilize the less than 30 percent of EU citizens that hold a negative attitude toward the EU to go to the polls and turn to the streets in protest. The rise of Euroscepticism (Hooghe and Marks 2007; McLaren 2006) has been fueled by the political and social consequences of the economic and financial crisis and globalization more broadly speaking (Risse 2015b; Börzel 2016). With pro-EU attitudes being rather stable and the mobilization of Euroscepticism increasing, we should see more rather than less noncompliance since the mid-1990s. Thus, variation in EU support over time cannot account for the identified temporal patterns of noncompliance.

To sum up, while support for the EU has overall remained stable, socialization and parliamentary involvement have increased since the 1990s and may therefore account for the decline in noncompliance. Yet the Southern European member states appear to be resilient to socialization effects. So are France and Italy, which are both founding member states of the EU but continue to rank among the worst compliers (chapter 3). The twelve most recent newcomers, in contrast, have been good compliers from the very beginning of their membership. Parliaments have become increasingly empowered in the shaping and taking of EU law at the EU and the domestic level. However, particularly the involvement of national parliaments remains limited and makes noncompliance more, not less, likely.

The PCP Model at Work: The Depoliticization of EU Law

The previous section has shown that the decline in noncompliance corresponds to changes in the nature of EU law, which the PCP model expects to reduce compliance costs and the risk of their politicization. In the following, I will use a statistical analysis to show that novelty and delegation—the two major properties of EU law that have changed over time—have a significant negative effect on noncompliance. The model will include the variables discussed in the previous section as controls.

Data and Method

Novelty and delegation are properties of EU law that have changed over time. To evaluate whether they have a significant effect on noncompliance, I use a data set of all 2,793 directives adopted between January 1978 and December 2009.[28] Unlike almost all research on noncompliance with directives, my sample includes not only those 1,791 directives that were subject to at least one official infringement proceeding. It also covers the other 1,002 directives the member states could have potentially violated but did not. The full sample enables me to avoid selection bias (cf. Toshkov 2010).

Overall, member states violated about 64 percent of the 2,793 directives the EU adopted between 1978 and 2009 at least once. Between 1978 and 2005, it was at least half of the adopted directives, with the exception of one year (1981). The share of infringed directives peaked in 1998, with 93 percent of the adopted directives being infringed. Since 2006, the ratio of infringed directives dropped below 50 percent (figure 4.11). This confirms once again that the accession of twelve additional member states in 2004 and 2007 has not inflated the level of noncompliance with directives adopted after 2004.

There is a mean of 3.33 official infringements per directive. The number of reasoned opinions based on a directive varies between 0 and 152. There are two extreme cases that drew more than one hundred official infringement proceedings: the fauna, flora, habitat directive (152)[29] and the directive on the common system of value added tax (114).[30]

The older a directive is, the more frequently it can be violated. This does not apply to the around 54 percent of the adopted directives that get repealed or replaced by new directives or that contain a sunset clause. It takes on average three years after the entry into force (4.5 years after adoption) until a reasoned opinion initiates the official stage of the proceeding. Directives are most likely to be violated relatively soon after they enter into force. This makes sense, since

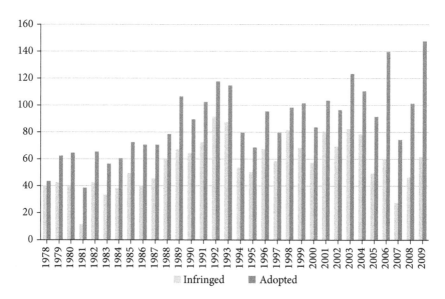

FIGURE 4.11. Adopted and infringed directives compared, 1978–2009
Source: Own compilation, using data obtained from the data set compiled by Dimiter Toshkov, "Legislative Production in the EU, 1967–2012," http://www.dimiter.eu/Data.html, last accessed 23 March 2020 and updated with EUR-Lex for adopted directives, combined with data from the Berlin Infringement Database for infringed directives.

around 80 percent of the infringements refer to delayed, incorrect, or incomplete transposition rather than improper application.

THE NATURE OF EU LAW: NOVELTY AND DELEGATION

EU directives that do not demand the introduction of new legislation at the domestic level require less capacity. I use a dummy variable dividing directives into new directives versus amending or modifying directives (Mastenbroek 2003; Kaeding 2006; Haverland and Romeijn 2007).

EU directives adopted as delegated legislation by the Commission are less likely to become politicized since they tend to deal with technical issues. The variable is coded as a dummy variable; it is either a Commission directive (1) or a Council or Council-EP directive (0).

CONTROLS

Complexity varies between directives and regulations (see above). There is no obvious reason why complexity should change over time beyond the type of legal act. I still include it in the model as an issue- or legal-act-specific variable that the PCP model would expect to increase compliance costs and require more capacity.

Complexity is measured by the number of *recitals* (Mastenbroek 2003; Kaeding 2006; Thomson 2007; Haverland and Romeijn 2007). Recitals are stated at the beginning of each directive and list the areas of application the directive affects.

Time for transposition is measured by the years between the adoption of the directive and the deadline set for the member states in the directive to notify the Commission of the transposition into national law. The length of the transposition deadline varies between a few days for minor delegated directives to up to thirty-six months in the case of substantial secondary directives.

A factor that is time sensitive and can increase compliance costs is workload and ministerial approval. The workload is defined by the number of directives the member states have to transpose in a given year. The more EU laws member states have to take, the more compliance costs they have to cope with and the more capacity they require (Mastenbroek 2003; Kaeding 2006; Haverland and Romeijn 2007). The variable is based on the average annual output of *adopted directives* in the period under observation. The difference between the annual and the average output is used to operationalize the workload. Directives adopted in years with less than average output numbers have negative values.

Ministerial approval taps into compliance costs due to preferential misfit (see chapter 3). There are various constellations in which the minister in charge of a member state has to implement an EU legal act that is not in line with his or her preferences (Börzel and Knoll 2015; König and Luig 2014). A change in government, for instance, can bring a new minister into office who has to transpose into national law a directive that was negotiated by her predecessor. Ministerial approval is operationalized by the distance of the outcome of the directive and the party preferences of the ministers in charge of transposition at the time of notified transposition or the transposition deadline (König and Luig 2014). The originally country-directive-specific variable from the PUCH data set was aggregated by the mean on the directive level. Positive values represent party preferences in line with the final text of the directive, and negative values indicate opposing preferences.

EU decision-making rules have changed over time but should increase rather than decrease compliance costs (see above). They are therefore only included as control variables. The *voting rule* in the Council is formally prescribed by the treaties. To distinguish between majority and unanimity voting, I use a dummy variable. Directives adopted by QMV (1) differ concerning possible outvoted member states from directives that were passed under unanimity (0).

The *voting outcome* refers to the actual voting behavior of member states. Directives adopted by all member states being in favor (0) are distinguished from those adopted with *dissent* in the Council because (a minority of) member states abstained or voted against (1).

Co-decision should increase compliance costs because the member states are likely to compromise with the EP. Unlike consultation and cooperation, the co-decision procedure gives the EP an absolute veto over any EU law, forcing the member states to accept its amendments or forgo EU legislation altogether. To distinguish between the three different legislative procedures according to the growing power of the EP, I weight them by giving the consultation procedure a value of 0.33, the cooperation procedure a value of 0.66, and the co-decision procedure a value of 0.99. Directives adopted by the Commission or the Council alone were coded as zero.

There is a high correlation between co-decision, on the one hand, and other variables related to EU decision making, such as QMV and Commission directives, on the other (see table A1.2). This should not be surprising, since the ordinary legislative procedure (previously Community Method) couples QMV in the Council with co-decision powers of the EP, while delegated legislation provides for neither any voting in the Council nor any involvement of the EP. I therefore drop co-decision. Instead, I use *inter-institutional EU level conflict* to tap into the compliance costs the EP creates for member states. It is measured by the degree to which the EP makes actual use of its power as co-legislator and pressures the Council to make concessions by accepting amendments to the legal act (Kreppel 1999, 2002; Selck and Steunenberg 2004). Minor and uncontroversial *EP amendments* may be accepted by the Council in the first reading. Substantial and controversial amendments, in contrast, provoke long-lasting conflicts between the Council and the EP, which need several rounds of negotiations to get settled. The values of the conflict variable follow a three-step scale, where (1) and (2) refer to EP amendments at first and second readings, respectively, increasingly reducing the Council's leeway. Directives passed without an EP amendment are coded as zero. Finally, co-decision procedures that include a conciliation committee and therefore reach the third reading were assigned the maximum value (3), as they force the Council to accept a compromise by QMV or risk the failure of the legislative proceeding.

Parliamentary involvement in the EU depends on the legislative procedure. For the EU level, it would be the same proxy as the one used for capturing compliance costs incurred by the need of the Council to compromise with the EP. For the *involvement of national parliaments* (König and Luig 2014), I use dummies for each member state in which the national legislature was involved and take the mean of those—that is, the share of member states in which the national legislator was involved. The information is published by the Commission in the EUR-Lex sector 7 database, which provides information on national implementation measures of EU directives (cf. König, Luetgert, and Dannwolf 2006).

EU support is usually measured at the country level. The Commission has been collecting public opinion data on European integration over a long time period in Eurobarometer surveys. To operationalize the attitude of the population toward EU legislative powers on a directive, I use *EU opposition*, measuring the percentage of replies opposing EU membership at the time of transposition of the directive as a proxy.

With the exception of *EU opposition, involvement of national parliaments*, and *ministerial approval*, the independent variables of the model were hand coded based on general information and the legislative document provided by EUR-Lex.[31] Specific information on the legislative proceeding was gathered from the Pre-Lex dossiers. Since Pre-Lex only offers information on inter-institutional legislation, data on Commission directives is not available. Data on the comitology procedures is available only since 2003, which does not match with the period of my study.

The dependent variable is of count nature. Because of overdispersion, I use a negative binomial regression model with robust standard errors. The summary statistics are provided in table A2.2. To control for violative opportunities, I include the age of the directive.

Results and Discussion

The results support the argument of the PCP model that the changing nature of EU directives drives the decline in noncompliance over time (table 4.1).

New directives produce higher compliance costs and lead to substantially more noncompliance than amending and modifying directives, since most of the adjustments have to be made when a policy is introduced at the EU level. Amending directives tend to update technical aspects of existing regulation. Major reforms in newly reregulated areas are scarce because of the necessity to find a new majority in the Council. The task of amending directives is often delegated to the Commission, to be passed by comitology. This finding confirms studies on transposition delays, which conclude that new directives need more time to get transposed (Borghetto, Franchino, and Giannetti 2006; Kaeding 2006; Luetgert and Dannwolf 2009; Steunenberg and Rhinard 2010).

As expected, delegated legislation has a negative but not significant influence on noncompliance. This is not too surprising, since Commission directives started to become more prominent only with the entering into force of the Maastricht Treaty (figure 4.7). Once I control for this change, the effect turns significant, while all the other results stay the same. *Commission directives* tend to be technical and therefore less visible and salient. This is in line with studies indicating that Commission directives cause less problems in the transposition phase (Borghetto, Franchino, and Giannetti 2006; König and Mäder 2014b; Mastenbroek 2003; Steunenberg and Rhinard 2010). Nearly all Commission directives

TABLE 4.1   Novelty, delegation, and noncompliance (EU-15, 1978–2009)

	(1)	(2)
Nature of EU law		
New directive	0.463***	0.494***
	(0.0607)	(0.0610)
Commission directive	–0.105	–0.149*
	(0.0831)	(0.0844)
Control variables		
Recitals	0.172***	0.173***
	(0.0398)	(0.0380)
Time	0.0846**	0.116***
	(0.0334)	(0.0334)
Adopted directives	0.0138	0.0748***
	(0.0154)	(0.0170)
Ministerial approval	–1.772***	–1.715***
	(0.345)	(0.349)
QMV (voting rule)	0.148	0.115
	(0.100)	(0.105)
Dissent (voting outcome)	–0.0261	–0.0536
	(0.0561)	(0.0559)
EP amendments	0.156***	0.132***
	(0.0439)	(0.0442)
Involvement of national parliaments	1.845***	1.860***
	(0.157)	(0.159)
EU opposition	–0.369***	–0.666***
	(0.104)	(0.114)
Age	0.0314***	0.0729***
	(0.00512)	(0.00819)
Maastricht		0.733***
		(0.129)
Constant	–0.0890***	–0.997***
	(0.232)	(0.280)
Observations	2,793	2,793

Robust standard errors in parentheses
*** $p < 0.01$, ** $p < 0.05$, * $p < 0.1$

are transposed into national law by ministerial decree, which deprives national parliaments of the possibility to politicize compliance costs (see below).

The two variables favored by the PCP model are significant and show the expected signs. This is also the case for some of the control variables, which relate to power, capacity, and politicization.

The complexity of a directive increases noncompliance because of higher costs. The broader the area of application of a directive, the more member states have to adjust existing laws in order to comply. Moreover, *recitals* are sometimes used by the member states to insert provisions they have failed to get into the text, by the Commission to insert normative provisions that have not attracted agreement (Kaeding 2006, 236), and by the EP to increase the political visibility of a directive (Steunenberg and Kaeding 2009; Steunenberg and Rhinard 2010). Finally, recitals indicate the number of issues that have remained unresolved during the decision making in the Council, since member states use them to express their reservations and to insert provisions they have failed to get into the text or to state clarifications (Kaeding 2006; Steunenberg and Rhinard 2010). Not surprisingly then, studies on transposition delay already concluded that a high number of recitals slows down transposition (Kaeding 2006; König and Mäder 2014b; Steunenberg and Rhinard 2010; Thomson 2007).

The *time* granted to the member states to comply with the directive matters too. Yet, more time leads to more noncompliance, not less. Studies of transposition delay have shown that member states take more time when more time is given to them by the deadline (Haverland, Steunenberg, and van Waarden 2011; Kaeding 2008; König and Luetgert 2009; Luetgert and Dannwolf 2009; Steunenberg and Rhinard 2010). The effect of annually *adopted directives*, which have to be transposed into national law, is positive as expected. Higher workload delays transposition.

The strong effect of *ministerial approval* corroborates the pivotal position member state governments have in the PCP model. Ministers appear to dodge the costs of compliance when a directive is not in line with their party preference. König and Luig (2014, 515) find that ministers try to keep the national parliament out and to pursue the ideological interests of their own political parties. It seems that they hide the transposition of unwanted or costly policies in their ministries to contain the risk of compliance costs becoming politicized.

Voting rule and voting outcome have no significant effect on noncompliance; *dissent* does not even take the expected sign. The result confirms the findings of previous research that majority voting and conflict in the Council do not delay transposition (Mbaye 2001; Kaeding 2006; Haverland and Romeijn 2007; Linos 2007; König and Luetgert 2009; Luetgert and Dannwolf 2009; Zhelyazkova and Torenvlied 2011). The extension of majority voting has not changed the consensual culture in the Council. The Council still tends to avoid dissenting votes even when the treaties would allow it to outvote member states (Hayes-Renshaw, Van Aken, and Wallace 2006; Kleine 2013).

The degree of inter-institutional EU-level conflict between the Council and the EP about the inclusion of an *EP amendment* seems to be a better indicator of compliance costs than voting rules and voting outcomes in the Council. By politicizing issues, the EP is able to move the final text in its favor and force some ministers to make concessions in order to achieve an agreement. EP amendments result in higher compliance costs at the shaping stage but also increase the propensity of their politicization at the taking stage. Raising public awareness is a prominent strategy of the EP to increase its influence in EU policy making

(Héritier et al. 2015, 77). Finding a consensus between two separate institutions is more difficult than in the Council alone, especially when the two institutions operate in different modes. In the Council, members of national governments can reach agreement by negotiating among themselves behind closed doors. The EP, by contrast, needs salience and publicity to influence legislative output. This finding supports the argument that noncompliance functions as opposition through the backdoor for overruled member states (Falkner et al. 2004; Thomson 2010)—but only if the compromises they had to strike get politicized. The involvement of the EP has a positive effect on noncompliance, *if* it forces the member states to compromise in public. This is in line with the finding of previous studies that an increased number of EU actors involved in the legislation process lowers the chances of a timely transposition by the member states because of the higher compliance costs caused by the concessions member states have to make (cf. König and Luetgert 2009, 189). I argue, however, that it makes a crucial difference for the noncompliance costs whether the involvement of the EP actually leads to concessions by the member states. Moreover, the role of the EP is an indicator, if not a driver, for the politicization of an EU legal act. The strong involvement of the European Parliament in the adoption of an EU directive fosters public visibility because of the political debates in the parliament (Häge 2010).

The positive effect *involvement of national parliaments* has on noncompliance corroborates the expectation of the PCP model that costs are particularly relevant for noncompliance if they are publicly visible. Public visibility and potential domestic opposition crucially depend on whether transposition is done by the ministerial bureaucracy hidden from the public or whether it is subject to parliamentary debate. Conversely, compliance costs are more likely to get politicized when the national parliaments are involved at the taking stage, since highly salient directives might mobilize political opposition (Dimitrakopoulos 2001; Falkner et al. 2005; Versluis 2004). Of the 1,569 directives that the member states transposed between 1986 and 2003, for instance, less than 15 percent involved legislative measures adopted by parliament (König 2007). For the time period of 1986 to 2009, it was around 20 percent (König and Mäder 2014a, 12). The UK, Ireland, Portugal, and Greece practically exclude their parliaments from the transposition process. Most of the other member states have enabling clauses that authorize executive agencies to enact implementation measures during particular time periods or for certain policy sectors. These measures are subject to parliamentary scrutiny to ensure some ex post control (Siedentopf and Ziller 1988; Steunenberg 2006). The *La Pergola* Law (86/1989), for instance, gave the Italian government the power to directly transpose directives by issuing a law via government regulation or ministerial decree, without requiring parliamentary approval. These measures are only subject to report to parliament. In the new member states, the parliaments were already marginalized in the legal adoption of the *acquis communautaire* during the accession process. Having all the essential EU laws on the books was a major precondition for membership. The Commission was willing to grant (temporary) exemptions only in exceptional cases. The immense workload, the time pressure, and the strict accession conditionality centralized the legal implementation of EU law in the hands of the core executives (Goetz 2005; Grabbe 2006; Börzel 2009a). The administrative standard operating procedures have not changed much after accession, which may explain why most of the new member states are top of the class in the transposition of directives (Sedelmeier 2008, 2012; Toshkov 2008).

Finally, more *EU opposition* leads to *less* noncompliance with directives, confirming the findings in the previous chapter on Eurosceptic member states being better compliers because they can tie their hands at the shaping stage.

This regression model refers to the EU-15. I ran it again adding five more years (2017), thereby also including violations by the thirteen member states that joined the EU in the 2000s (see table A4.3). The results are robust, with one exception: voting rule turns significant This could be related to the subsequent extension of qualified majority rule that started with the Maastricht Treaty. After the Lisbon Treaty, which made QMV the ordinary procedure, took effect, the share of directives adopted by qualified majority increased from 24 percent to 39 percent.

New and Not Delegated

The findings of the statistical analysis are further corroborated by comparing the ten directives adopted between 1978 and 2012 that have received more than fifty reasoned opinions (table 4.2). All of them are new directives. None was delegated to the Commission for adoption.

The ten directives are extreme cases, since only 9 percent of the infringed directives have received more than ten reasoned opinions. Four of the "top 10" concern the environment, including the fauna, flora, habitat (FFH) directive adopted in 1992, which is the most violated legal act in the history of the EU.[32] Closely related to FFH is the wild birds directive, passed in 1979.[33] These two policies aim at protecting biodiversity in Europe. The urban waste water directive of 1991 requires the collection and treatment of waste water in agglomerations with a population of over two thousand, and more advanced treatment in agglomerations with more than ten thousand inhabitants in sensitive areas.[34] The EIA directive of 1985 prescribes administrative procedures that shall ensure that public authorities take into account the environmental consequences of a plan, policy, program, or project requiring a license. Moreover, the public is to be informed and heard in the process.[35]

TABLE 4.2 The 10 most infringed directives

CELEX	SUBJECT MATTER	N_RO	NEW	COM.DIR	QMV	CON.VOTE	EPINTER	NP	MIN.AP	WORK	RECT	TIME	EPPOW	EUOPP
31992L0043	Fauna-flora-habitats (FFH)	152	1	0	0	0	1	0.67	0.05	29.6	21	2.06	1	0.12
32006L0112	Value-added tax (VAT)	114	1	0	0	0	0	0.73	0.17	51.6	67	1.09	1	0.14
31992L0050	Public service contracts	86	1	0	0	0	2	0.25	0.12	29.6	27	1.04	2	0.12
31979L0409	Wild birds	74	1	0	0	0	0	1.00	0.17	-25.4	17	2.02	1	0.15
31993L0037	Public works contracts	72	1	0	1	0	0	0.18	-0.02	26.6	14	0.06	2	0.13
32004L0018	Public works, supply & services contracts	72	1	0	1	0	3	0.50	0.14	22.6	51	1.84	3	0.15
31985L0337	Environmental impact assessment (EIA)	60	1	0	0	0	1	0.80	0.14	-14.4	13	3.02	1	0.09
32005L0036	Recognition of professional qualifications	60	1	0	1	2	2	0.87	0.19	3.6	44	2.12	3	0.13
31991L0271	Urban waste water treatment	59	1	0	0	0	1	0.50	0.13	14.6	11	2.11	1	0.10
31983L0189	Technical harmonization	57	1	0	0	0	0	0.20	0.15	-30.4	12	1.01	1	0.11
Min		0	0	0	0	0	0	0.00	-0.26	-49.4	1	0.00	0	0.06
Max		152	1	1	1	2	3	1.00	0.29	59.6	142	11.55	3	0.18
Mean		3.12	0.64	0.40	0.64	0.08	0.48	0.13	0.02	7.3	10.2	0.97	0.92	0.13
Median/p50		1	1	0	1	0	0	0.00	0.01	8.6	7	0.81	0	0.13

The second-most-infringed directive is the VAT directive of 2006.[36] If we control for time, the VAT directive tops the FFH directive; the latter has thirty-eight more violations but has been in force three times longer. The VAT directive aims at the harmonization of value added tax law in the EU.

There is a cluster of three directives related to the coordination of procedures for the award of public service contracts (1992),[37] public works contracts (1993),[38] and public works, supply, and service contracts (2004).[39] Together, they account for 230 reasoned opinions. In a similar vein, the technical standards and regulations directive of 1983 aims at harmonizing technical standards and regulations.[40] It has been amended in 1988[41] and is the only amending directive among the "top 20" in the data set.

The directive on the recognition of professional qualifications (2005), finally, sets up the legal framework for the recognition of professional qualifications not ruled by specific legal provisions. It is intended to enable the free movement of professionals, such as doctors or architects, within the EU.[42] The directive has already drawn sixty reasoned opinions in the first ten years.

In all, the most infringed directives either seek to advance the Internal Market by harmonizing national regulations that may impair competition (market making), or they aim at protecting the environment against negative externalities of market activities (market correcting). Altogether, ten of the twenty most infringed directives relate to the environment and account for slightly less than half of all reasoned opinions. Internal Market accounts for about 20 percent of both directives and infringements (cf. chapter 5).

Besides confirming that new and non-delegated directives are more prone to noncompliance, the sample corroborates some of the other (non)findings. Only a third of the directives were adopted by QMV, and all but one (recognition of professional qualifications) were not contentious. This confirms that voting in the Council has no significant influence on compliance costs. Conflict between the EP and the Council, in contrast, occurred in all those cases in which the EP had at least a formal voice, if not a vote, in decision making, with the exception of the 1993 directive on the award of public works contracts. The involvement of national parliaments in the transposition was above average. Ministerial approval shows a less clear pattern, being higher than we would expect.

The ten directives practically cover the entire spectrum of possible workload (from almost the maximum of adopted directives to close to the minimum) and vary significantly in transposition deadlines (from three weeks to more than three years). What they share is a high level of complexity. The FFH directive may feature only 21 recitals and 24 articles, compared to the VAT directive, with 67 recitals and 414 articles. The annex, however, contains an endless list of plants and animals that merit protection.[43] All directives were adopted with the maximum EP involvement the treaties provided for at the time of adoption. Finally, opposition to EU membership is around 13 percent, corroborating the counterintuitive results of the statistical analysis.

The combined results of the multivariate regression analysis and the closer examination of the ten most violated directives confirm that declining noncompliance with EU law is driven by its changing nature, reducing compliance costs and rendering their politicization less likely.

Research on noncompliance in the EU has focused on violations of EU law by the member states. Despite an ongoing debate on whether the EU suffers from a compliance problem, little attention has been paid to changes in noncompliance over time. Eastern enlargement led many to expect an increase in noncompliance. Yet this is not what the data shows. Noncompliance had started to decline more than ten years before twelve new member states got admitted to the EU, and their accession has done nothing to reverse the declining trend.

Member state properties cannot account for this secular trend, since they have remained largely constant. The causes lie with systemic or EU-level factors. The PCP model identifies the changes in the nature of EU law as the key driver. With the completion of the Internal Market and the establishment of the EMU by the Maastricht Treaty in the mid-1990s, the EU has increasingly adopted technical rules in the form of directly applicable regulations, on the one hand, and of Commission directives that execute or amend existing laws, rather than enact new legislation, on the other. Implementing technical amendments is less costly for the member states and requires less capacity. Compliance costs of amending legislation are also less likely to become politicized since their adoption tends to be delegated to administrative bodies. Delegation reduces the role of both the European Parliament and the national parliaments at the shaping and the taking stage, respectively. Since the Maastricht Treaty, both have been continuously empowered to interfere at the shaping stage of the compliance game. Yet these attempts at the parliamentarization of EU policy making, with the aim to address the democratic legitimacy deficit of the EU, have been counteracted. Depoliticization and delegation strengthen the executive at all levels of the EU's system of multilevel governance (König 2007; Börzel and Sprungk 2009). At the same time, delegation does not only disempower the EP at the shaping stage. National parliaments are only involved in the taking of about a fifth of EU directives. Where directives amend existing rather than create new legislation and are (therefore) delegated to the Commission, member states tend to delegate implementation to their administrative bodies that have the necessary expertise and can draw on previous legislation as the legal basis. Some national variation notwithstanding, the "trend towards bureaucratic implementation of directives is visible for almost all member states over time and across most policy sectors" (König 2007, 421).

Somewhat paradoxically, the changes introduced by the Lisbon Treaty to boost the role of national parliaments in EU law making, on the one hand, and the right of the Council and the EP to object or revoke delegation, on the other, have empowered the Commission in using delegation. The Council shares the Commission's preferences for delegation de facto undermining parliamentary involvement (Héritier, Moury, and Granat 2016). Since member states have lost their influence in the adoption of delegated acts, they support the use of implementing acts, where the comitology is still involved and the EP has no right of objection or revocation. The PCP model thereby accounts for the ambivalent findings in the literature on the effect of parliamentary involvement on noncompliance. National parliaments only tend to delay or water down transposition, if they have not been involved at the shaping stage, are required to give their approval at the taking stage, *and* deal with highly politicized issues (Sprungk 2011, 2013). Since directives are increasingly technical, tend to amend existing legislation, and are adopted by the Commission, national parliaments are only marginally involved at the taking stage. If they are involved, however, these directives are likely to be of high issue salience and therefore are prone to flawed transposition, owing to the politicization of compliance costs.

Whether less politicization results in more delegation, or vice versa, is not clear. Council and Commission seek to avoid politicization by using delegation (Bergström, Farrell, and Héritier 2007). Likewise, the Commission is more likely to initiate delegated acts if it anticipates legislative gridlock in the Council or the EP (Junge, König, and Luig 2015). This seems to suggest that delegation is an instrument rather than the result of depoliticization. Findings on the management of the euro crisis corroborate the supposition that delegation drives depoliticization and not the other way round (Börzel 2016). To avoid political controversy, the governments of the euro group delegated far-reaching competencies to the European Commission (e.g., European Semester) and the ECB (e.g., banking supervision), circumventing the involvement of both the European Parliament and national legislatures (Schimmelfennig 2014b; Genschel and Jachtenfuchs 2016; cf. chapter 6).

In any case, my analysis suggests that the effect of depoliticization through delegation has reduced noncompliance by making EU law less costly for the member states and the politicization of compliance costs less likely. This is not to deny that EU laws have been subject to domestic politicization. If citizens, companies, interest groups, or advocacy networks become aware of the economic, social, or political costs market integration may incur, denouncing Brussels and the European Commission for its "obsession with regulation" provides a useful argument in the political debate. For instance, trade unions and large parts of industry have effectively joined forces in blocking the EU-induced liberalization of the German service sector (Eckert 2015). The pan-European outcry against the Bolkestein directive[44] that aims at establishing an Internal Market for services offered them a formidable pretext to curb and contain attempts of the federal government to open the German service sector to foreign competition (Crespy 2012). Such politicization, however, tends to arise already at the shaping stage, resulting in a substantial revision or, as in the case of the infamous regulation banning olive oil jugs in restaurants,[45] the ultimate withdrawal of the proposed EU legislation. Politicization is less pronounced at the taking stage, and if so, less related to the EU origin of the law. Improper application of directives and regulations on the ground may give rise to local contestation, which, however, often remains isolated and confined to a specific case with its particularities. More often than not, "once transposed, Community Law is applied no better or worse than domestic law" (Ciavarini Azzi 2000, 58). While violations of the wild birds directive and the FFH directive have made headline news in many member states, EU legislation has provided environmental groups with an additional weapon to protect nature against economic interests. Attempts of transnational mining companies or local developers to expand their activities into nature conservation areas would have outraged the public irrespective of whether there were some EU laws that protected these areas (Börzel and Buzogány 2010).

Finally, improving compliance through delegation comes at a price. While multilevel executive federalism helps ensure the effectiveness of EU law, it exacerbates the "parliamentary deficit" (König 2007) in EU policy making and the democratic deficit of the EU more broadly speaking. The treaties of Maastricht, Amsterdam, Nice, and Lisbon may have continuously empowered the European Parliament and national parliaments in EU policy making. Parliamentarization, however, has done little so far to undermine the dominance of supranational and national bureaucrats. Quite on the contrary, the financial crisis has further increased their roles. The marginalization of the European Parliament and the national parliaments produces "policy without politics" (V. Schmidt 2006). The depoliticization of EU policies stands in stark contrast to the growing politicization and contestation of the EU as a polity. "Politics without policy" is increasingly replaced by "politics about polity" (De Wilde, Leupold, and Schmidtke 2016, 14). EU citizens have not only become more aware of the EU and its policies; they increasingly care and mobilize against the technocratic logic of EU policy making (De Wilde and Zürn 2012, 140; cf. Chalmers, Jachtenfuchs, and Joerges 2016). Depoliticization has fueled Eurosceptic populism in the member states, which in turn undermines the capacity of the EU to take forceful action in areas in which its competencies are limited, the migration crisis being a case in point (Börzel 2016). The backlash against depoliticization has made it increasingly difficult for member state governments to honor the commitments they made to manage the historic influx of migrants. Overall compliance with EU law, however, has not been affected yet.

WHY NONCOMPLIANCE IS SECTOR SPECIFIC

Policy matters to noncompliance in the EU. Only five of twenty-three policy sectors account for two-thirds of member state violations of EU law (figure 5.1). The first part of this chapter maps the sector variation in noncompliance in more detail. In the absence of an established theory on sector-specific noncompliance, the second part reviews the field of public policy analysis for arguments that allow us to address sector variation. I link these arguments to the three principal components of the PCP model, showing that different types of policy and their regulatory logic affect compliance costs differently. Unlike distributive and redistributive policy, regulatory policy that seeks to harmonize national regulations at the EU level to correct failures of the Internal Market produces higher costs at the taking stage of the compliance game. While market making is mostly about deregulation, EU harmonization requires the member states to set up new or change existing regulation, to which domestic actors have to adapt their behavior. A statistical analysis in the third part of the chapter evaluates the significance of the different policy factors for noncompliance, controlling for alternative influences. The chapter demonstrates that the EU's noncompliance problems are concentrated in sectors that seek to protect the rights of EU citizens in an increasingly integrated Internal Market. The fourth part of the chapter uses the case of the EU's migration crisis to corroborate the findings of the previous two chapters that politicization renders noncompliance even more likely. The failed attempts to depoliticize the handling of the refugee and migration flows by delegating it to EU institutions also demonstrate the limits of regulatory policy in an increasingly politicized EU. While EU law may have become less costly for

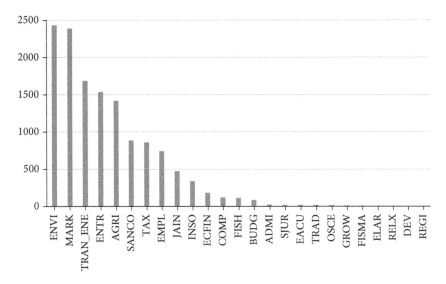

FIGURE 5.1. Total number of reasoned opinions per policy sector, 1978–2017
Source: Own compilation, with data from the Berlin Infringement Database.
Note: ADMI = Administration; AGRI = Agriculture; BUDG = Budget; COMP = Competition; EMPL = Employment & Social Affairs; ENTR = Enterprise & Industry; ENVI = Environment; FISH = Fisheries & Maritime Affairs; INSO = Information Society & Media; JAIN = Justice & Home Affairs; MARK = Internal Market & Services; OSCE = Organisation of Security and Cooperation in Europe; REGI = Regional Policy; RELX = External Affairs; SANCO = Health & Consumer Protection; SJUR = Legal Service; TAX = Taxation & Customs Union; TRAD = Trade; TRAN_ENE = Transport & Energy.

member states over time, the rise of populism has rendered political conflict surrounding EU regulatory policy more likely. Noncompliance may be declining overall, but market-correcting policy is likely to remain the linchpin of noncompliance in the EU.

Policy Matters!

Five sectors account for the lion's share of violations against EU law. Two of them, Internal Market and Agriculture, have anchored the European integration project from the beginning. The European Economic Community of 1957 was built around the goals of creating an Internal Market, while providing affordable food for European citizens and a fair standard of living for European farmers through a common agricultural policy (Pinder 1968; Dinan 2004). The other three sectors have been important in flanking the Internal Market. Enterprise & Industry aims at promoting the competitiveness of European industry mostly by means of harmonizing product standards. Closely related to the Internal Market, this sector obtained an independent legal basis in the Maastricht Treaty and became part of the Directorate-General for Internal Market, Industry, Entrepreneurship and SMEs (small and medium-size enterprises) in 2015. The Transport & Energy sector relates to the regulation of network utilities that are crucial to the Internal Market. The free movement of goods and people depends on transport utilities that can rely on a Europe-wide infrastructure and free access to national transport markets (rail, air, roads). Since services and infrastructure used to be state owned, member states were reluctant to grant the EU any regulatory power. The Maastricht Treaty laid the institutional and budgetary foundations for a common transport policy, breaking up the state monopolies. It also introduced the plan for creating a Europe-wide infrastructure for transport, energy, and telecommunications (Trans-European Networks). Energy became a proper EU competence even later. Before the Lisbon Treaty, the EU had legislated on energy policy. However, it had to draw on its Internal Market and Environment powers to promote the creation of a common energy market, which provides citizens and business with affordable energy and energy services at competitive prices. The Energy Union, officially launched in 2015, is intended to ensure a secure and safe energy supply, reducing the reliance on Russia. Finally, Environment, similar to Enterprise and Transport & Energy, became a proper competence of the EU rather late, in 1986, with the Single European Act. By that time, however, the EU had already established a comprehensive body of environmental legislation to prevent member states from using national regulations as nontariff barriers in the Internal Market.

The frequent violations of EU law in five core areas of European integration have fueled concerns about a (growing) compliance problem in the EU (see chapter 4). The picture changes, however, when we control for violative opportunities and focus on those eleven sectors that have a substantial number of laws that member states could infringe on. The EU has comprehensively regulated on Environment and Health & Consumer Protection for more than three decades. Agriculture is among the oldest policy sectors and, naturally, more densely regulated than the younger Environment sector. EU agricultural law is ten times more comprehensive than EU environmental law. JAIN (Justice & Home Affairs) and Information Society & Media together total less than one-third of the legislation passed in Environment. Controlling for violative opportunities not only paints a more realistic picture of the leading noncompliance sectors; it helps ensure that noncompliance is driven by sector-specific rather than issue-specific factors (figure 1.5).

The following analysis of sector-specific noncompliance focuses on directives. We lack data on regulations and treaty articles that would allow us to control for violative opportunities (see chapter 1). Analyzing directives still yields generalizable results, since the EU's compliance problems are largely confined to directives (see chapter 4).

Once we control for violative opportunities, JAIN and Environment compete for the rank of the no. 1 noncompliant sector (figure 1.5). They are followed at some distance by Information Society & Media and Health & Consumer Protection. In the four sectors leading the noncompliance ranking, the vast majority of infringements involve violations of directives. Directives also account for the lion's share of noncompliance in other sectors—with the exceptions of Taxation, Agriculture, and Competition. Legislation in Agriculture is based on regulations to a greater extent than in other sectors (think about the infamous milk quota). In Competition and Taxation, many prescriptions and prohibitions are laid down in treaty articles. Article 102 TFEU, for instance, prohibits monopolies, price discrimination, and exclusive dealing. Likewise, Article 101 bans anticompetitive agreements, including price fixing. According to Article 107, states must not aid or subsidize private parties in distortion of free competition. Because of the EU's limited competencies on taxation, tax-related EU law is heavily based on the free movement of capital (payments), people (workers), services (right of establishment), and goods (customs union). The four freedoms build the core of the Internal Market and therefore are directly protected by treaty articles.

Directives account for at least two-thirds of official infringements in the leading noncompliance sectors. Between 1978 and 2012, EU member states violated on average more than 80 percent of the directives adopted in each of these sectors. In the case of JAIN, every directive has been violated at least once (figure 5.2). The following section briefly outlines the five top noncompliance sectors.

The objective of JAIN is to establish an "area of freedom, security and justice." Its core is the border-free Schengen area. The abolishment of mutual border controls among the twenty-six participating countries, four of which (Iceland, Liechtenstein, Norway, and Switzerland) are not members of the EU, has created the necessity for a common policy on asylum, immigration, and external border control. Within the EU, the freedom of movement has led the member states to coordinate their fight against terrorism, human trafficking, sexual exploitation, illicit drug trafficking, money laundering, corruption, counterfeiting, and computer crime. Finally, JAIN legislation is intended to ensure EU citizens' fundamental rights, including access to the local justice system, and protect them against discrimination on the grounds of sex, racial or ethnic origin, religion or belief, disability, age, or sexual orientation. The most frequently violated directive is the citizens' right directive to guarantee free movement and residence of EU citizens throughout the EU.[1] The majority of the other front-runners for violation involve the rights of immigrants and the treatment of asylum seekers,

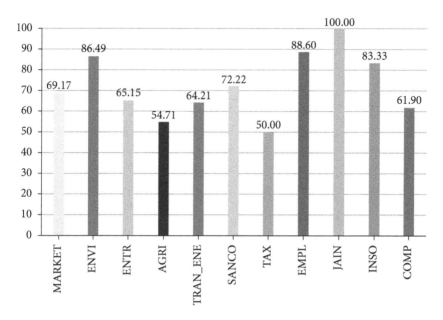

FIGURE 5.2.   Percentage share of officially infringed directives in relation to all directives adopted by policy sector, 1978–2012
Source: Own compilation, with data from the Berlin Infringement Database.

for instance in regard to the status of third-country nationals and minimum standards for legal recognition.[2] With the migration crisis, noncompliance has intensified in this area. In 2015, the Commission took legal action against virtually all member states for not applying the five directives the EU had adopted between 2001 and 2011 (European Commission 2016, 19–20). Individual rights of nondiscrimination in employment and occupation and the protection of personal data also figure prominently. This includes the retention-of-data directive of 2006, which required member states to store citizens' telecommunications data for a minimum of six months and at most twenty-four months.[3] In 2014, the ECJ annulled the directive, since it considered the general and blanket retention of data a violation of fundamental rights. Finally, the harmonization of criminal law with regard to environmental pollution has gained prominence.[4] Given its younger age and lower regulatory density, JAIN is likely to remain the least-complied-with policy sector in the EU.

Environment (ENVI) started as trade policy, since the Treaty of Rome did not foresee any competence for the EU in this sector. Yet, from the very beginning, the European Commission pushed policies that went beyond harmonizing national regulations to prevent their use as nontariff barriers. The wild birds directive was adopted as early as 1979—before the Single European Act conferred on the EU the power to legislate on the environment.[5] It was the first piece of EU legislation on nature conservation and got a complete overhaul thirty years later.[6] Together with the much younger fauna, flora, habitat directive passed in 1992, it accounts for almost a fifth of all infringements in Environment; nature conservation is the least-complied-with area of EU law in the history of the EU.[7] Environmental impact assessment (EIA) and urban waste water treatment (UWWT) are two other front-runners, not only in Environment but in the EU as a whole (see chapter 4). EIA, which came into force in 1985, prescribes procedures for the licensing of public and private projects with significant effects on the environment.[8] UWWT was adopted in 1991 under Article 130(s) of the Single European Act, which granted the EU the power to enact proper environmental legislation. It sets standards for the treatment and discharge of waste water from cities and certain industrial sectors.[9] Some of the other least-complied-with directives conform more to the original idea of EU environmental policy as promoting free trade, for instance by setting common limit values for air and water pollutants, such as sulfur oxide or nitrate.

Information Society & Media (INSO)[10] aims at creating the Digital Single Market by 2018. It is an advancement of the Internal Market, which was officially completed in 1992. The free movement of data entails free and fair access to electronic communications services and electronic communications networks, for both providers and consumers. Accordingly, EU legislation seeks to harmonize user rights, the processing of personal data, and the protection of privacy. The most infringed directives, which account for more than 80 percent of all infringements in this sector, concern the EU's attempt to set up a common regulatory framework on electronic communications networks and services (Nijenhuis 2013). By far the least-complied-with directive is the universal service directive adopted in 2002[11] and amended in 2009.[12] It seeks to ensure the availability of a minimum set of good-quality electronic communications services accessible to all users at an affordable price, which member states have to ensure, including to those users who do not yet have a connection to public communications networks (telephone, internet) because they live in a remote area. Low-income users are entitled to special tariffs. Consumers also receive the right to change their phone company while keeping their old number and to be informed of changes in prices and tariffs.

Health & Food Safety (SANCO) is the core area of consumer protection. It entails a series of laws on food and product safety, consumer rights, and public health. The most infringed directives seek to protect consumers against unfair terms in consumer contracts,[13] unfair business-to-consumer commercial practices,[14] or against health risks emanating from foodstuffs, particularly those entering from third countries that are not members of the EU. Some directives are about animal protection, for example the laying-hens directive, which sets minimum standards for the welfare of laying hens.[15] Such regulations are also to prevent distortions of competition between producers in different member states.

The literature has not paid much attention to variation in noncompliance between policy sectors, even though research shows that variation is not random and may be even larger than between member states (Steunenberg 2007; Börzel et al. 2007; Börzel, Hofmann, and Panke 2011; Zhelyazkova, Kaya, and Schrama 2016). The neglect of the policy dimension in compliance research may be related to the lack of clear or intuitive patterns, as we find with regard to time (decline since the 1990s) and member states (North v. South; West v. East). The majority of the eleven most infringed sectors follow the secular trend of declining noncompliance analyzed in chapter 4. Only in JAIN and Transport & Energy have infringements increased.

The increase in JAIN and Transport & Energy seems to be at least partly driven by the new member states that joined in 2004 and 2007. Overall, eastern enlargement has mitigated rather than exacerbated the EU's compliance problems (see chapters 3 and 4). In most sectors, the new member states range among the top compliers. In JAIN, however, nine of the twelve newcomers are leading the noncompliance ranking. In Transport & Energy, the CEE countries still diverge from their exemplary compliance behavior, mingling with the old member states.

What do JAIN, Information Society & Media, Environment, and SANCO have in common? What renders these four most noncompliant sectors different from the other sectors that do comparatively better and conform to the general patterns of cross-time and cross-country variation?

Unlike compliance research in IR, implementation studies on EU policy making have paid more attention to variation in violations of EU law across sectors than across member states (Treib 2008; Knill 2015). These studies tend to be variable driven, though. There are no theories (yet) to account for policy-related variation in noncompliance behavior. Similar to implementation research in the field of public policy analysis, various case studies have identified a multitude of factors that may cause problems of noncompliance at the sector level. These studies provide important insights into the causes of policy noncompliance. However, they tend to compare (if at all) only two or three policy sectors, usually concentrating on social and environmental policy, while other sectors have remained largely unexplored (Luetgert and Dannwolf 2009; Toshkov et al. 2010; Zhelyazkova, Kaya, and Schrama 2016, 2017). Thus, the external validity of qualitative research tends to be limited (Haverland, Steunenberg, and van Waarden 2011). This has started to change with the quantitative turn in EU research.

A growing number of studies have been using statistical methods to test explanations similar to those of case studies across a larger N. The majority of them still focus on the transposition of a limited number of directives in a limited number of sectors by a limited number of member states (Borghetto, Franchino, and Giannetti 2006; Berglund, Grange, and van Waarden 2006; Toshkov 2007b, 2008; Haverland and Romeijn 2007; Thomson 2007; König and Luetgert 2009; Luetgert and Dannwolf 2009). These studies narrow the dependent variable to timely transposition by a subset of member states in selected sectors. They usually do not develop genuine policy explanations either. Rather, the literature uses dummy variables and relies otherwise on factors that are derivative of issue-specific or country-specific variables discussed in chapter 3 and 4, respectively.

In short, there is solid empirical evidence that policy matters, but we do not know exactly why and how. Rather than drawing on explanations that focus on issue-specific and country-specific factors (dis)aggregated at the sector level, this chapter uses the PCP model to develop a genuinely sector-specific explanation to solve the puzzle of why noncompliance is concentrated in a handful of sectors.

Policy Matters—but Why?

While often criticized for its complex models, public policy research offers theoretical arguments for why noncompliance varies across policy sectors. These arguments focus on the costs of compliance at the shaping stage.

Sector-Specific Explanations

REGULATORY VERSUS NONREGULATORY POLICY

"Policy determines politics," said Theodore Lowi (1972, 299). To state his argument, he distinguished four different types of policy in terms of the likelihood and applicability of coercion. With regard to the PCP model, policy types vary in the extent to which they produce compliance costs for the member states (König and Luetgert 2009). *Constituent policy* refers to the structures of government and administration. In the case of the EU, this would mostly include treaty reforms rather than directives and regulations. Affecting primary rather than secondary EU law, constituent policy is not so relevant for explaining sector variation in noncompliance. The remaining three policy types, in contrast, carry different implications for compliance costs. *Distributive policy* allocates public resources among alternative users (Majone 1996, 63). Examples include public security, education, and infrastructure. Their costs are borne by the collectivity of taxpayers rather than by a specific group (Schumann 1991). Distributive policy is also less costly in its enforcement, since actors do not have to change their behavior to ensure compliance. Their implementation is mostly a question of capacity. This is also true for *redistributive policy*, such as Agriculture and Regional Policy. Yet, unlike Research or Education, *redistributive* policy transfers resources from specific social groups, member states, or regions to others. It creates clear winners and losers, which renders agreement at the shaping stage difficult. Once the policy is adopted, however, its taking should not be much of an issue. *Regulatory policy*, finally, prohibits or prescribes certain behavior. Unlike distributive and redistributive policy, regulatory policy does not involve direct public expenditure costs. However, prohibiting mergers, price collusions, state subsidies, unfair terms in consumer contracts, or discrimination on grounds of sex, racial or ethnic origin, religion or belief, disability, age, or sexual orientation entails benefits for the broader society but incurs significant costs for some parts of it (Wilson 1980). So do mandating the reduction of environmental pollution, the application of certain licensing procedures, the access to public communication networks, or the protection of personal data. Air pollution control regulations, for instance, reduce public health risks but require industry to introduce new abatement technologies. Since actors are likely to resist such costs, regulatory policy requires enforcement, which is not only a matter of capacity but also politicization when actors mobilize against the costs they have to bear.

A few scholars have worked with Lowi's typology to address issues of implementation and compliance. Most prominently, Majone argued that the costs of policy formulation and decision making for regulatory policy are relatively low at the shaping stage but often significant—in material and political terms—at the taking stage. (Re)distributive policy (Agriculture, Regional Policy) require direct public expenditures; these costs need to be dealt with at the stage of decision making. Regulatory policy (Internal Market, Competition, Environment, SANCO), in contrast, shift the costs to implementation at the domestic level, where implementing authorities and societal actors might be neither willing nor able to bear them (Majone 1993, 1996). Accordingly, noncompliance with EU law should be higher in regulatory as compared to nonregulatory policy sectors.

The difference between (re)distributive policy and regulatory policy with regard to the costs arising at the shaping versus the taking stage explains why the EU has developed into a "regulatory state," one that lacks the power to make truly (re)distributive policy (W. Wallace 1983; Majone 1993, 1994). The EU's tax and spending capacity is limited. The one exception is Agriculture, which has always accounted for a significant share of the EU budget (more than two-thirds until the 1990s), benefiting less than 5 percent of the EU population. Still, the EU's (re)distributive capacity is less than 5 percent of what its member states do. The vast majority of EU law is regulatory in nature. This may explain why more than

90 percent of official infringements refer to violations of regulatory policy, and the most noncompliant sectors are predominantly regulatory.

With the establishment of the political union in the Maastricht Treaty, the EU began to go beyond classical regulation, moving into the area of internal security and the individual rights of its citizens. Its competencies for (re)distribution have remained limited (Scharpf 2003). At the same time, EU law has increasingly interfered with national sovereignty on (re)distribution. The convergence criteria of the Maastricht Treaty, the Stability and Growth Pact, the Fiscal Compact, and the European Semester circumscribe the fiscal powers of the member states (Scharpf 2015; Streeck and Elsässer 2016). The EU's attempt to manage the sovereign debt crisis has significantly constrained domestic economic and social policy, producing or at least exacerbating redistributive effects that are increasingly attributed to the EU (Hix 2015; Scharpf 2015; Polyakova and Fligstein 2016). Moreover, the financial guarantees, assistance, and interventions of the European Stability Mechanism and the ECB have directly or indirectly caused massive redistribution among and within the member states. The euro crisis has definitely turned the EMU into a redistributive issue by increasing the financial scale and the public visibility of redistribution.

Despite the redistributive consequences of the common currency, the member states have remained unwilling to change the treaties to give the EU substantial redistributive authority. They continue to have difficulty in finding the necessary consensus on the structures and goals of the EU as a polity—for example, with regard to the degree of state intervention into markets (W. Wallace 1983; Majone 1994). Agreement on regulatory policy, in contrast, is easier, since costs only become salient in the implementation. Genschel and Jachtenfuchs (2016) contend that EU regulatory policy is still *less* prone to noncompliance because it is less likely to be politicized. While EU regulatory standards may incur costs at the domestic level, their redistributive implications are concealed since they impose uniform legal obligations on all member states—everybody should have to bear the same costs. Moreover, regulatory policy does not directly interfere with core state powers required for distributive and redistributive policy, such as public security, taxation, or welfare; the latter policies lie at the heart of state sovereignty, where EU law is more likely to meet domestic opposition (Genschel and Jachtenfuchs 2016).

In sum, regulatory policy is likely to entail higher compliance costs than distributive and redistributive policy. This facilitates policy adoption at the shaping stage but creates problems at the taking stage, making noncompliance more likely. Philipp Genschel and Markus Jachtenfuchs (2016) argue the opposite—noncompliance with regulatory policy should be lower because compliance costs are less likely to become politicized at the taking stage. Regulatory policy is less publicly visible and does not concern politically sensitive issues. Public visibility and political sensitivity are central to the PCP model. Regulatory policy may or may not interfere with core state powers. The fauna, flora, habitat directive or the services in the Internal Market directive do not, but they still became politicized in virtually all member states (chapter 4). The redistributive consequences of regulatory policy make politicization more likely. As a result, the PCP model expects noncompliance with regulatory policy to be higher than with nonregulatory policy.

MARKET-CORRECTING VERSUS MARKET-MAKING REGULATORY POLICY

Given the predominance of regulatory policy in the EU, Zürn (1997) refined Majone's argument on compliance costs. His starting point was the distinction within regulatory policy between regulations aimed at market making (negative integration) versus market correcting (positive integration). The distinction was originally introduced by Pinder (1968) in his analysis of the European Economic Community. Negative integration refers to the opening of existing markets to foreign competition by eliminating tariffs, taxes, quotas, and other protectionist policies, such as state subsidies. Negative integration also entails the creation of new markets by breaking up state monopolies as they traditionally existed for utilities, such as telecommunications or energy (Pinder 1968). While negative integration is about deregulation and privatization at the national level, positive integration aims at reregulation at the EU level, removing nontariff barriers. To create and maintain a level playing field for suppliers and consumers, member states agree on common European standards on the quality, safety, and labeling of products and production processes (e.g., regulations on food standards, packaging, the use of chemicals, working hours).

Nine years after its ratification, the Treaty of Rome, Pinder concluded, was "strongly biased in the direction of negative integration and away from positive integration" (Pinder 1968, 99). About thirty years later, Scharpf confirmed the structural asymmetry between negative and positive integration and related it to different dynamics in EU decision making and the market-friendly jurisdiction of the ECJ (Scharpf 1996, 1997b, 2001a). The member states agreed to create an Internal Market in 1957. They have shared an interest in harmonizing national regulations at the EU level to prevent them from being used as nontariff barriers to protect certain sectors of the national economy against foreign competition. At the same time, member states have found it difficult to agree on the extent to which the Internal Market should be reregulated concerning the internal economic competition unleashed by EU-induced deregulation at the domestic level. The ECJ interpreted the treaties in a way that elevated the four market freedoms to the status of economic liberties to be protected not only against protectionist discrimination but also nondiscriminatory constraints, for instance in the form of collective labor rights (Scharpf 2016b). "Integration through law" (Cappelletti, Seccombe, and Weiler 1986) reinforced the asymmetry of market making over market correcting. Majone saw the main difference between regulatory and nonregulatory policy in the costs the former incurs at the taking stage and the latter at the shaping stage. Scharpf contended that market-correcting policy has redistributive consequences that already materialize at the shaping stage of the compliance game, making its adoption as difficult as in the case of (re)distributive policy.

Zürn systematically extended the distinction between positive and negative integration to the taking stage. He hypothesized that member states are more likely to infringe on positive or market-correcting policy (Zürn 1997; cf. Börzel, Hofmann, and Sprungk 2003; Toshkov 2008). The taking of EU policy designed to facilitate negative integration may incur costs for some domestic actors, such as companies that are not internationally competitive. However, market-making policy does not require member states to take action or develop and police the application of new legislation. In order to remove obstacles to market integration, member states mostly have to abstain from interfering with the free flow of market forces by not levying import tariffs and export fees and not controlling borders. Compliance is less a matter of capacity. Market-correcting policy, in contrast, explicitly requires states to actively interfere in market and society (Scharpf 1999; H. Wallace 2005). The implementation of common environmental, health, or labor standards demands more capacity and is more prone to politicization than the control of mergers, price collusions, or state subsidies. Member states have to enact new legislation, invest additional administrative resources, and strengthen administrative coordination to enforce it. At the same time, the "regulatory competition" (Héritier 1996) among the member states makes any compromise at the EU level likely to become subject to domestic opposition, for instance by business sectors that face higher production costs because they have to invest in new abatement technology or pay higher wages. Taking market-correcting policy requires more capacity to cope with the costs and is more likely to become politicized.

In sum, the PCP model proposes that regulatory policy carries a greater risk of noncompliance than other policy types, particularly if its regulatory logic is market correcting rather than market making. There are a few other factors identified in the literature that provide sector-specific explanations for noncompliance with EU law. They have not always been linked back to some theoretical framework. Nor are they inherent to specific policy types. However, the number of years the EU has had the competence to legislate on a sector, the level and scope of its competencies and their public (nonacceptance), and the regulatory density of EU legislative action vary across sectors, affecting compliance costs. They therefore serve as control variables.

AGE

The "EU age" of a sector—that is, the length of time the EU has had the competence to adopt laws—may matter for the capacity of member states to cope with compliance costs (Börzel, Hofmann, and Panke 2011). Agriculture, Internal Market, or Competition have been subject to EU policy making since the early days of European integration. The member states have had sixty years to build up the capacity to implement EU legal acts (Berglund, Grange, and van Waarden 2006; Haverland, Steunenberg, and van Waarden 2011). They also have gained more administrative experience with the implementation of EU law (Steunenberg and Rhinard 2010). JAIN, in contrast, is one of the youngest sectors. It was introduced with the Maastricht Treaty in 1992 and only became fully supranationalized with the Lisbon Treaty of 2010. As older sectors, Agriculture, Internal Market, or Competition should see more noncompliance than younger sectors, such as JAIN and Employment & Social Affairs.

EU COMPETENCIES

The more competencies the EU has to legislate in certain policy sectors, the more likely member states are to face EU laws that do not reflect their preferred outcome, imposing compliance costs. To measure the range of the EU competencies, Lindberg and Scheingold distinguished between scope and locus (level) of decision making (Lindberg and Scheingold 1970, 67–71). While scope relates to the initial expansion of EU authority to new policy areas, locus or level stresses "the relative importance of Community decision-making processes as compared with national processes" (1970, 68; cf. Börzel 2005). Policy sectors such as Internal Market, Competition, or Environment, in which the EU has comprehensive legislative competencies (broad level and wide scope), are expected to come with higher costs than policy sectors such as Taxation, in which the EU can legislate only on selective or minor issues. The broader the level and the wider the scope of EU competencies, the more member states might be unwilling or unable to bear the costs that come with the implementation and enforcement of comprehensive and far-reaching EU policies.[16] Given the EU's comprehensive competencies in Internal Market, Competition, or Environment, we should expect more noncompliance in these sectors than in Taxation or Employment & Social Affairs.

OPPOSITION TO EU COMPETENCIES

Public attitudes toward the EU vary not only across member states (chapter 3). EU citizens also differ in the extent to which they support or oppose EU competencies over policy sectors (Zhelyazkova, Kaya, and Schrama 2016). Public opinion data shows that citizens are supportive of the EU legislating on Environment but prefer their member states to remain in charge of Employment & Social Affairs. We should expect more noncompliance in the latter sectors owing to the greater opposition against the EU as the rule-making institution, rendering politicization more likely. I already found that higher EU opposition leads to less rather than more noncompliance (see chapters 3 and 4). We shall see whether this counterintuitive finding also holds when sector-specific factors are included in the analysis.

REGULATORY DENSITY

Another factor that shapes the costs of compliance across different sectors is regulatory density. The more European laws that exist in a policy sector, the lower the need in the member states to adapt already harmonized (or Europeanized) domestic laws to newly passed directives (Mastenbroek 2003; Kaeding 2006; Haverland and Romeijn 2007). Taking EU policies in sectors with high regulatory density, like Agriculture and Enterprise & Industry, should be less costly and require less capacity and domestic power as compared to JAIN, Information Society & Media, and Taxation.

Issue-Specific Explanations

Some studies aggregate issue-specific explanations of noncompliance at the sector level. Rather than including the entire list of issue-specific factors, I will limit myself to the factors that chapter 4 found to be significant in explaining temporal variation in noncompliance and that are unequally distributed across sectors (cf. Haverland, Steunenberg, and van Waarden 2011; Steunenberg and Rhinard 2010; Berglund, Grange, and van Waarden 2006; Toshkov 2008; Luetgert and Dannwolf 2009).

NOVELTY

New legislation is more demanding than amending legislation. The former creates a greater misfit with existing domestic legislation, which needs to be adapted, imposing higher compliance costs that member states may not be willing or able to bear. Environment and Employment & Social Affairs, which have a higher share of new legislation, should be more prone to noncompliance than Agriculture and Competition.

COMPLEXITY

Complex legislation is more demanding on the capacities of the member states. Highly complex sectors, such as Information Society & Media and JAIN, should show more noncompliance than Agriculture and Enterprise.

DELEGATION

Delegation reduces the risk of politicized implementation, requiring less domestic power for enforcement. Agriculture, Enterprise, and Competition, with their higher share of delegated legislation, should feature less noncompliance than Environment, Employment & Social Affairs, or JAIN.

EU-LEVEL CONFLICT

The amendments the European Parliament introduces during the adoption of directives increases the risk of those directives being politicized in their implementation. Environment and Health & Consumer Protection, where parliamentary interference is higher, are more likely than Competition and Agriculture to face domestic opposition to compliance.

While controlling for issue-specific factors, I do not include country-based explanations in the sector models. Partisan preferences (König and Luetgert 2009), bureaucratic quality (Steunenberg and Rhinard 2010), or organized interests (Steunenberg and Rhinard 2010; Luetgert and Dannwolf 2009; König and Luetgert 2009) and subnational authorities (Borghetto and Franchino 2010; Steunenberg and Rhinard 2010) may vary significantly within member states, producing legislative and bureaucratic drift "within sector-specific boundaries" (Steunenberg and Rhinard 2010, 497). This is not the same, however, as to argue that all member states are similar with regard to these sector-specific differences, resulting in similar noncompliance patterns. There are neither theoretical reasons nor empirical evidence suggesting that the capacity or the power of member states is higher in particular sectors than in others. Party preferences do not converge along sectors either. Parties belonging to the same side of the political spectrum seldom share the same preference for how to deal with an entire policy sector. The German Christian Democrats and the Hungarian Fidesz are members of the European Peoples Party, the conservative group in the European Parliament. Yet their preferences on individual rights, rule of law, asylum and migration, or environmental and social standards greatly diverge (Scully, Hix, and Farrell 2012). The same is true for the social democratic parties in France, Spain, Germany, Sweden, and Eastern Europe that are members of the Party of European Socialists.

Finally, member states also vary with regard to their ability to shape policy outcomes as to reduce compliance costs, as well as in the power to resist them. Yet no single member state is in the position to dominate at the shaping stage of the compliance game (Héritier, Knill, and Mingers 1996; Börzel 2002a). It makes little sense, therefore, to disaggregate country-specific power and capacity at the sector level.

The control variables can be grouped into factors that affect the compliance costs of a sector and factors that render politicization more likely. With regard to the former, noncompliance becomes more likely owing to higher compliance costs the broader and deeper a sector is integrated (*EU competencies*); the more directives the EU adopts, which set new rather than amend existing legislation (*novelty*); and the more issues these directives regulate (*complexity*). The number of years the EU has been active in a sector mitigates the expected positive effect of costs on noncompliance (*age*). So does the number of already existing laws member states have to comply with (*regulatory density*). The adoption of a directive by Council and EP (*non-delegation*), the interference of the EP in the adoption of a directive (*EU conflict*), and low domestic support for the EU legislating on a sector (*EU opposition*) increase the likelihood of politicization.

Evaluating Factors Influencing Policy Variation

Since I am interested in policy explanations, I focus the statistical analysis on policy type and regulatory logic as genuine sector characteristics. The more indirect sector variables and issue-specific factors that are assumed or empirically observed by the literature will be included in the analysis as control variables.

Data and Methods

The regression models in chapters 3 and 4 took member states[17] and individual directives[18] as their unit of analysis, respectively. The ensuing analysis includes annual observations per policy sector and employs the number of infringements per policy sector per year as its dependent variable. More specifically, the dependent variable is based on 10,135 observations concerning infringements against directives between 1978 and 2012, as allocated to eleven policy sectors in the Commission sources.

The EU publishes data on its legislation on EUR-Lex, including information and search options on the type of legal act, period of validity, and other characteristics. However, it does not provide for a clear categorization of policy sectors. The multilingual thesaurus EuroVoc, maintained by the Publications Office of the European Union,[19] links numerous topics, subject matters, and directory codes to a legal act. I therefore apply the categorization of infringement proceedings, which the European Commission uses in its Annual Reports on Monitoring the Application of EU Law. It clearly indicates the (main) policy sector concerned by listing infringements according to the Directorate-General responsible for handling the proceeding. The categorization of sectors by the DG in charge of the infringement comes closest to the categories used for coding the infringements by sectors. It also has an advantage over the treaty base in general. Enabling treaty articles, such as Article 100 EC Treaty, served as the legal basis for many enterprise and environment directives, before a proper primary legal base was established by treaty reforms. The structure of most policy sectors has changed over time. The eleven sectors under investigation have remained rather constant, though. The DGs for Health & Consumer Protection and Transport & Energy were separated in 2004 and 2010, respectively, because of the growing number of member states. I continue to aggregate them.

Using the directory codes allows me to draw on the data set *Legislative Production in the EU, 1967–2009* compiled by Dimiter Toshkov to compute the number of *adopted* directives per sector and year as a proxy for the legislation in force. A lag of three years matches adoption and official infringement of a directive controlling for the six to twelve months it takes for a directive to enter into force, and the twenty-four to thirty-six months that elapse between the Commission registering a possible infringement and sending out a reasoned opinion.

POLICY TYPE

The coding of policy sectors as *regulatory* vs. nonregulatory is a challenge. EU law is predominantly regulatory owing to the limited competencies the EU has for redistribution (Börzel 2005; Genschel and Jachtenfuchs 2016). Fishery is clearly redistributive, as it sets limits to what member states are allowed to fish. So is Regional Policy with regard to the fiscal transfers member states receive. Both sectors, however, are not included in the sample because of the low number of adopted directives (less than one directive in two years). For the same reason, I dropped Research and Education, which are redistributive policies. Agriculture is the one policy sector in the sample that contains a substantial redistributive dimension, in the form of farm subsidies, which still account for a third of the EU budget. EU price and market support has been politically justified by considerations of food security, declining living standards of farmers, and structural and natural disparities between the various agricultural regions in the EU (Knudsen 2009). While some member states benefit more than others, redistribution is more indirect and, as expected by Majone, becomes an issue of contention every seven years when the EU's budget is negotiated at the EU level rather than in everyday implementation (De la Fuente and Doménech 2000; Aksoy 2010).

REGULATORY LOGIC

Internal Market, Competition, and Taxation & Customs Union are the three sectors that are predominantly market making. Internal Market aims at removing obstacles to trade in goods and services, such as tariffs, taxes, quantitative restrictions on imports (e.g., quotas) and measures having equivalent effect. EU competition law (Articles 101–109 TFEU) seeks to prevent behavior of states and companies that harms competition in the Internal Market. This entails the control of state aid, mergers and acquisitions, and the formation of cartels, collusion, and other forms of anticompetitive practices. The customs union protects the external borders of the Internal Market by setting common external tariffs. The coordination of taxation policy across the EU is intended to prevent indirect state aid, such as offering tax credits to (foreign) businesses. A prominent example is the European Commission ordering the Irish government to collect more than €14 billion in taxes, including interest, from Apple in 2018.

Employment & Social Affairs has clearly *market-correcting* goals (Article 151 TFEU) since it aims at improving living and working conditions to protect workers' health and safety. In a similar vein, Environmental and Health & Consumer Protection are designed to correct market failures by setting production and product standards to fight environmental pollution (Article 191 TFEU) and protect the health in general (Article 168 TFEU), for workers (Article 153 TFEU) and consumers (Article 169 TFEU).

The other sectors are more difficult to classify and entail some broad generalization. Every policy sector or, in fact, every EU legal act may entail regulatory elements or some elements of *market correcting* and market making. This is why previous studies have primarily analyzed policies or EU laws that are straightforward in their categorization (Scharpf 1996, 1997a; Zürn 1997, 2002). Yet even on the level of individual legal acts, things may become at times difficult. Surrendering to the methodological challenge might be tempting but would make the theoretical distinctions of policies made by Lowi or Scharpf empirically irrelevant. I try to tackle the challenge by analyzing the general goals the EU aims to achieve within a certain policy sector, its underlying problem-solving approach, and the policy instruments mainly invoked to achieve these goals. This allows me to determine the predominant character of a policy sector. My categorization is certainly not beyond criticism but provides a first cut into an important research area (cf. Börzel, Hofmann, and Sprungk 2003; Börzel, Hofmann, and Panke 2011).

Agriculture was meant to be part of building a common market. While the member states subsequently removed tariffs on agricultural products, they set up a system of agricultural subsidies, which has prevented free competition. Being predominantly redistributive, the EU has heavily regulated production to bring rising production down and stabilize prices—the milk quota regime was only abolished in 2015. The increasingly contested regulatory dimension of the common agricultural policy, which also shows in the most infringed legal acts being regulatory, is market correcting in the sense that it aims at protecting the farming sector against the free market.

Enterprise & Industry had no clear legal base until the Treaty of Maastricht introduced the rather broad goal to ensure conditions necessary for the competitiveness of the industry (Article 173 TFEU). A closer look at the directives adopted in this policy sector shows that the main goal appears to be the approximation of laws regarding product standards. One could argue that Enterprise & Industry is reregulating the market created by Internal Market-making policies. Its policies, however, seek to eliminate nontariff barriers, such as different technical standards, rather than correcting market failures. The most infringed legal act in this sector is a directive laying down a procedure for the provision of information in the field of technical standards and regulations. Article 28 TFEU prohibits quantitative restrictions on the movement of goods and measures having an equivalent effect, such as technical standards and regulations. Member states may still issue them where they are necessary in order to meet essential requirements and are in the public interest. The directive obliges the member states to notify the Commission about their intent to adopt a technical provision to give the Commission time to voice its objection, make amendments, or to consider the adoption of an EU directive.[20]

Information Society & Media seeks to establish a Digital Single Market (Articles 179–180 TFEU). A range of regulations is intended to remove barriers to competition. Similar to Transport & Energy, however, (tele)communications used to be a public service, so as to guarantee universal access even in remote or otherwise unprofitable areas. With the creation of the Internal Market, state monopolies were subsequently privatized, requiring some reregulation of the provision of services at the EU level to ensure that customers and businesses have fair and affordable access to networks and services, and that their data is protected. Accordingly, the two sectors have become predominantly market correcting, protecting consumer rights. Network neutrality is a prominent example. It is part of the universal service framework. Providers of internet access must not discriminate between services offered online, or give one preferential treatment over the other. Several network providers have started to offer their users subscription plans that would allow them to continue using certain services, such as WhatsApp and Spotify, even if their monthly data allowance expired. Competing chat apps and streaming services are blocked. While this is about fair competition, network neutrality is an individual and enforceable right of EU citizens as end users.[21]

CONTROL VARIABLES

The *age* of a sector is easy to determine. It is measured in the number of years the EU has had the competence to legislate. Not surprisingly, the EU had obtained competencies in most market-making sectors, as well as in Agriculture, already with the Treaty of Rome (1958), while market-correcting competencies only came later with the Single European Act (1986). The youngest sectors are JAIN and Employment & Social Affairs, which were only created by the Maastricht Treaty (1992).[22]

Rather than the length of time the EU has held the competence to legislate on a sector, *EU competence* captures the level and scope of the EU's legal authority. The formal allocation of EU competencies and the institutional decision-making procedures as they evolved in the various treaty reforms provide an adequate operationalization (cf. Scharpf 2001b). The integration index developed by Börzel (Börzel 2005; cf. Schimmelfennig and Winzen 2014; Nanou, Zapryanova, and Toth 2017) captures the level (breadth) of integration by the number of issues in a given policy sector for which the EU has the power to legislate. The scope (depth) is measured in terms of the procedures according to which policy decisions are taken, focusing on the involvement of Commission (agenda setting) and European Parliament (consultation, cooperation, co-decision) and Council voting rules (unanimity, majority voting). For each of the two dimensions, a five-point scale is applied. In order to come to a more differentiated assessment, the scale also allows for half points. Since there is no theoretical reason to weigh level and scope differently, the average of the two scores is used. Agriculture and Internal Market are the sectors where the EU received a broad range of competencies subject to supranational decision making early on. In Enterprise, Environment, Consumer & Health, and Employment & Social Affairs the EU broadened its regulatory powers with every treaty reform, and directives became increasingly passed under what now is the ordinary procedure. The Commission has the exclusive right to introduce EU legislation, on which the Council votes by majority; the Parliament's approval is necessary to pass the bill, which is subject to the judicial review of the ECJ. Taxation,[23] Transport & Energy, and Information Society & Media are at the other end of the integration spectrum, where the EU's formal powers have remained more limited and it is more difficult to form a consensus in the Council because of often-still-required unanimity (the unanimity requirement does not apply to Information Society & Media).

EU support for the EU is usually measured at the country level in terms of public support for membership in the EU (see chapter 3). To tap into *EU opposition* against the EU's legal authority in a sector, I use Eurobarometer time series data on public support for transferring legislative competences in a specific policy sector to the European level.

As for the regulatory density of policy sectors, I look at the latitude of the EU's regulatory activities. This can be measured in two ways: first, by the rate of directives adopted in one sector in relation to all eleven sectors, and second, by the number of *adopted directives* in one sector in a given year. The second indicator is dynamic, varying by year. The two indicators highly correlate. I chose the second indicator for it is dynamic.

For the four issue-specific control variables, misfit (new directives), complexity (recitals), delegated legislation (Commission directive), and EU-level conflict (EP amendments), I draw on the data sets developed for the analysis in chapter 4. For misfit and delegated legislation, I use the annual number of *new directives* and *directives not delegated* to the Commission, respectively, adopted in a sector three years prior to the official infringement. For complexity, I multiply the annual average of *recitals* based on directives in a sector by the number of directives adopted in the sector and divide the result by ten for reasons of rescaling. EU-level conflict is measured by the average stage at which the *EP interferes* in the adoption of a directive, pressuring the Council to make concessions by accepting amendments.

Finally, I use two dummy variables as controls for the effect of the *Maastricht Treaty* and the growing number of *member states*. More than any other treaty reform, the Maastricht Treaty substantially broadened and deepened the competencies of the EU, giving it the power to legislate on several new policy sectors, extending QMV in the Council, and empowering the European Parliament in the adoption of EU law. Between 1981 and 2012, the number of member states grew from ten to twenty-seven, increasing the violative opportunities.

The dependent variable is the absolute number of infringement proceedings per year and sector officially opened between 1981 and 2012 against violations of directives adopted three years before in the same sector. It is a count variable that is over-dispersed. The summary statistics can be found in table A1.5. Similar to what I did in chapter 4, I estimate a negative binomial regression with random effects to account for the pooled structure of the data. The Hausman test showed that unit-specific differences between years and sectors are coincidental. It is therefore not necessary to include fixed effects. Several of the issue-specific control variables check for violative opportunities.

Four control variables influencing compliance costs significantly correlate with each other since they are all linked to the number of adopted directives in a given year (see table A2.3). Regulatory density, misfit, delegated legislation, and complexity are therefore put into separate models. A fifth and six model control for the effect of the Maastricht Treaty and the growing number of member states, respectively.

Results and Discussion

POLICY TYPE AND REGULATORY LOGIC

The effect of *regulatory policy* is positive and significant in all models (table 5.1). The finding that regulatory policy is more prone to noncompliance finds further

TABLE 5.1 Policy type, regulatory logic, and noncompliance (EU-15, 1981–2012)

	REGULATORY DENSITY	MISFIT	COMPLEXITY	POLITICIZATION
Policy				
Regulatory policy	**1.015***	0.362	**0.924***	**0.612***
	(0.270)	(0.229)	(0.253)	(0.220)
Market-correcting	**0.436***	**0.299**	**0.392***	**0.445***
	(0.145)	(0.142)	(0.141)	(0.140)
Control Variables				
Costs				
Age	-0.000153	-0.000254	-0.00206	-0.000945
	(0.00444)	(0.00461)	(0.00439)	(0.00432)
EU competencies	0.0262	0.0111	0.0224	0.0700
	(0.0517)	(0.0511)	(0.0517)	(0.0525)
Directives adopted	**0.0291***			
	(0.00509)			
New directives		**0.0725***		
		(0.0129)		
Recitals			**0.0378***	
			(0.0569)	
Politicization				
Council/Council-EP directive				**0.0668***
				(0.00802)
EP amendments	**0.514***	**0.502***	**0.483***	**0.459***
	(0.0670)	(0.0693)	(0.0678)	(0.0697)
EU opposition	**-2.036***	**-1.970***	**-2.052***	**-1.678***
	(0.507)	(0.527)	(0.508)	(0.520)
Constant	-1.108**	-0.346	-0.971*	-0.960*
	(0.526)	(0.511)	(0.503)	(0.497)
Observations	308	308	308	308
Number of years	32	32	32	32

Standard errors in parentheses
*** p<0.01, ** p<0.05, * p<0.1

support by the omission of four nonregulatory sectors from the analysis. I did not include Fisheries & Maritime Affairs, Regional Policy, Development, and Education & Culture because violative opportunities are very low (less than one adopted directive in two years). These nonregulatory sectors hardly feature non-compliance (figure 5.1).

Likewise, *market-correcting* regulation has a positive and significant effect on noncompliance. Three of the four most infringed sectors, JAIN, Environment, and Health & Consumer Protection, seek to harmonize national standards meant to protect individuals and their rights. Information Society & Media has become increasingly concerned with data protection and universal access. By contrast, the lesser infringed sectors are predominantly market making or nonregulatory.

In sum, member states are more likely to violate regulatory policy, particularly if it aims at correcting market outcomes. Policy type and regulatory logic have a substantial effect on noncompliance.

COMPLIANCE COSTS

The results on the control variables confirm that sectors differ in the compliance costs they impose on the member states at the taking stage. The greater the level and scope of the *competencies* the EU has to set legislation and the higher the misfit (*new directives*) and the complexity (*recitals*) of the adopted legislation in a sector, the more noncompliance we are likely to see. Regulatory density (*adopted directives*) is significant, too, but appears to increase costs rather than alleviate them. This could be explained by regulatory density resulting in a higher workload, straining the capacity of the member states in taking EU directives (see chapter 4).

Age, in contrast, has a negative but not significant effect. This may have to do with *EU competencies*. On the one hand, extending the level and scope of EU competencies usually takes several treaty reforms. The older a sector, the more issues the EU is likely to be able to legislate on (level) and the more likely decision making is to be supranational (scope). On the other hand, market-correcting sectors tend to be younger. While market making has been at the core of European integration since its beginning, the Treaty of Rome of 1957 hardly conferred any market-correcting powers to the EU. This only started to change with the Single European Act. Environment is a case in point. The EU had selectively legislated on the sector more than ten years before the Single European Act of 1986 granted it the formal competence to do so. While the level of Article 130 (s) was already rather broad, member states had to decide by unanimity. Only the Maastricht Treaty of 1992 introduced qualified majority voting and gave the European Parliament a say in the adoption of EU environmental law.

POLITICIZATION

Higher compliance costs result in more noncompliance. So does higher politicization. In the regression model, directives adopted by the Council and the EP increase the number of infringements (*Council/Council-EP directive*). Noncompliance becomes even more likely if conflict arises between the two co-legislators (*EP amendments*). With each additional stage of EP amendments, the expected infringements increase.

EU opposition, in contrast, makes noncompliance, if at all, *less* likely. It is the only variable that decreases the expected number of infringements. Its effect is significant in five of the six models. Similar to member state noncompliance, this counterintuitive correlation may be related to the effect of public opinion on EU decision making. Member state governments that face public opposition are empowered to shape EU law according to their preferences. They can also tie their hands when negotiating the transfer of new or the extension of existing competencies of the EU. These decisions require unanimity. Eurosceptic UK blocked the conferral of comprehensive competencies in Employment, Health & Consumer Protection, JAIN, and Taxation. Opt-outs and other forms of differential integration have allowed the EU to eventually move forward with integrating these policy sectors (see chapter 4). Yet the scope and level of its competencies remain more limited compared to policy sectors where EU opposition is lower, such as Environment. The legal acts the EU has managed to pass tend to be frequently violated, particularly in market-correcting sectors. This explains why, despite the EU's more limited competencies, Health & Consumer Protection and JAIN are among the most infringed policy sectors when controlling for violative opportunities. They have fewer legal acts than Environment; the member states, however, are equally likely to violate them because they are market-correcting regulatory policies and tend to get politicized, which may explain why the negative effect loses significance in politicized sectors.

The results on the variables influencing compliance costs and politicization support the findings of chapter 4. Declining noncompliance is driven by the decreasing propensity of the EU to adopt new and complex directives, and the growing tendency of the member states to delegate the adoption of amending legislation to the Commission, which renders conflict between Council and EP impossible. These factors also seem to vary across sectors without leveling the effect of policy type and regulatory logic. Regulatory policy and market-correcting policy correlate negatively with the four variables related to compliance costs as well as with the adoption of directives by Council and EP, which all have a significant positive effect on noncompliance. Likewise, they show a positive correlation with EU opposition. EU conflict is the only factor conducive to noncompliance that correlates positively with the regulatory policy and market-correcting logic of a sector.

As in the country and the directive models, the explanatory power of PCP variables is rather robust in the sector model when including another five years (table A5.1).

Policy Matters! The EU's Migration Crisis

As expected by the PCP model, the policy type and the dominant regulatory logic of a sector have a significant effect on that sector's propensity for noncompliance. EU regulatory policy is more prone to violations, particularly if its regulatory logic is market correcting. The substantial costs incurred at the taking rather than the shaping stage of the compliance game are more likely to become politicized. While market-correcting policy creates winners and losers by opening markets, the domestic actors who have to bear the costs of EU market-correcting policy have to change their behavior to ensure compliance. This renders politicization of compliance costs more likely. The migration crisis, which hit the EU in 2015, is a powerful illustration of how politicization affects noncompliance with EU regulatory policy that incurs high costs at the domestic level.

In 2015, the EU found itself confronted with over 1.2 million refugees and migrants who had entered its territory. In order to cope with the historic influx, the majority of the member states agreed in September 2015 on an obligatory relocation quota. However, rather than many states sharing the burden, the vast majority of refugees and migrants ended up in a few member states. The failure of a common European solution is a clear demonstration of how difficult it is for member states to ensure compliance with EU regulatory policy that has redistributive costs at the domestic level when these costs become highly politicized. Even Germany and Sweden, which did not renege on their initial commitment to accept refugees, made available only a fraction of the places they had pledged.[24] Three weeks before the relocation scheme expired on 26 September 2017, only 27,695 refugees (less than a quarter) out of the 120,000 legally foreseen in the Council decision of September 2015 had been relocated.[25] Malta and Norway (a non-EU member state) are the only ones that fully met their relocation quota. With the exception of Finland, Ireland, Lithuania, Luxembourg, Malta, and Sweden, all other member states underperformed by more than 50 percent. The Commission officially opened infringement proceedings against Hungary, the Czech Republic, and Poland for neglecting their legal obligation to accept refugees from Greece and Italy.[26] In 2015, it had already taken legal action against all twenty-eight member states for not applying the five directives the EU had adopted between 2001 and 2011 to provide minimum standards on asylum procedures and reception conditions for asylum seekers, temporary protection and recognition of refugees, and for the deportation of illegal migrants, as well as observing the Dublin and Eurodac fingerprinting regulations (European Commission 2016, 19–20). The increasing politicization of migration and asylum policy has made it more difficult to take the costs of complying with EU asylum and migration law. The regulatory measures substantially affect the allocation of refugees and migrants in the EU. Protecting their rights renders member states more attractive recipients, as the cases of Sweden and Germany demonstrate. Conversely, poor humanitarian conditions in reception centers and the setting up of detention camps where people are treated as criminals have a deterring effect.

As the PCP model would have expected, noncompliance with EU asylum and migration law had started well before the historic influx of more than a million refugees and migrants in 2015. Since the completion of the EU Common European Asylum System (CEAS) in 2005, the Commission had already sent more than three hundred reasoned opinions. Germany, Sweden, and Austria as primary destinations had hoped to make countries of first entry and transit countries more attractive for refugees and asylum seekers by shaping EU law as to harmonize standards for their reception, protection, and recognition. While those three countries had succeeded in uploading their policies to the EU level, Greece, Italy, Spain, Hungary, and Bulgaria have lacked the capacity to deal with rising numbers of persons in search of protection.[27]

Greece and Italy as member states of first entry stopped registering and accommodating migrants and refugees when their numbers started to increase in 2014. They have never really managed to return migrants not qualifying for asylum or refugee status to their country of origin (European Commission 2016, 9–10). Returning migrants to Greece as a country of first entry (Dublin transfers) has not been possible since 2010, not least because the European Court of Human Rights and the ECJ raised concerns about the human rights situation and the treatment of migrants in the reception centers (European Commission 2016, 10).[28] Rather than sharing the costs as required by EU law, Austria, France, Denmark, Sweden, and Germany reintroduced border controls. In the face of rising populism, member state governments felt unable to overcome the mounting public opposition to the reception and integration of refugees. While temporary border controls are admissible under the Schengen regime, the introduction of daily caps to restrict access of refugees in Austria and the building of razor-wire fences by Hungary and Bulgaria to stop them altogether are a blatant violation of both EU Schengen rules and international law.

The migration crisis is an exceptional example of noncompliance with market-correcting policy in the EU. As an extreme case, however, it illustrates clearly the underlying causal mechanisms specified by the PCP model. Market-correcting policy is more likely to become politicized because of its redistributive costs. Member state governments have used politicization fueled by populist parties to shape EU law in the EU's initial response to the migration crisis. At the same time, growing politicization had made compliance with the mandatory relocation scheme increasingly difficult, and not only in those countries that had been outvoted in the Council. Polarized public controversy over how to handle the refugee and migrant flows in the member states, as well as polarization in the European Parliament, has rendered any attempts at arriving at a common European solution through depoliticization by delegation futile.

In September 2015, Hungary, Slovakia, the Czech Republic, and Romania opposed the adoption of a temporary and exceptional mechanism to relocate 120,000 refugees from Italy and Greece to other member states over two years, on top of the 40,000 the member states had already decided to relocate.[29] Germany, France, Austria, and Sweden had successfully tied their hands to the electoral success of right-wing populist parties that vigorously opposed the reception of further refugees and migrants. Since the Council passed the relocation decision under the non-legislative procedure, the EP was only consulted. In view of the urgent situation, the EP gave its consent to the Commission proposal without proposing any amendment, which would not have been binding for the Council anyway. The EP stressed, however, that it expected the Commission to prepare a proposal for a regulation of the European Parliament and of the Council to establish a crisis relocation mechanism.[30] A third of the parliamentarians either voted against or abstained, which indicates that relocation has been controversial in the EP, too. Particularly the Eurosceptic European Conservatives and Reformists Group has been opposed to any relocation scheme.

The EU-Turkey agreement on the resettlement of Syrian refugees required an amendment of the Council Decision of 2015. The resettlement agreement introduced a one-in, one-out policy. In exchange for each "irregular" migrant that Turkey took back from Greece, the EU would resettle one Syrian refugee from Turkey. Moreover, the EU allotted altogether €6 billion to help Turkey provide temporary protection for Syrians (European Commission 2016). The Council Decision of 2016 enabled member states to subtract from their allocated number of relocated applicants the number of Syrians admitted to their territory through resettlement from Turkey. The majority of EP members rejected that resettlement should take place at the expense of relocation. They also sought to extend the scope of the decision to Iraqis, Eritreans, and Afghans. Finally, the EP called on the member states to comply with their relocation commitments and agree on a holistic EU approach to migration. The EP introduced twenty-four amendments, which the Council chose to ignore.[31]

All attempts to institutionalize a permanent solution to deal with the continu-ing influx of migrants have failed so far. It has been impossible for the member state governments to ignore the increasing politicization of relocating even refu-gees. In line with the PCP model, the frontline states have continued to struggle with their lack of capacity to cope with compliance costs incurred by already agreed decisions and EU asylum and migration laws. In transit and destination countries, their taking has been undermined by mounting domestic opposi-tion against receiving refugees. Even liberal Sweden has responded to the grow-ing support for the right-wing populist Sweden Democrats by announcing a more restrictive approach. Germany has faced the rise in the polls of the anti-immigration party Alternative für Deutschland, resulting in the reneging on the *Willkommenskultur* (welcome culture) Chancellor Angela Merkel had advocated when Germany welcomed over 890,000 refugees in 2015 at the height of the crisis. As the most resourceful member state with a potent administration, it still has not been able to process the massive amount of pending applications for asylum, not to mention the proper housing and integration into the German labor market of the more than 1.2 million migrants Germany received in 2015 and 2016.

Facing mounting politicization at the EU level (EU-level conflict) and the domestic level (EU opposition), member state governments sought to delegate the regulation of migration to EU institutions. In 2016, the Commission pro-posed the computerized relocation of refugees enforced by an independent EU agency (cf. Börzel 2016). The European Asylum Support Office (EASO) would be turned into the European Union Agency for Asylum, with new powers to evalu-ate member states' policies. Moreover, the EU Border and Coast Guard Agency (EBCG) would monitor the EU's external borders to ensure that the member states effectively implemented EU legal standards for border management. In case of failure to do so, the EBCG would have the authority to intervene directly, without the consent of the member state concerned. A European Return Office, created within EBCG, would deploy European Return Intervention Teams to return illegally staying third-county nationals. The EU border guards would also enforce the mandatory and semiautomatic mechanism for redistributing asylum seekers and refugees, which the Commission suggested as part of the planned reform of the Dublin Regulation.[32] The proposed distribution system would be activated whenever a member state faced a disproportionate number of asylum applications, namely more than 150 percent of its capacity. It would reflect the relative size, wealth, and absorption capacities of member states and would be monitored by the EASO. Member states refusing to accept asylum seek-ers would have to pay a €250,000 "solidarity contribution" to the hosting mem-ber state. A new regulation would amend the so-called Dublin III Regulation, circumventing the consent of national parliaments (European Parliament / European Council 2013).

The growing politicization of migration prevented the member states from delegating the handling of refugees and migrants to independent EU regulatory agencies. Instead, they have reverted to national solutions, comprehensively violating EU law. The reform of the EU's internal asylum system has deadlocked. The member states have not been able to agree on Commission proposals on how to grant and withdraw international protection, a list of safe third countries, reception conditions, labor market access for asylum seekers, residency permits for refugees and people with subsidiary protection status, guarding unaccompanied minors, and entering fingerprints of children into the Eurodac biometric database. The Salzburg Summit of September 2018 officially abandoned the idea of mandatory relocation. The new Commission president Ursula von der Leyen had promised a "fresh start on migration."[33] Yet the Commission announced it would shelve its attempts at replacing the rule of first entry by a relocation mechanism because of the resistance of the Czech Republic, Hungary, and Poland. Its proposal for reforming the Common European Asylum System has focused on fortifying the EU's external border by increasing the budget and the personnel of the EBCG (cf. Börzel 2020).

Most Europeans consider immigration, together with terrorism, the most important issue for the EU and the member states. In 2017, some 68 percent of EU citizens supported a common migration policy; in only four of the twenty-eight member states was a majority opposed.[34] Yet member state governments are unwilling to confer on the EU the necessary competencies to effectively deal with the problem of protecting its external borders, of fighting human trafficking, and of preventing thousands of people from drowning in the Mediterranean. The times in which the EU could adopt regulatory policy without politics appear to be gone.

Policy determines the politics of noncompliance. Regulatory policy entails higher costs that are more likely to become politicized because of their redistributive consequences at the domestic level. This is particularly the case if the better part of regulatory policy aims at correcting market failure. Compliance research focuses on country variation and has not systematically explored nor explained sector-related noncompliance. The PCP model specifies how policy determines the politics of noncompliance by focusing on the differential effects of policy type and regulatory logic on compliance costs. First, because of the regulatory diversity of the member states with regard to the level of regulation but also their underlying regulatory philosophy, member states that have the power to shape EU market-correcting regulations according to their regulatory preferences are likely to face lower compliance costs. This is a function of public support for the

EU. Eurosceptic member states are better shapers of the laws the EU adopts, as well as of its political authority to do so. Second, actively applying and enforcing EU regulations is more costly for the member states than simply abolishing national regulations or refraining from enacting new ones. Third, domestic resistance against compliance is more likely since domestic actors have to engage in costly change, and compliance costs tend to be unevenly distributed. The higher tendency of politicization may explain why the adoption of market-correcting policy is more likely to be delegated to the Commission, and why domestic opposition to EU competencies for market-correcting policy tends to be higher. If, however, market-correcting directives are adopted by the Council and the European Parliament instead of the Commission, conflict is likely to arise between the two co-legislators, increasing the propensity of the national parliaments to get involved in the transposition process, as shown in chapter 4.

Monetary policy and immigration are two prominent examples of how member states have tried to address the redistributive implications of regulatory policy by depoliticizing them through delegation (cf. Börzel 2016). In both sectors, member states have not been willing to confer redistributive power to the EU. At the same time, EU regulations on the Monetary Union and the borderless Schengen area substantially constrain the member states in making redistributive policy at the domestic level. The convergence criteria and the Stability and Growth Pact deprive euro countries of key instruments of macroeconomic management without providing the EU with the tax and spending capacity to deal with external shocks and structural asymmetries within the Monetary Union. In a similar vein, the Schengen regime requires the participating countries to abolish internal border controls without creating a common external border control and a common administration to handle asylum seekers and refugees.

Unable to agree on a transfer mechanism to bail out member states in sovereign debt or at the front line of immigration, governments of creditor and nonrecipient member states have framed the euro and the Schengen crises as problems of too lenient rules and too lax enforcement. The solution, as they see it, is not fiscal transfer and relocation of refugees but compliance with stricter austerity, immigration, and border control rules, as well as structural reforms monitored and enforced by the Commission and independent EU agencies, such as the ECB, the ECBG, and the EOS. Compliance with EU rules is supposed to enable debtor and frontline countries to become self-sufficient in dealing with external shocks. Financial assistance is only a temporary means to buffer adjustment costs and help build reform capacities.

One could argue that EU monetary policy and immigration policy interfere with core state powers, which would explain why EU regulatory policy became so politicized, causing exceptional levels of noncompliance by which member states try to escape an equal distribution of costs. JAIN relates to internal security and is indeed the most infringed policy sector when controlling for violative opportunities. However, the degree to which EU environmental, health, and consumer regulations are contested in the member states and not complied with tells a different story. Member states have been very reluctant to grant the EU competencies to regulate issues that would directly interfere with their core powers (security, taxation, welfare). When not measured against the number of laws member states can potentially violate, JAIN ranks much lower on the sinners list (figure 5.1). The EU's noncompliance problems are concentrated in policy sectors the EU has comprehensively regulated because they are at the core of its mission to realize the four freedoms constituting the Internal Market. Ignoring their redistributive implications or trying to mask them as regulatory problems that need to be depoliticized has merely fueled the politicization of the EU (Börzel and Risse 2018). Isolating controversial policy from democratic politics by delegating its adoption to independent EU agencies has emboldened the calls of right- and left-wing populists to restore the sovereignty of the member states as the most effective way to protect citizens against financial markets, migration, civil rights activism, or terrorism. Market correction has ultimately turned into policy with politics.

THE LIMITS OF REGULATORY GOVERNANCE

The concluding chapter re-assembles the PCP model with the specifications generated by the empirical analyses in chapters 3–5. Power, capacity, and politicization matter in the two-level compliance game, which plays out across the two stages of EU law making. While power and capacity figure prominently in the literature, the PCP model specifies which conceptualizations are most relevant and how they interact in making noncompliance more or less likely. Moreover, the PCP model introduces politicization as a factor that has been largely neglected in compliance research but is crucial in understanding why some member states comply less than others, why noncompliance has declined over time, and why market-correcting policy is more prone to be violated.

I argue that the PCP model provides for a comprehensive account of variation in noncompliance with EU law across twenty-eight member states, eleven policy sectors, and more than forty years of European integration. Built within a rational institutionalist framework, the model is generalizable enough to explain the politics of noncompliance in areas of EU law not subject to infringement proceedings, as well as in other regional and international organizations. I then propose areas for future research where the PCP model could provide new insights, particularly with regard to the increasing relevance of politicization and the redistributive nature of law beyond the nation state. I conclude by considering the implications of my theoretical arguments and empirical findings for the effectiveness and legitimacy of the EU, and international governance more broadly. The increasing politicization of international trade, security, and climate change policy shows the limits of international regulation in dealing with redistributive issues.

International institutions lack sufficient tax and spending capacity to engage in meaningful redistribution. At the same time, they increasingly constrain states in making social adjustments to compensate those of their citizens who do not profit from globalization. The rise of nationalist movements and populist parties in Europe and in the US challenging the liberal foundations of Western societies and the international order alike may be the harbingers of post-regulatory politics. States need to tackle redistribution directly and decide who gets what in a transparent and accountable way instead of leaving this decision to independent agencies or the global markets.

The Politics of Noncompliance: Power, Capacity, and Politicization

The book set out to answer the following research question: Why has noncompliance in the EU not increased, or even decreased since the mid-1990s, despite a growing number of member states with weak compliance capacities and waning enthusiasm for European integration and with EU legislation expanding in sectors that are particularly prone to noncompliance? The research question consists of three empirical puzzles. To solve them, chapter 2 set out the PCP model, which conceptualizes compliance as a two-level game played across two stages. Unlike existing studies, it focuses on three variables that affect both the shaping and the taking of international and EU law. The model combines power and capacity in explaining noncompliance, while also specifying which conceptualizations matter in the shaping and taking of EU law. Finally, the PCP model brings in politicization, which compliance research has largely neglected. Counterintuitively, politicization explains why popular support for the EU increases noncompliance. Politicization also accounts for the declining noncompliance in an ever deeper and wider European Union.

The compliance game starts at the shaping stage. As rational actors, member state governments seek to minimize compliance costs by shaping EU laws according to their policy preferences. They differ, however, in the ability to do so. Rather than economic size or voting power in the Council, it is the Euroscepticism of their population that allows big and small member states alike to negotiate for policy outcomes that incur lower compliance costs on their domestic constituencies. Euroscepticism increases the chances of politicization in the implementation of costly EU laws. The anticipated risk of politicization, which may spill over to other member states, allows the governments of Eurosceptic countries to assert that their hands are tied by domestic opposition and therefore to negotiate for legal acts that entail lower compliance costs, to enable them to overcome such opposition. The differing propensity for domestic politicization explains why countries with efficient bureaucracies and similar voting power vary in their noncompliance with EU law, depending on how much their publics support and oppose the EU.

Chapter 3 confirmed the expectations of the PCP model that big, inefficient, and EU-supportive member states are worse compliers than small, efficient, and Eurosceptic member states. Combining power, capacity, and politicization, the PCP model can also explain why equally big and equally small member states substantially differ in their noncompliance with EU law (France versus UK; Denmark versus Luxembourg). Big states have the power to resist compliance with costly EU law, while small states have little choice but to comply. Both differ, however, in their ability to reduce compliance costs at the shaping stage and to cope with costly EU law at the taking stage. Eurosceptic member states, big or small, can tie their hands in negotiating policy outcomes close to their policy preferences. With efficient bureaucracies, they have less difficulty in coping with compliance costs at the taking stage if they have not been able to reduce them at the shaping stage in the first place. The combination of power, capacity, and politicization explains why Italy tops the list of noncompliers. The quality of its bureaucracy is as low as that of Greece or Portugal. So is its ability to reduce compliance costs at the shaping stage. What makes its performance even worse is Italy's power to resist compliance pressure. Denmark's bureaucracy is not only more efficient in both shaping and taking EU law. As one of the most Eurosceptic countries (until recently at least), Denmark holds an advantage, also over other member states with equally efficient bureaucracies and little power of recalcitrance, such as Belgium or Luxembourg. Likewise, big but efficient UK performed better than equally big and efficient Germany because its government could credibly tie its hands to the most Eurosceptic public in the EU, which voted to leave in 2016.

The PCP model can also explain why eastern enlargement, which brought in twelve member states with low administrative capacity that had no possibility to shape the vast part of EU laws they have to comply with, has not reversed the negative trend in noncompliance. Not only do the newcomers have little power to resist compliance costs. Pre-accession assistance and conditionality helped them build the specific administrative capacity to take EU law. Finally, the centralized taking capacity built during the accession phase has shielded the governments of the new member states against the politicization of costly EU laws in their implementation at the domestic level, particularly in the early days of their membership.

Figure C.1 reassembles the PCP model in light of the empirical findings. It is powerful in explaining country variation. Austria is the only member state

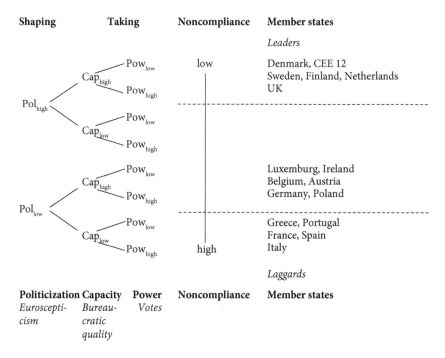

FIGURE C.1. The PCP model reassembled

whose level of noncompliance is lower than expected. Its bureaucratic quality is as high as its power is limited compared to the other Eurosceptic member states that head the list of compliers. Nevertheless, Austria's performance puts it in the middle field, on a par with the more Europhile Belgium and Luxembourg. Politicization is a major part of Austria's noncompliance with EU law (Falkner et al. 2005, 271, 333). Having joined in 1995, the Austrian government has had less opportunity to tie its hands to its Eurosceptic public to shape new EU law, since the EU has increasingly passed amending legislation adopted by the Commission rather than the Council and the EP. Yet this is also the case for Sweden and Finland, which comply much better.

The PCP model not only explains why some states comply less than others. By bringing in EU institutions, it also tackles variation in noncompliance across time and policy sectors, two dimensions that the literature has woefully neglected. While more EU opposition (anticipated politicization) increases the ability of member states to shape EU laws, the actual politicization of costly EU laws renders their taking more difficult. This is the reason why delegated legislation, in whose shaping and taking parliaments have no say either at the European or at the domestic level, is less prone to noncompliance. Likewise, market-correcting regulatory policy has a greater propensity of being violated, as its compliance costs are more likely to become politicized at the taking stage.

As suggested by IR theory, temporal variations in noncompliance are driven by changes in international institutions. Yet rather than enforcement, management, or legitimacy, it is the delegated decision-making power of international institutions that allows states to abide (more) with international and EU law. Delegating the adoption of international and EU laws to "regulatory bureaucracies" (Pollack 1997a, 106), such as the European Commission, entails lower compliance costs, which are also less visible to domestic constituencies. On the one hand, states opt for delegation to achieve policy outcomes that otherwise may get caught in time-consuming and complex international negotiations or become politicized at the domestic level (Moravcsik 1998). On the other hand, state principals seek to retain control over their international agents by administrative and oversight procedures (Pollack 1997a). As a result, delegated legislation tends to be secondary legislation amending existing rules and procedures rather than the setting new ones. Moreover, being executive acts, delegated legislation does not involve parliaments. Compliance costs are less visible to the public and therefore less likely to become politicized in implementation and enforcement at the domestic level. This is why noncompliance has decreased since the mid-1990s. Chapter 4 demonstrated that with the completion of the Internal Market, the EU started to pass more and more amending legislation, whose adoption is delegated to the Commission. Despite a growing body of EU law and an increasing number of member states that have to comply with it, noncompliance has declined.

As regards the third puzzle, violations of EU law are concentrated in a handful of policy sectors. Market-correcting policy is more frequently violated because it entails higher compliance costs that are more likely to become politicized. Unlike distributive and redistributive policy, regulatory policy incurs costs at the taking rather than at the shaping stage. Therefore, states are more likely to agree on regulatory as opposed to redistributive policy—they only have to face the costs when it comes to implementing and enforcing their agreements (Majone 1993, 1994). This explains why international and EU law tends to be regulatory rather than redistributive. At the same time, the regulatory nature makes international and EU law more prone to noncompliance, particularly when it seeks to protect and advance citizen rights. Chapter 5 validated the argument that EU laws that seek to harmonize regulatory standards to prevent market failure and correct politically undesired market outcomes are costlier than EU laws that aim at opening markets for foreign competition. To protect the environment or consumer and citizens' rights, member state government have not only to refrain from collecting tariffs and taxes. They have to enact or change existing legislation, which requires administrative capacity. Moreover, market actors have to often make costly adjustments to their behavior to comply with EU social and environmental standards. Accordingly, market-correcting law is more demanding on member states' enforcement capacity. Also, its compliance costs tend to be more visible and salient, making domestic opposition more likely.

In sum, the PCP model combines factors privileged by different compliance approaches and thereby provides for a comprehensive explanation of noncompliance in the EU regarding variation across countries, time, and policy sectors. Instead of treating power, capacity, and EU support as alternative explanations, the PCP model integrates them as complementary accounts of member state noncompliance. Drawing on concepts of general compliance theories and testing alternative conceptualizations allowed me to accommodate many of the explanatory factors considered in EU research without inflating the PCP model.

The Politics of Noncompliance: Europe and Beyond

The book develops a model of noncompliance with EU law whose enforcement and, increasingly, whose adoption the member states have delegated to the European Commission and the ECJ. This raises the questions of whether the PCP model also applies to areas that are not subject to infringement proceedings, and whether it travels to other international institutions where states largely control the enforcement and management of compliance.

From Market to Economic and Political Integration

The theoretical arguments of this book are based on a comprehensive empirical analysis of noncompliance with EU law. The Berlin Infringement Database covers thousands of violations of EU laws that form the core of the European integration project to which infringement proceedings apply. Article 258 TFEU entitles the European Commission to bring legal action against member states for failing to fulfill their obligations under EU law. There are three areas of EU law, however, that are not subject to the infringement proceedings of Article 258: competition law, economic and monetary policy, and the fundamental values.

First, Article 105 TFEU grants the Commission direct and exclusive enforcement authority to ensure free and fair competition in the Internal Market. This entails extensive investigative powers, including the authority to carry out dawn raids on the premises of suspected undertakings and private homes and vehicles in the member states (cf. Jones and Sufrin 2016).[1] These exceptional powers also show in the possibility of the Commission to refer cases to the ECJ without open-ing infringement proceedings if member states refuse to comply with its decision. Since competition law is treaty law, member states have no shaping possibilities to reduce compliance costs. In the taking of a Commission decision, however, capacity and politicization should still matter. What makes the case interesting is the attempt of the Commission to extend its enforcement authority for com-petition law to areas in which it has only limited competencies, such as taxation. In the summer of 2016, the Commission sought to force the Irish government to collect more than €13 billion in taxes from Apple.[2] Ireland refused to comply, so the Commission referred the case to the ECJ. The Irish government claimed that the Commission had overstepped its competencies by dictating tax laws and imposing them on a tax deal of twenty-five years ago. The Commission con-tended that Ireland had granted Apple tax credits that were far too generous (less than 1 percent) and therefore amounted to state subsidies. It withdrew the case in October 2018 after the Irish government had caved in and collected the money from Apple.[3]

Second, while the Commission enjoys extraordinary powers to enforce com-petition law, it has only a subsidiary role in guarding the EMU. The member states have created the Stability and Growth Pact and the Excessive Deficit Pro-cedure Protocol to impose fiscal discipline and prevent the building up of unsus-tainable national deficits. To ensure compliance with the limits on budget deficit (3 percent of GDP) and state debt (60 percent of GDP) set by the convergence criteria of the Maastricht Treaty, EU member states have to submit every year a compliance report for the scrutiny and evaluation of the Commission and the Council of Ministers. While the Commission is in charge of monitoring, sanc-tions have to be decided by the member states, which they considered in only three cases (Portugal, Spain, and Italy) and have never actually imposed so far.[4] Overall, the excessive deficit procedure is at best a soft policy tool for monitoring budget reforms rather than a hard mechanism for enforcing budgetary discipline on the member states.[5]

Third, the reluctance of the member states to have the EU interfere with core state powers (Genschel and Jachtenfuchs 2016) also explains why infringement proceedings do not apply to violations of fundamental values laid down in Arti-cle 2 TEU. The deterioration of democracy and the rule of law in Hungary since 2010, Romania in 2012, and in Poland since 2015 violates the liberal democratic founding values of the EU (Sedelmeier 2014; Keleman 2017; von Bogdandy and Sonnevend 2015). Yet the member states have refused to make the Commission the sole guardian of those values. While accession candidates are subject to strict political conditionality, the Commission has limited powers to monitor and enforce compliance with human rights, democracy, and the rule of law within the EU (van Hüllen and Börzel 2015). In response to the participation of right-wing populist parties in member state governments (Alianza Nazionale in Italy, Freiheitliche Partei Österreich in Austria), the Treaty of Amsterdam established with Article 7 a sanction mechanism, which provides for the suspension of membership rights in the event of a "serious and persistent breach" of EU values. The Treaty of Lisbon amended Article 7, allowing action against a "clear risk" of a breach (Sadurski 2012).

The design of Article 7 renders it a rather blunt instrument, though. The Commission and the member states consider it an instrument of last resort or a "nuclear option." They have been reluctant to use it as means to prevent a major crisis at an early stage of eroding compliance (Jakab and Kochenov 2016). The Commission, the European Parliament, and one-third of the member states can initiate the Article 7 procedure. Any decision on a risk and the adoption of recommendations addressed to the offending government requires a four-fifths majority in the European Council and a simple majority in the European Parliament. A breach has to be determined by unanimity (minus one) in the European Council and approved by simple majority in the EP. Sanctions have to be supported by a qualified majority in the Council. The majority requirements in Council and Parliament have so far proven an insurmountable institutional hurdle for the application of Article 7. National governments and members of the European Parliament alike seek to protect members of their respective European party family (Sedelmeier 2014). To lower the bar, the Commission adopted a new framework in 2014 to address systemic threats to the rule of law in the member states (Kochenov and Pech 2016).[6] The rule-of-law framework is based on dialogue rather than punishment. If the framework fails to produce a solution, Article 7 TEU is to be triggered. The Commission activated the framework for the first time against the newly elected Polish government, seeking to counteract its attempts to undermine the independence of the Polish Constitutional Tribunal and the public broadcasters.[7] Since Polish authorities refused to cooperate on its opinions and recommendations, the Commission invoked Article 7 sanctioning procedures for the first time in December 2017. In September 2018, the European Parliament voted to launch Article 7 against Hungary for controlling media, restricting academic freedom, compromising the independence of the judiciary, and targeting civil society organizations. As in the case of Poland, the Council has yet to decide that there is a clear risk of a serious breach of EU values. Any sanctions that could follow would most likely be prevented by the Polish and Hungarian governments, respectively.

Seeking to circumvent political stalemate built into the Article 7 procedure, the European Commission has tried to interpret violations of fundamental values as noncompliance with the four freedoms of the Internal Market. This way it could open infringement proceedings against France for expelling Sinti and Roma in 2012 as a violation of the free movement of persons. The Commission also brought Hungary before the ECJ, which ruled against the Orbán government for violating the independence of the central bank and the data protection authority, as well as for changing the mandatory retirement age for judges.

More than sixty infringement proceedings related to the rule of law are still pending. Two of the most spectacular cases concern the attempt of Viktor Orbán to close down the Central European University in Budapest. Amid the unwillingness of the member states to consider the curbing of academic freedom as a threat to EU essential values, the Commission interpreted the changes in the Hungarian Higher Education Law as violations of the freedom to provide services and the freedom of establishment.[8] Its invoking Article 7 for a serious breach of the rule of law notwithstanding, the Commission filed infringement proceedings against Poland over gender discrimination in the legal reforms Poland's ruling PiS party had initiated to seize control of the judiciary. One of the four controversial laws adopted by the Polish parliament set different retirement ages for female and male judges. The Commission asked the ECJ to issue an injunction in which the ECJ ordered Poland to halt its forced retirement of Polish Supreme Court judges and to restore all judges that had been forced out.[9] After some initial defiance, the Polish government announced an amendment to the original law and reinstated the forced-out judges.[10] In October 2019, however, the Commission referred Poland again to the ECJ over new disciplinary procedures and sanctions on ordinary court judges that would undermine their judicial independence from political control.[11] The Commission launched yet another infringement proceeding against Poland in April 2020 for adopting a law that would allow Polish judges to be disciplined for referring cases to the ECJ. Only a few weeks before, the ECJ had suspended the activities of the newly created disciplinary board when it was about to waive the immunity of a Polish judge, a fierce PiS critic, to have him prosecuted for inviting reporters to a closed court hearing.[12] The Polish government rejected the judgment immediately, arguing that the ECJ had no authority to assess the legality of constitutional bodies in a member state. Rather than responding to the EU's enforcement pressure, Warsaw and Budapest have used the Covid-19 pandemic as a pretext to further undermine the EU's fundamental principles by employing extraordinary emergency powers and compromising democratic elections, respectively. A major blow to the EU's legal order, however, came from the highest court of the most powerful member state. In May 2020, the German Constitutional Court dismissed the ruling of the ECJ on the legality of the European Central Bank's bond-buying scheme. Germany's top court considers the stimulus program beyond the ECB's power because the ECB did not prove that it took into account the broader economic effects of its bond-buying scheme (e.g., on people's savings or rents). Since the ECJ ruled in 2018 that the ECB's action conform with EU law, the German Constitutional Court explicitly challenges the primacy of EU law and the ECJ as its final arbiter. This could set a dangerous precedent for other national constitutional courts to defy the EU's authority to set and enforce law. At the same time, the decision of the German Constitutional Court may end, or at least seriously constrain, the member states' attempts to depoliticize controversial decisions by delegating them to independent EU bodies, such as the ECB.

In sum, the book covers violations of central parts of EU law around which European integration has emerged and where the EU (therefore) has developed a centralized compliance system. Budgetary rules or fundamental principles, including the rule of law, in contrast, have to be enforced by the member state governments, which have been reluctant to do so. The Commission has therefore sought to interpret legal obligations outside its enforcement authority as issues related to the Internal Market, making them subject to infringement proceedings. Transforming political rights, such as the freedom of the press, into market freedoms has allowed the Commission to circumvent member state control of enforcement. The diverging power of the member states to resist compliance remains, however, an issue. More importantly, Brussels bureaucrats directly interfering with decisions of democratically elected national parliaments to (re)design the separation of powers or to allocate social benefits risks politicizing the EU's authority to make and enforce laws. Populist parties in Hungary, Poland, Greece, Italy, and the UK have successfully mobilized the issue of popular sovereignty, contesting the EU's authority to enact laws even within its core purview (free movement of people). So does the German Constitutional Court when it challenges the ECJ's authority because the EU's top court did not curb the powers of the ECB in trying to keep the eurozone's economy afloat. This points to the limits of the EU as a regulatory polity and of regulatory governance beyond the nation state in general, to which I will return at the end of this chapter.

De-centering the EU

What does the EU teach us about noncompliance in international politics? The EU is often regarded as a system sui generis, whose unique supranational properties, including the supremacy and direct effect of EU law (Alter 2001), preclude generalizations to other international institutions. EU scholars and experts of other regions alike used to treat the EU as if it represented an *n* of 1, which required its own theories (Caporaso 1997; cf. Börzel 2013; Acharya 2016). Research on comparative regionalism has found that the EU exhibits an extraordinary degree of pooling and delegation of national sovereignty (Lenz and Marks 2016; cf. Hooghe et al. 2017). Compared to other regional organizations and international institutions, EU member states have relinquished ever more control over decision making, implementation, and dispute settlement. However, if we adopt a perspective that is fine-grained enough, any political institution will ultimately be one of its kind. Beyond the nation state, the EU is the most legalized system of governance in the world (Alter 2000, 490). At the same time, institutionalized mechanisms to manage and enforce compliance can be found in other international institutions, too (Mitchell 1996, 17–20; Smith 2000, 139–140; Peters 2003). This allows us to apply insights and theoretical arguments from the broader IR literature to the EU. The PCP model has four important implications for noncompliance with law beyond the nation state.

First, states with both weak capacity and strong power are compliance laggards and delimit the power of law beyond the nation state. They lack the bureaucratic quality to swiftly comply with international law and have the power to resist enforcement pressure. Studies differ in what they consider to be the source of state power in international institutions (Barnett and Duvall 2005; Baldwin 2016). The extent to which a state can use its superior military capabilities or the size of its economy and population to impose its preferences on others in international institutions is questionable, not only in the highly supranationalized EU (P. Haas 1998, 22–23; on the "fungibility problem" of power see Baldwin 2013, 278). At the same time, capabilities or resources often define the institutional power of a state (Barnett and Duvall 2005, 51–52). The permanent members of the United Nations Security Council are five nuclear powers. In the International Monetary Fund, the quota systems link financial contributions from member governments to their voting power. In the EU, the four largest member states pay more than 60 percent of the EU budget. While budget contributions are based on economic size (GDP), the votes in the Council of Ministers are weighted according to a member state's population. Even though the system has been skewed in favor of smaller member states, the four most populous member states, France, Germany, Italy, and the UK, used to have almost ten times more votes than Malta, whose population is less than 0.05 percent of the German population. Under the double majority rule introduced by the Lisbon Treaty's ordinary legislative procedure, population size still matters. Each member state has only one vote now. However, majority decisions require 55 percent of member states representing at least 65 percent of the EU population (Article 238 TFEU). The largest member states can block the adoption of EU laws in the Council. In other words, rather than weighted votes, it is the pooling of national sovereignty in the form of majority decisions that distinguishes the EU from other international institutions when it comes to the politics of noncompliance. Interestingly, though, many regional and international institutions, including the African Union, the Council of Europe, the Organization of the Petroleum Exporting Countries (OPEC), the World Trade Organization (WTO), and the World Health Organization (WHO), display a much higher degree of pooling than the EU (Hooghe et al. 2017, 128). In any event, the EU offers important insights on how institutional power affects the propensity of states to defect from their legal commitments that travel beyond Europe.

The EU's exceptionally high degree of delegation does not preclude generalization either. Monitoring and sanctioning may be more decentralized in the WTO, the North American Free Trade Agreement (NAFTA), or the West African Economic Community (ECOWAS). At the same time, the WTO, for instance, has authorized financial sanctions much more frequently than the EU, where the ECJ ruled on member states to pay lump sums for noncompliance only in a dozen or so cases. WTO penalties can also be much more severe in terms of their economic impact (Bronckers and Baetens 2013). This is not to deny that the delegation of enforcement authority is exceptional in the EU. However, if anything, this renders the EU a least likely case for the power to resist compliance. Big member states are able to resist EU enforcement pressures despite the strong authority and independence of the Commission and the ECJ in monitoring and sanctioning noncompliance. The EU puts claims about the importance of independent enforcement authorities into perspective.

Second, the twinning of management and enforcement is an effective way to restore compliance (Tallberg 2002, 632). The combination of managerial dialogue, capacity building, and penalties addresses the source of noncompliance identified by most compliance approaches. States need to be both willing and able to cope with compliance costs. The managerial instrument of capacity building, however, is not sufficient in restoring compliance if it merely entails the transfer of resources to noncompliant states. It is essential to foster bureaucratic efficiency, for instance by encouraging the establishment of coordination mechanisms and by promoting anticorruption measures as part of public-sector reforms. Bureaucratic efficiency is decisive for the capacity of states to absorb financial and technical assistance of international institutions. By promoting good-governance reforms, including the fight against corruption, international institutions can help reduce the risk of noncompliance (Dimitrova 2005; Börzel and van Hüllen 2014).

Third, politicization is on the rise, not only in the EU. The authority of international institutions is increasingly contested (Zürn, Binder, and Ecker-Ehrhardt 2012). National publics have become more and more aware of international institutions, such as the WTO, the International Criminal Court, or NATO, exercising authority. Public resistance against international authority has grown, too, resulting in opposing political preferences for international policies on free trade, financial regulation, climate change, or nuclear arms control. The politicization of international authority is likely to undermine compliance with international law, particularly by big states, such as the US, Russia, India, or Brazil. It may also affect the adoption of new international agreements. If concluded at all, they may become "thinner" (Downs, Rocke, and Barsoom 1996) or less demanding, once status quo and rising powers tie their hands to the growing public resistance against international authority. President Trump's attempt to renegotiate NAFTA into the United States-Mexico-Canada Agreement (USMCA) in the name of his "America First" policy, in whose name he also abandoned the Paris Agreement on climate change and the Iran nuclear deal, are only part of what many have described as a general crisis of the liberal international order (Ikenberry 2018; Zürn 2018; Lake, Martin, and Risse, 2021).

Fourth, the findings of the book highlight the regulatory nature of international law as a driver of noncompliance that has not received sufficient attention in the literature. IR approaches treat noncompliance as an issue of international cooperation. Defection is at the core of the collective-action problems that render agreement among states difficult even if they share common interests. In line with the functionalist-institutionalist thinking that has informed many IR theories, compliance approaches focus on institutional design. Enforcement prioritizes institutional mechanisms for monitoring and sanctioning, while management stresses capacity building and dispute settlement. Legitimacy, finally, points to international institutions as arenas of socialization. Consequently, IR theories have largely been used to account for variation in compliance across international institutions (Keohane, Moravcsik, and Slaughter 2000; Abbott et al. 2000). Since they diverge on assumptions about what motivates states to cooperate and defect, enforcement, management, and legitimacy approaches have been reformulated in a way to account for country-based explanatory factors, such as power (enforcement), capacity (management), and the acceptance of international rules and institutions (legitimacy). While international and domestic drivers of noncompliance are well understood, they are institutional and structural rather than policy related. There seems to be little variation as most international regimes and organizations make regulatory policy. The book, however, demonstrates that regulatory policy may vary with regard to the redistributive consequences that regulatory policy produces at the domestic level, making noncompliance more or less likely. Somewhat ironically, setting international standards aimed at correcting politically undesired market outcomes, such as social or environmental dumping, may be more likely to become politicized than classical market-making free trade agreements. In Europe, the latter fall under the exclusive competence of the EU. The former involve competencies, such as environment and consumer protection, which the EU shares with the member states. As "mixed agreements," they require ratification by all member states, which renders politicization, and thus ultimate failure, much more likely. The EU-Mercosur trade agreement, for instance, signed in June 2019 after twenty years of negotiations, will not only establish the largest free trade area in the world by removing tariffs. It will also strengthen workers' rights, improve environmental protection, uphold high food safety standards, and protect intellectual property rights. Nevertheless, the agreement faces major opposition in several member states, including France and Ireland.

In sum, institutional power, bureaucratic quality, and politicization are neither specific to EU market integration nor to the EU as a highly legalized international institution. The PCP model is general enough to capture noncompliance with all law beyond the state.

The Politics of Noncompliance: Avenues for Future Research

The findings of the book give rise to some suggestions for future research. It is important to disentangle specific variants of the different compliance approaches. Power matters mostly at the taking rather than the shaping stage. Moreover, instead of economic size and population per se, votes in the Council account for the power to resist enforcement pressure. Likewise, it is not the endowment with resources but the capacity of a government to mobilize them that is relevant for coping with costly EU laws. As the PCP model is based on a rational institutionalist framework, it has treated legitimacy variables only as controls. Bringing in politicization allows the model to account for the counterintuitive finding that more EU support correlates with more, not less, noncompliance. The causal mechanism is the ability of member state governments to tie their hands to Eurosceptic publics, which make the politicization of compliance costs more likely. Socialization and democratic accountability yield equally counterintuitive results. There are, however, other factors related to legitimacy, such as procedural fairness, support for the rule of law, or peer pressure. The literature has found little support for these variables. However, this may be related to the lack of time series data. There is room for a constructivist model of noncompliance that systematically explores the constitutive effect of norms, such as the rule of law, the role of socialization processes at the EU level, or the relevance of cultural factors at the domestic level.

Within its rational institutionalist framework, the PCP model neglects a number of factors, owing to the liberal intergovernmentalist conceptualization of the link between the EU and the member state level. While domestic actors influence the formulation of policy preferences, member state governments gate-keep access to EU negotiations. We know that organized interests, companies, and citizens are an important part of the EU's decentralized monitoring system providing the Commission with information about possible violations of EU law. They can also block or at least delay compliance when they mobilize against costly EU laws. However, to what extent do they directly interfere with the compliance game, seeking to prevent costly EU laws or at least lower their compliance costs? Likewise, the literature has focused on pro-compliance coalitions at the domestic level, which try to push their governments toward compliance, raising the costs of noncompliance at the taking stage. To what extent do domestic actors seeking to extend their rights under EU law already interfere at the shaping stage, through allying with the Commission as the key agenda setter, as suggested by supranational institutionalist theories of European integration (Sandholtz and Stone Sweet 1998; Pollack 1997b)? Finally, what about the courts of the member states? They are obliged to enforce EU laws, even if those laws contradict existing national legislation. This may empower lower domestic courts vis-à-vis their superior courts because they have the right to directly address the ECJ for a ruling on the compatibility of EU and national law (Burley and Mattli 1993; Alter 2001; Conant 2002). Domestic courts provide important arenas for the legal internalization of EU law in the member states (Koh 1996; Panke 2007). At the same time, their effectiveness depends on the mobilization of societal actors that use legal claims to pressure for the necessary domestic changes to ensure rule-consistent behavior (Conant 2002; Cichowski 2007; Kelemen 2006), as well as their own capacity to deal with the legal claims (Dyevre, Glavina, and Atanasova 2019). Rather than treating preliminary rulings as an alternative measurement of noncompliance with EU law, though, it could be fruitful to investigate whether preliminary rulings increase the chances of noncompliance by making EU laws costlier after their adoption or whether they bring noncompliance down by socializing domestic actors. Finally, the dismissal by the German Constitutional Court of the ECJ decision on the ECB's bond-buying power, which the German Constitutional Court itself had sought from the ECJ, indicates that preliminary ruling may become an object of noncompliance rather than work as a mechanism to induce compliance. Future research should explore more society-centered models of noncompliance, which give domestic and transnational actors a greater role beyond influencing national preference formation at the shaping stage and acting as potential veto players at the taking stage. De-centering national governments could also involve unpacking national parliaments. Compliance research has started to explore the role of party composition, electoral rules, and institutional culture for noncompliance with EU law (Steunenberg 2006; König and Luetgert 2009; König 2007; Luetgert and

Dannwolf 2009; Sprungk 2011; Auel and Raunio 2014; Auel, Eisele, and Kinski 2016). It would be interesting to see whether these factors influence the degree to which national parliaments politicize compliance costs. This could also help explain why some costly market-correcting EU laws become more politicized than others. One issue-related factor could be the concentration of compliance costs (Siegel 2011). These are much more concentrated, for example, in the case of the fauna, flora, habitat directive as compared to the directive on the quality of water intended for human consumption.

This book demonstrates that different compliance approaches can and should be combined to account for variation in noncompliance across countries, time, and policy sectors. Across the board, countries with high power (to be recalcitrant) are more likely to violate EU law than less powerful ones. Countries with inefficient administrations are worse compliers than those of high bureaucratic quality, no matter what legal act they have to transpose, implement, and enforce. Likewise, all member states violate legal acts in market-correcting policy sectors more often than legislation in policy sectors that are mostly aimed at market making. Also, all member states infringe on new EU legal act more often than on amending and delegated legislation. The PCP model specifies how these country-, policy-, and rule-specific characteristics jointly affect noncompliance at the two different stages of the compliance game. At the same time, the PCP model suggests potential interaction effects that are supported by the empirical findings. Politicization reduces the positive effect of power and enhances the negative effect of capacity on noncompliance. Figure A5.1 in appendix 5 exemplifies the interactions of voting power, bureaucratic quality, and opposition to the EU (Euroscepticism). The plot shows that voting power increases the number of reasoned opinions—the slope and the level of this effect, however, vary depending on the level of bureaucratic quality and Euroscepticism. Member states with high bureaucratic quality and Eurosceptic publics comply quite well, even when they wield substantial voting power in the Council. This is even the case (although to a lesser extent) for countries with low bureaucratic quality and Eurosceptic publics (middle line). The impact of voting power on noncompliance is greatest, as expected, in member states with low bureaucratic quality, Euro-supportive publics, and strong voting power. Similar interaction effects may be observed between EU institutions, policy sector, and politicization. If market-correcting policy is more likely to be violated because its compliance costs are more visible and salient, a higher number of political constraints should magnify the positive effect of market-correcting policy on noncompliance. Delegated legislation, in contrast, should reduce this positive effect, since the lack of parliamentary involvement renders the politicization of compliance costs less likely. The empirical testing of the PCP model also yields some findings that point to possible interaction or conditional effects that may lie outside its explanatory logic. In the EU-25 model, for instance, some variables, such as EU support and regional authority, change their sign and/or significance (see chapter 3). There is nothing in the PCP model to suggest that the effect of EU support or opposition on noncompliance is conditional upon a factor that systematically varies between old and new member states.

Finally, the PCP model is generalizable enough to explain noncompliance in other regional and international organizations. However, there is one caveat. Even though there is a gap in power and capacity between most of the old and most of the new member states, the EU consists of a group of relatively homogeneous states, which face a globally unique level of political and economic integration. The membership of other international organizations and regional integration projects, such as the Association of Southeast Asian Nations (ASEAN) or NAFTA/USMCA, is much more heterogeneous in terms of economic size, resources, or bureaucratic quality (compare the US and Mexico within NAFTA/USMCA). This applies even more to the regime types of member states, their economic development, and their respect for the rule of law and human rights. This book could not explore the role of these potential background variables since they are largely constant within the data set. Future research should focus on these factors and inquire whether they affect the explanatory value of the PCP model and to what extent they account for unexplained variation.

The Limits of Regulatory Governance beyond the State

The EU governs the largest market in the world. It does so through the adoption of market-making and market-correcting regulation. Rather than directly providing public goods and services, the EU regulates states, private actors, and markets. Accordingly, Majone has described the EU as a "regulatory state," which lacks the power to make truly (re)distributive policy (Majone 1993, 1994). With the subsequent deepening and broadening of its regulatory authority, the EU has established a comprehensive regulatory framework that has successfully prevented and corrected market failures (Eckert 2015; Finger 2011). Besides opening national markets to foreign competition by eliminating tariffs, taxes, quotas, and other protectionist policies, such as state subsidies, EU law has broken up state monopolies as they traditionally existed for utilities, such as telecommunications or energy. It has also created a level playing field for suppliers and consumers by harmonizing standards on the quality, safety, and labeling of products and production processes (e.g., regulations on food standards, packaging, the use of chemicals, working hours).

When it came to developing the Internal Market into an EMU, the EU opted again for a regulatory approach. Despite the massive (re)distributive implications of a common currency, this was arguably the only way to give the EU any authority over core state powers, such as fiscal policy (Genschel and Jachtenfuchs 2016). Shifting costs to the domestic level facilitated agreement at the EU level. An equal distribution of costs suggested by imposing uniform legal obligations on all member states promised to mitigate the risk of politicization.

Not surprisingly then, the multiple crises the EU has faced over the past decade are often considered a regulatory failure (Jachtenfuchs 2018), a major cause of which is noncompliance. Indeed, member states had violated EMU rules even before they were hit by the collapse of US investment banks in 2008. They also broke the Schengen rules long before the historic influx of refugees and migrants in 2015. However, as this book suggests, a certain level of noncompliance does not necessarily undermine the functioning of the EU. In fact, a polity seeking to integrate a growing number of states, which are ever more heterogeneous with regard to their policy preferences, power, capacity, and politicization, may need a certain amount of noncompliance or "institutionalized hypocrisy" (Iankova and Katzenstein 2003) to allow for the flexibility necessary to balance unity and diversity. Similar to escape clauses or safeguards in international treaties, noncompliance provides the necessary flexibility to prevent the breakup of otherwise too rigid regulatory arrangements (Rosendorff and Milner 2001; Pelc 2009). In other words, noncompliance ain't always a bad thing. It only turns into a systemic risk when states refuse to incur compliance costs altogether by contesting the authority of the Commission as the guardian of the treaty, the ECJ as its ultimate umpire, or the validity of EU law as such.

With the euro and the migration crises, noncompliance has gained a new quality in the EU—it has become a way for member states to dodge the costs of redistribution, which regulatory policy shifts to the domestic level, where costs become politicized. Accordingly, noncompliance with euro and Schengen rules differs from the noncompliance analyzed in this book in three important ways. First, by establishing a common currency and abolishing border controls, member states have given up rather than transferred authority to the EU level. EMU deprives euro countries of key instruments of macroeconomic management without creating a common fiscal and economic policy. The EU is a monetary but not an economic union. Likewise, the Schengen states did away with internal border controls but have refused to set up common external border controls and common rules and procedures to handle asylum seekers and refugees. This is different from traditional regulatory policy, which seeks to establish and enforce common EU regulations to correct market failure and politically undesired outcomes. Second, compliance costs are not evenly distributed among states. Export-led economies, including Germany and the Netherlands, have less difficulty with the budgetary rules of the Stability and Growth Pact than the demand-led economies of France, Italy, or Greece, which rely on deficit spending to generate growth and employment (Scharpf 2016a). Likewise, in immigration, frontline states (Greece, Italy, Spain) as well as target countries (Germany, Austria, Sweden) face greater challenges than transit countries in meeting the requirements of the Dublin regime, because of the much higher number of refugees and migrants they have to cope with (see chapter 5). Third, the euro and Schengen are about identity politics. The political controversies over the euro crisis have centered predominantly on questions of order—that is, what constitutes Europe as a community, and how much solidarity members of the community owe to each other and under which conditions. The mass influx of migrants and refugees changed identity politics into questions of borders: who belongs to Europe as a community, with Eurosceptic populist parties advocating for an exclusionary fortress Europe (Börzel and Risse 2018).

These differences explain why compliance with EU law has become increasingly politicized. Nationalist populist politicians do not only resent the euro and Schengen. Viktor Orbán, Marine Le Pen, Jarosław Kaczyński, Alexander Gauland, Geert Wilders, or Nigel Farage deny the EU the authority to make and enforce rules on issues that interfere with national sovereignty, which could also include large-scale logging in one of Europe's last primeval forests in Poland.[13] This is not the place to discuss the rise of nationalist populism in Europe and other parts of the world (cf. Hutter, Grande, and Kriesi 2016; Hooghe and Marks 2018). There is little doubt that the politicization of international authority will continue. The findings of the book indicate that politicization is likely to intensify if governments seek to mask and address redistributive issues as regulatory problems, which require stricter rules and tougher enforcement. CEE member states shirking their obligation to take in refugees under the temporary relocation mechanisms adopted in 2015 is a case in point (see chapter 5). Germany dragging its feet in setting up the Single Resolution Fund (SRF) is another. The Banking Union, established after the financial crisis of 2008, prohibits the bailing out of insolvent banks by states. The Single Resolution Mechanism (SRM) and SRF are intended to regulate and finance the restructuring of troubled banks (de Rynk 2016). Yet the German government anticipates major opposition to German banks bailing out banks of crisis countries, which is one of the reasons why the SRF is still not operational. As a result, the Italian government had to use €17 billion of its taxpayers' money to rescue two of its major banks, which the ECB had sent into insolvency proceedings. The intervention violates a core rule of the Banking Union that private creditors have to cover bank failure costs, rather than taxpayers. The Commission approved the state aid for the liquidation of the two Italian banks because of the serious economic impact their breakdown would have had.[14]

The UK's decision as the first member state ever to leave the EU could be seen as the ultimate act of systemic noncompliance. No other member state has obtained so many opt-outs (see chapter 4). Still, 51.9 percent of the British electorate chose exit over voice. Rather than a massive declaration of noncompliance with core principles of the EU, such as the free movement of people, Brexit seems the logical continuation of the UK's approach to avoid legal obligations the majority of British citizens would not want to comply with. In light of the consistently low support for EU membership and the exemplary compliance record, this seems to be only consequential. Tying hands has reached its limits. The other member states have not been willing to reduce the European integration project to the regulation of free trade in goods and financial services. At the same time, many of them do not seem to be willing to comply with essential EU laws that go beyond regulating markets. While this seems paradoxical, it has to do with the limits of EU regulatory governance.

A common policy on refugees, asylum seekers, and migrants is the flip side of the free movement of people in a borderless Europe. Likewise, a common currency as the next step of economic integration requires some common economic and fiscal policy to ensure the necessary convergence of national economies. More regulatory governance is not only inadequate to deal with the ensuing redistributive conflicts that come with such common policies (Majone 1994). Seeking to mask the allocation of adjustment costs or refugees as a regulatory issue undermines both the effectiveness and the legitimacy of EU governance. The EU's failure in the financial crisis to recognize the need for a different governance mix to tackle redistribution that does not rely on non-majoritarian supranational institutions has further politicized the EU as a system of governance. Its democratic credentials are not only questioned by populist politicians and citizens rallying against the socioeconomic effects of the financial and the migration crises (Börzel 2016). The constitutional courts of several member states have also reserved the right to review and, if necessary, nullify changes in the EU's governance mix, by which EU law is allowed to override the will of the majority produced by democratic elections (Fabbrini 2014; Joerges 2016). The German Constitutional Court has been the first to do so. Germany's top court nullified the ECJ decision that the ECB had acted within its power with its bond-buying scheme. Thereby, it not only challenged the ECJ's exclusive right to rule on EU institutions and interpret EU law. It may also put a stop to the member states relying on the ECB to offset economic shocks because of their own unwillingness to raise and allocate the necessary financial resources. The member states' attempt to depoliticize redistributive issues through delegating them to supranational institutions has backfired. The delegation of more political authority to the ECB, the Commission, or the European Border and Coast Guard to avoid or escape politicization at the domestic level has fueled opposition to an increasingly intrusive and undemocratic EU and empowered Eurosceptic populist forces at both ends of the political spectrum (Börzel and Risse 2018). Abolishing or severely constraining national sovereignty can be no longer legitimized by the need to strengthen the EU's problem-solving capacity. On the contrary, delegating authority to ensure compliance with controversial EU law is not only likely to result in more (fundamental) violations of EU law, particularly if there is increasing disagreement among member state governments (König and Mäder 2013, 2014b). It also undermines public support of the EU as a whole (Fjelstul and Carrubba 2018).

There is neither the political will nor the public support for creating a genuine social and political union, which would have the legal and fiscal authority to protect and support specific social rights (Habermas 2013) of both EU citizens and third-country nationals in need of protection. The controversy over "corona bonds" to finance the EU's emergency and recovery measures in managing the Covid-19 pandemic illustrates one more time that member states are unwilling to develop a common fiscal policy to cope with external shocks. The €0.5 trillion infusion to help governments, businesses, and workers to cope with economic crisis will be funded through the European Stability Mechanism, the European Investment Bank, and the Pandemic Emergency Purchase Programme of the ECB. The disagreement, notably between France and Germany, on giving the EU more redistributive power, at least partly explains why the EU has become a monetary but not an economic union (Dyson 1994). The debate on how to strengthen the eurozone indicates that the disagreement continues to exist more than fifteen years after the Maastricht Treaty created the Economic and Monetary Union. The proposals for a euro finance ministry with its own budget to strengthen the euro zone are not new. Since the proposal was taken up by France's President Emmanuel Macron in 2017, Germany no longer outright rejects the idea. However, rather than a way to kick-start the economies of Southern European crisis countries through European investments, Germany conceives of the euro finance minister as another institution to supervise and enforce solid budget management in these countries. The EU agreement on a USD $870 billion stimulus package to cope with the COVID-19 pandemic notwithstanding, the persisting lack of consensus between Germany and France on a European social model is a major impediment to EU redistributive policy. Attempts to establish a common asylum system have equally stalled as member states cannot agree on whether and how to share the responsibility for receiving and integrating people seeking international protection (Börzel 2020).

The EU is likely to remain what it used to be good at—a regulatory state. What has been undermining its effectiveness and legitimacy is not so much the lack of redistributive authority. While its regulatory institutions constrain the member states in their redistributive capacity, the problem lies in the attempt of member state governments to depoliticize redistributive issues by delegating them to independent regulatory agencies, such as the Commission, the European Central Bank, or the European Border and Coast Guard. Ironically, this has ultimately led, at the domestic level, to more rather than less politicization that contests not only specific EU policy but the authority and legitimacy of the EU as such (Börzel 2016; Börzel and Risse 2018).

While being an extreme case of regulatory governance beyond the state, the EU offers some important lessons to other international institutions. Rising public resistance against deep and comprehensive international trade and investment agreements, such as CETA, TPP, or TTIP, which are not only about market making but entail some substantial elements of market correction (Kim, Mansfield, and Millner 2016), clearly demonstrate that the compliance costs of regulatory policy are redistributive and increasingly likely to be politicized. Rather than masking redistribution as a regulatory problem to be best delegated to independent agencies, such as investor state dispute settlement bodies or international courts, national policy makers may have to engage in public debates about who should get what within and beyond the nation state. National parliaments could play a key role in this regard. The book has found them to be agents of politicization by increasing the salience of the EU and its policies. However, this does not necessarily have to result in policy blockage and noncompliance (Auel, Eisele, and Kinski 2016). Public debates about the EU and EU policies can increase democratic accountability (Auel 2007; Auel and Höing 2015) and thus the legitimacy of the EU, thereby fostering voluntary compliance. The EU has to start relying on the social acceptance of its citizens to ensure compliance.

Appendix 1

SUMMARY STATISTICS

TABLE A1.1 Official infringements (reasoned opinions) against directives by member states, 1978–2012

	N	MEAN	MEDIAN	STD. DEV	MIN	MAX	VARIANCE
Austria (A)	17	25.8824	23	11.4175	10	51	130.3603
Belgium (B)	34	29.4706	31.5	10.8467	5	53	117.6506
Germany (D)	34	24.5294	23	11.9221	7	51	142.1355
Denmark (DK)	34	5.4118	5	2.7974	0	13	7.8253
Spain (E)	26	27.5000	27.5	11.1185	9	60	123.6200
Greece (EL)	31	39.0645	35	15.6332	4	67	244.3957
France (F)	34	32.8235	29.5	14.3727	12	62	206.5740
Finland (FL)	17	13.4706	12	6.1249	7	29	37.5147
Italy (I)	34	45.4118	47.5	17.6397	14	80	311.1586
Ireland (IR)	34	19.4118	19	10.4101	2	44	108.3708
Luxembourg (L)	34	21.5000	20	11.1171	3	46	123.5909
Netherlands (NL)	34	14.5294	14	6.6114	5	32	43.7112
Portugal (P)	26	34.8077	34.5	17.2024	6	71	295.9215
Sweden (S)	17	12.8235	12	5.0773	4	21	25.7794
United Kingdom (UK)	34	17.2059	16	8.7552	3	35	76.6533
EU-15	**440**	**24.7000**	**22**	**15.7762**	**0**	**80**	**248.8893**
Cyprus (CY)	8	14.1250	14	7.0597	4	26	49.8393
Czech Republic (CZ)	8	17.7500	18	7.8148	7	29	61.0714
Estonia (EE)	8	11.3750	10	6.0930	5	20	37.1250
Hungary (HU)	8	12.0000	11.5	4.9570	6	21	24.5714
Lithuania (LT)	8	6.5000	5.5	4.3095	1	13	18.5714
Latvia (LV)	8	7.1250	6	5.4363	2	16	29.5536
Malta (MT)	8	11.8750	6	9.8769	2	25	97.5536

(Continued)

TABLE A1.1 (Continued)

	N	MEAN	MEDIAN	STD. DEV	MIN	MAX	VARIANCE
Poland (PL)	8	25.0000	24	7.9102	14	36	62.5714
Slovenia (SL)	8	11.5000	10	5.3452	5	20	28.5714
Slovakia (SK)	8	10.1250	10	5.0551	4	17	25.5536
2004 enlargement	**80**	**12.7375**	**11.5**	**8.0501**	**1**	**36**	**64.8036**
EU-25	**520**	**22.8596**	**20**	**15.4614**	**0**	**80**	**239.0535**

TABLE A1.2 Independent variables and their transformation (country)

	N	MEAN	MEDIAN	STD. DEV	MIN	MAX	TRANSFOR-MATION*
Intra-EU trade/ GDP (in US$) eu_trade_ gdp_p100	440	29.95342	24.9249	22.3344	4.3723	160.7732	in percent
Net recipient (in €)	440	–21.5233	–7.5273	282.5044	–1109.234	885.94	/100.000
net_recip_ 100.000	520	–1.8877	0.7782	273.5420	–1109.234	1097.508	
Ministerial approval per year min_app_x100	440	9.2463	8.9455	4.0244	0.3924	29.3849	x100
EU support	440	13.1639	11	9.3003	2	49	in percent
eu_oppose_ p100	520	13.0515	11	8.8328	2	49	
Voting power (SSI)	440	7.1945	5.71	4.5775	0.95	17.86	x1
voting_ssi	520	6.4734	5.52	4.6086	0.82	17.86	
POLCON III	440	44.8909	44.6689	13.6218	12.0006	72	x100
polcon_iii_x100	520	45.1954	46.3455	13.1656	12.0006	72	
Regional authority index	440	15.7000	12.2474	11.6879	0	36.9899	x1
regional_rai	520	13.9248	11.2467	11.6424	0	36.9899	
Parliamentary scrutiny	440	12.7177	11.3924	9.1508	0	70.8333	in percent
parl_scrutiny_ p100							
GDP per capita (in US$)	440	32.2581	30.9425	12.7437	11.2038	87.7727	/1000
gdp_capita_ p1000	520	29.3875	28.1950	13.6681	6.7470	87.7727	
Bureaucratic quality	440	36.6316	40	5.4128	7.5	40	x10
icrg_bq_x10	520	35.5425	40	5.8326	7.5	40	
Years of membership	440	27.3682	27.0	14.3353	2	55	x1
ms_year	520	24.0039	23.5	15.3950	2	55	

EU-15 model; EU-25 model
* Values in the table are already transformed

194

TABLE A1.3 Official infringements (reasoned opinions) per directives, 1978–2009

	N	MEAN	MEDIAN	STD. DEV	MIN	MAX	VARIANCE
EU-15	2,793	2.9474	1	5.9961	0	137	35.9532
EU-27	2,793	3.3315	1	6.8891	0	152	47.4602

TABLE A1.4 Independent and control variables and their transformation (issue)

	N	MEAN	MEDIAN	STD. DEV	MIN	MAX	TRANSFOR-MATION*
Policy misfit (new)	2,793	0.3509	0	0.4773	0	1	
Preferential fit (minister_dir)	2,793	0.0209	0.0091	0.0825	−0.2633	0.2902	
Voting rule (qmv_fill0)	2,793	0.2467	0	0.4312	0	1	
Voting outcome (content_vote)	2,793	0.0895	0	0.3877	0	2	
EU conflict (ep_inter)	2,793	0.4948	0	0.8118	0	3	
Complexity (recitals_d10)	2,793	1.0448	0.7	1.0246	0.1	11.8	/10
Time for transition (years_transpose)	2,793	1.0067	0.8849	0.9047	0	11.5452	
Workload (workload_fill_d10)	2,793	0.8446	1.0625	2.4890	−4.9375	5.9625	/10
Delegated legislation (com_dir)	2,793	0.4228	0	0.4941	0	1	
Bureaucratic implementation (napa_dir)	2,793	0.1284	0	0.2157	0	1	
Democratic accountablity (ep_power)	2,793	0.9123	0	1.1392	0	3	
EU oppposition (eu_opp_yadopt1_x10)	2,793	1.3001	1.2901	0.2815	0.6359	1.8318	%/10

* Values in the table are already transformed

TABLE A1.5 Official infringements (reasoned opinions) against directives by policy sector, 1981–2012

POLICY SECTOR	N	MEAN[1]	MEDIAN	STD. DEV.	MIN	MAX	VARIANCE
Market (MARK)	32	51.21875	44	34.0301	7	139	1158.047
Environment (ENVI)	26	76.61538	75	27.86119	32	136	776.2462
Agriculture (AGRI)	32	37.59375	19.5	50.39576	0	203	2539.733
Enterprise (ENT)	32	40.59375	42	23.34435	0	90	544.9587
Transport & Energy (TRAN_ENE)	32	39.03125	30	40.26964	0	156	1621.644
Taxation (TAX)	32	13.15625	11	7.849838	2	34	61.61996

(Continued)

TABLE A1.5 (Continued)

POLICY SECTOR	N	MEAN[1]	MEDIAN	STD. DEV.	MIN	MAX	VARIANCE
Employment (EMPL)	19	19	15	10.44031	7	44	109
Health & Consumer Protection (SANCO)	26	31.11538	19.5	30.44645	1	97	926.9862
Justice&Home Affairs (JAIN)	19	17	5	25.63418	0	92	657.1111
Information Society & Media (INSO)	26	10.92308	6.5	12.00641	0	37	144.1538
Competition (COMP)	32	1.8125	1	2.66927	0	10	7.125
Total	308	31.2922	17.5	34.80273	0	203	1211.23

1 The mean is different from graph 4.2 since the period covered by the data used in the regression is shorter (1981–2012) due to the three-year lag. Moreover, observations in which age is 0 are eliminated. The ranking of the sectors remains unaffected.

TABLE A1.6 Independent and control variables (sector)

	N	MEAN	MEDIAN	STD. DEV	MIN	MAX
Policy type (reg_pol)	308	0.8961	1	0.5072	0	8
Regulatory logic (m_corr)	308	0.5844	1	0.4936	0	1
Age (age)	308	29.2760	30	15.6819	1	55
EU competence (eu_comp)	308	2.9091	3	1.0134	0.5	4.5
EU opposition (EU_opp_sector_lag3)	308	0.4320	0.3777	0.1282	0.2167	0.7367
Regulatory density (adopted_dir_lag3)	308	8.8799	4	11.0972	0	45
Misfit (misfit_absolute3)	308	3.0390	2	3.6765	0	23
Complexity (compx_mean_X_adopt3_d10)*	308	9.2030	5.8541	9.2251	0	38.1095
Delegated legislation (polit_absolute3)	308	5.0487	3	5.4618	0	34
EU level conflict (EU_conflict_lag3)	308	0.6005	0.4694	0.6543	0	3
Maastricht control (maas)	308	0.6786	1	0.4678	0	1
Member state control (ms)	308	17.3766	15	6.3897	10	27

* Divided by 10

CORRELATION OF INDEPENDENT VARIABLES

TABLE A2.1 Member states

EU-15

	INTRA ~E	NET RE~T	MIN APP	EU OPP~E	VOTING~I	POLCON~I	REGIO ~I	PARL	_S~Y	GDP_
intra eu t~e	1.0000									
net recipi~t	-0.0477	1.0000								
min app	-0.0555	0.1363	1.0000							
eu oppose	-0.1455	-0.1421	-0.2590	1.0000						
voting ssi	-0.5587	-0.2558	0.0065	-0.0387	1.0000					
polcon iii	0.4904	-0.0866	0.0825	-0.3365	-0.1231	1.0000				
regio rai	0.0629	-0.3204	-0.0368	-0.1310	0.4449	0.2570	1.0000			
parl scrut~y	0.1110	-0.1691	-0.1018	0.0469	-0.1564	0.1337	0.2435	1.	0000	
gdp capita	0.5283	-0.2527	0.0112	0.0531	-0.4584	0.1200	-0.1900	0.	2252	1.
burqual icrg	0.3368	-0.2959	-0.0554	0.1711	-0.1197	0.1492	0.0780	0.	2053	0.

EU-25

	NET RE~T	EU OPP~E	VOTING~I	POLCON~I	REGIO ~I	GDP CA~A	BURQUA~G
net recipi~t	1.0000						
eu oppose	-0.1452	1.0000					
voting ssi	-0.2483	-0.0374	1.0000				
polcon iii	-0.0707	-0.3397	-0.1265	1.0000			
regio rai	-0.3242	-0.1138	0.5228	0.2028	1.0000		
gdp capita	-0.3008	0.0714	-0.1879	0.0625	0.0188	1.0000	
burqual icrg	-0.3168	0.1777	0.0689	0.0829	0.2184	0.6248	1.0000

TABLE A2.2 Time

	NEW	QMV	EP CON~T	COM_DIR	NATIONAL	MIN_APP	WORKLOAD	RECITALS	TIME T-E E
new	1.0000								
qmv	0.2023	1.0000							
ep conflict	0.2940	0.4882	1.0000						
ccm dir	-0.3848	-0.4898	-0.5218	1.0000					
nation parl	0.3358	0.3080	0.4605	-0.3763	1.0000				
min app	0.1261	-0.0704	0.0787	-0.3001	0.1670	1.0000			
workload	0.0319	0.2369	0.0949	0.0621	0.0948	-0.1558	1.0000		
recitals	0.3711	0.4278	0.4777	-0.3074	0.5738	0.0304	0.2220	1.0000	
time trans~e	0.3026	0.1512	0.3366	-0.3050	0.3853	0.0884	-0.0856	0.2647	1.0000
ep power	0.3306	0.7375	0.7278	-0.6856	0.4259	0.0828	0.1665	0.4930	0.2452
eu oppose	-0.0110	0.1955	-0.0240	0.1211	0.0618	-0.0086	0.2953	0.1569	-0.0790

TABLE A2.3 Policy sectors

	AGE	REG POL	M CORR	EU COMP	EU OPP~E	ADOPTE~R	NEW DIR	POLIT ~R	COMPX ~S E
age	1.0000								
reg pol	-0.2224	1.0000							
m corr	-0.5507	-0.2871	1.0000						
eu comp	0.1910	-0.2225	-0.0709	1.0000					
eu oppose	-0.4330	0.0545	0.4808	-0.2293	1.0000				
adopted dir	0.4448	-0.5838	-0.0638	0.1573	-0.2957	1.0000			
new dir	0.2513	-0.2254	-0.0539	0.0755	-0.2691	0.7248	1.0000		
polit dir	0.3409	-0.3736	-0.1121	0.0479	-0.3596	0.8438	0.8504	1.0000	
compx reci~s	0.4324	-0.4923	-0.0632	0.1722	-0.3118	0.9648	0.7672	0.8700	1.0000
ep conflict	-0.1467	0.2415	0.1800	0.0095	0.1028	-0.1330	0.0566	0.0082	-0.0254
maas	0.2106	0.0618	0.1532	0.2920	0.3524	0.0383	0.0376	-0.0627	0.0687
ms	0.3314	0.0435	0.1076	0.2620	0.3422	0.0644	0.0164	-0.0554	0.1026

DEPENDENT AND INDEPENDENT VARIABLES AND THEIR OPERATIONALIZATION

TABLE A3.1 Member states

	OPERATIONALIZATION	EXPECTED EFFECT ON NONCOMPLIANCE	DATA SOURCE
DEPENDENT VARIABLE			
Official infringements	Reasoned opinions per member state and year of the infringement proceeding (YearIN)		Berlin Infringement Database (1979–2012)
INDEPENDENT VARIABLES			
Power			
Voting power	Proportion of times when a member state is pivotal in the Council, in percent	+/–	Shapley & Shubik Index (SSI) (1979–2012)
Capacity			
GDP per capita	Gross domestic product per capita (constant 2005 US$), divided by 1,000	–	World Bank (1979–2012)
Bureaucratic quality	Ability and expertise to govern without drastic changes in policy or interruptions in government services, bureaucracy is autonomous from political pressure and has an established mechanism for recruitment and training, also evaluates policy formulation and day-to-day administrative functions, multiplied by 10	–	PRS Group: International Country Risk Guide (1985–2012)[1]
Politicization			
Political constraints	Number of independent branches with veto power and the distribution of political preferences across these branches, multiplied by 100	+	Political Constraints Index (POLCON III) (1979–2012)
Regional authority	Regional Authority Index (RAI)	+	Hooghe et al. 2016[2] (1979–2011)[3]
Parliamentary scrutiny	Average proportion of (notified) national transposition measures involving national parliaments, per member state and year, in percent	+	PUCH (1979–2010)[4]
EU opposition	Share of replies that EU membership is "a bad thing," in percent	+	Eurobarometer (1979–2012)

202

Controls

Intra-EU trade	Sum of exports and imports of goods within the EU-15 as share of the GDP (US$), in percent (quotient x 100)	OECD, World Bank (1979–2011)[5]
Net recipient	Operational budgetary balance (€), divided by 100.000	Annual EU Budget Financial Reports (1979–2012)
Ministerial approval	Annual average distance of national ministers' party preferences to the outer limits of the Council core, all EU directives adopted in a given year, multiplied by 100. Inside the core > 0 Outside the core < 0	PUCH (1979–2010)[6]

---

1 Data on bureaucratic quality is available for years 1984–2011. As we are lagging independent variables by one year, this leaves missing observations for the early years of 1979–1984. However, due to the low dynamics of the variable over time, we consider an imputation of values from 1984 for each member state unproblematic.

2 Hooghe et al. 2016.

3 Data on the RAI is available until 2010. As we are lagging independent variables by one year, this leaves one missing observation per member state for 2012, each of which was filled with the preceding year's value.

4 Data on national transposition (PUCH) is available until 2009. As we are lagging independent variables by one year, this leaves two missing observations per member state for 2011 and 2012, each of which was filled with the 2009 value.

5 Data on Intra-EU trade was taken from the OECD International Trade by Commodity Statistics (SITC Revision 2) and is available for the EU-15 until 2010. As we are lagging independent variables by one year, this leaves one missing observation per member state for 2012, each of which was filled with the preceding year's value. Furthermore, there are only combined numbers for Belgium and Luxembourg for the years 1978–92 and no separate values for Luxembourg until 1999. Thus, for years 1979–93 the combined volume of intra-EU trade was divided by the combined GDP of Belgium and Luxembourg, while missing values for Luxembourg (1993–98) were imputed with the mean of the preceding and subsequent ten years. Data on GDP was taken from the World Bank's World Governance Indicators.

6 Data on ministerial approval (PUCH) is available until 2009. As we are lagging independent variables by one year, this leaves two missing observations per member state for 2011 and 2012, each of which was filled with the 2009 value.

TABLE A3.2 Issue

	OPERATIONALIZATION	EXPECTED EFFECT ON NONCOMPLIANCE	DATA SOURCE
DEPENDENT VARIABLE			
Official infringements of directives	Reasoned opinions per directive[1]		Berlin Infringement Database (Directives 1978–2009)
INDEPENDENT VARIABLES			
Nature of EU law			
New directive	New directive[2] 1 Amending directive[3] 0	+	EUR-Lex (Directives 1978–2009)
Commission directive	Commission directive 1 Council/Council+EP directive 0	–	EUR-Lex (Directives 1978–2009)
Control variables			
Recitals	Number of recitals, divided by 10	+	EUR-Lex (Directives 1978–2009)
Time for transposition	Years between adoption and transposition deadline[4]	–	EUR-Lex (Directives 1978–2009)
Adopted directives	Annual minus average number of directives adopted, divided by 10	+	EUR-Lex (Years 1978–2009)
Ministerial approval	Average distance of national ministers' party preferences to the outer limits of the Council core Inside the core > 0 Outside the core < 0	–	PUCH (Directives 1978–2009)
Qualified majority voting	(Qualified) majority 1 Unanimity 0	+	Monthly Summaries of Council Acts/Pre-Lex (Directives 1978–2009)

Variable	Categories	Coding	Direction	Data source
Dissent	All MS in favor	0	+	Monthly Summaries of Council Acts (Directives 1994–2009)[5]
	Abstentions and/or Negative votes	1		
Co-decision	No EP participation	0	−	Pre-Lex (Directives 1978–2009)
	Consultation	1		
	Cooperation	2		
	Co-decision	3		
EP amendments	No amendments	0	+	Pre-Lex (Directives 1978–2009)
	Amendments at 1st reading	1		
	Amendments at 2nd reading	2		
	Conciliation Committee	3		
Involvement of national parliaments	Share of member states (EU-15) involving parliament in the transposition process (if duly notified), quotient (= percent divided by 100)		+	PUCH (Directives 1978–2009)
	Involvement	1		
	No involvement	0		
EU opposition (institutional legitimacy)	Share of replies opposing EU Membership ("a bad thing") in the year of transposition[6], quotient multiplied by 10 (= percent divided by 10)		+	Eurobarometer (Directives 1978–2009)

1 Number of infringement proceedings opened between 1978 and 2012, having reached a reasoned opinion until February 2016.

2 According to title: no reference to another directive OR including formulations such as "implementing" (= Implementing directives)

3 According to title: including formulations such as "amending," "repealing," "adapting to technical progress," "granting derogations from."

4 The notification deadline was coded according to the "Date of transposition" on EUR-Lex. If it is missing, we used the "Date of notification," "Date of effect," or "Date of document," in order of priority.

5 For years 1979–1993, all missing cases were coded "0" because even if member states had voted against a legal act before 1994, this would not have been published (and thus known to the public).

6 Quotient multiplied by 10 (= percent divided by 10) > Year of adoption + 1 (mean years of transposition deadline = 0.972 [2984exPUCH] or 1.006 [2793incPUCH]).

TABLE A3.3 Sector
Dependent and independent variables and their operationalization

	OPERATIONALIZATION		EXPECTED EFFECT ON NONCOMPLIANCE	DATA SOURCE
DEPENDENT VARIABLE				
Official infringements of directives	Official infringement proceedings per year, 1981–2012			Berlin Infringement Database, EUR-Lex
INDEPENDENT VARIABLES				
Policy				
Regulatory	Regulatory	1	+/−	Legal base (EU treaties)
	Non-regulatory	0		
Market-correcting	Market-correcting	1	+	Legal base (EU treaties)
	Market-making	0		
Control variables				
Age	Years of EU legislative competence		−	Legal base (EU treaties)
EU competence	Average score of level and scope		+	Integration Index (Börzel 2005)
EU opposition	Share of replies in favor of national decision-making, per sector, per year		−	Eurobarometer (1978–2012)
Adopted directives	Number of directives adopted per year		−	PUCH (1978–2009)
New directives	Number of new directives adopted per year		+	EUR-Lex (1978–2009)
Recitals	Number of adopted directives X average number of recitals per sector, divided by 10 (rescaled for better comparability)		+	EUR-Lex (1978–2009)

Council/Council-EP directive	Number of directives not delegated to the Commission per year	–	EUR-Lex (1978–2009)
EP amendments	Annual average interference of EP during the adoption of directives, using 0 for missing observations	+	Pre-Lex (1978–2009)
Maastricht control	Before entering into force of the Maastricht Treaty (1978–1993) 0	+	
	After (1994–2012) 1		
Member state control	Number of member states per year	+	

Appendix 4

ROBUSTNESS TESTS

TABLE A4.1 Power, capacity, and politicization (EU-15, 1979–2017)[1]

	COEFFICIENT
Power	
Voting power (SSI)	**0.0653*****
	(0.00734)
Capacity	
GDP per capita	–0.00157
	(0.00182)
Bureaucratic quality (ICRG)	**–0.0397*****
	(0.00421)
Politicization	
Political constraints	**0.00371***
	(0.00191)
Regional authority	**–0.00588*****
	(0.00258)
Parliamentary scrutiny	**0.00602****
	(0.00258)
EU opposition	**–0.0179*****
	(0.00287)
Controls	
Intra-EU trade	**0.00654*****
	(0.00132)
Net recipient	**0.000129***
	(6.98e-05)
Ministerial approval	0.00135
	(0.00518)

(Continued)

TABLE A4.1 (Continued)

	COEFFICIENT
Constant	2.982***
	(0.195)
Observations	515
Number of years	39

Standard errors in parentheses
*** p < 0.01, ** p < 0.05, * p < 0.1

1 Values for the following variables are based on projections: ministerial approval (2010), parliamentary scrutiny (2010), regional authority (2011), EU opposition (2011), net recipient (2015), political constraints (2015), and bureaucratic quality (2011). Variables based on GDP (US constant 2005) were recoded using GDP (US constant 2010). Such an approach is acceptable since most of these variables have not undergone significant reform during the added five years.

TABLE A4.2 Power, capacity, and politicization (EU-27, 1979–2017), with EU-15 dummy[1]

	COEFFICIENT
Power	
Voting power (SSI)	**0.0545***
	(0.00601)
Capacity	
GDP per capita	0.000822
	(0.00179)
Bureaucratic quality (ICRG)	**−0.0259***
	(0.00373)
Politicization	
Political constraints	**0.00612***
	(0.00166)
Regional authority	−0.00203
	(0.00209)
EU opposition	**−0.0173***
	(0.00273)
Controls	
Net recipient	**0.000245***
	(6.23e-05)
EU-15	**0.524***
	(0.0807)
Constant	1.961***
	(0.150)
Observations	665
Number of years	39

Standard errors in parentheses
*** p < 0.01, ** p < 0.05, * p < 0.1

1 Values for the following variables are based on projections: regional authority (2011), EU opposition (2011), net recipient (2015), political constraints (2015), and bureaucratic quality (2011). Variables based on GDP (US constant 2005) were recoded using GDP (US constant 2010). Such an approach is acceptable since most of these variables have not undergone significant reform during the added five years.

TABLE A4.3 Novelty, delegation and noncompliance (EU-28, 1978–2015)

		MAASTRICHT DUMMY
Nature of EU law		
New directive	0.571***	0.580***
	(0.0641)	(0.0646)
Commission directive	−0.131	−0.228*
	(0.0834)	(0.0847)
Control variables		
Recitals	0.295***	0.312***
	(0.0306)	(0.0299)
Time	0.186**	0.210***
	(0.0367)	(0.0379)
Adopted directives	0.0557***	0.0675***
	(0.0147)	(0.0156)
QMV (voting rule)	0.342***	0.257**
	(0.0987)	(0.105)
Dissent (voting outcome)	0.00848	−0.00615
	(0.0497)	(0.0504)
EP amendments	0.221***	0.182***
	(0.0458)	(0.0454)
EU opposition	−0.421***	−0.564***
	(0.118)	(0.119)
Age	0.0285***	0.0498***
	(0.00483)	(0.00653)
Maastricht		0.587***
		(0.110)
Constant	−0.0913	−0.655**
	(0.272)	(0.300)
Observations	3,236	3,236

Robust standard errors in parentheses
*** p < 0.01, ** p < 0.05, * p < 0.1

TABLE A4.4 Policy type, regulatory logic and noncompliance (EU-28, 1981–2017)

	REGULATORY DENSITY	MISFIT	COMPLEXITY	POLITICIZATION
Policy				
Regulatory policy	0.690***	0.193	0.658***	0.395***
	(0.257)	(0.230)	(0.245)	(0.238)
Market correcting	0.334**	0.257*	0.290**	0.325**
	(0.139)	(0.140)	(0.138)	(0.149)
Control variables				
Costs				
Age	−0.000616	−0.00715*	−0.00909**	−0.00336
	(0.00420)	(0.00431)	(0.00431)	(0.00425)
EU competencies	−0.0422	−0.0526	−0.0463	−0.0502
	(0.0498)	(0.0500)	(0.0506)	(0.0491)
Directives adopted	0.0176***			
	(0.00509)			

(Continued)

TABLE A4.4   (Continued)

	REGULATORY DENSITY	MISFIT	COMPLEXITY	POLITICIZATION
New directives		0.0423***		
		(0.0108)		
Recitals			0.0264***	
			(0.00583)	
Politicization				
Council/Council-EP directive				0.0104*
				(0.00599)
EP amendments	0.530***	0.521***	0.496***	0.530***
	(0.0672)	(0.0687)	(0.0696)	(0.0670)
EU opposition	−2.579***	−2.577***	−2.618***	−2.639***
	(0.461)	(0.472)	(0.469)	(0.457)
Constant	−0.188	0.428	−0.0487	0.124
	(0.471)	(0.474)	(0.469)	(0.461)
Observations	363	363	363	363
Number of years	37	37	37	37

Standard errors in parentheses
*** $p < 0.01$, ** $p < 0.05$, * $p < 0.1$

INTERACTION EFFECTS

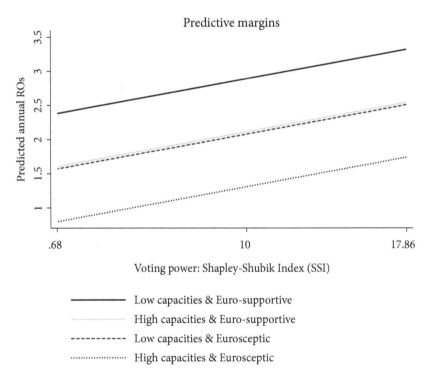

FIGURE A5.1 Voting power, bureaucratic quality, and Euroscepticism

Notes

INTRODUCTION: THE POLITICS OF NONCOMPLIANCE

1. "Almost all nations observe almost all principles of international law and almost all of their obligations almost all of the time" (Henkin 1968, 479; italics in original).

1. INFRINGEMENT DATA AND NONCOMPLIANCE

1. For real icebergs, more than 90 percent is submerged.

2. Treaty provisions and regulations are generally binding and directly applicable, while decisions are administrative acts aimed at specific individuals, companies, or governments, for which they are binding.

3. Member states may also fail to comply with judgments of the court on the four types of violations. The EU's court is the final arbiter concerning violations of EU law. Its judgments are as legally binding as treaty provisions, regulations, directives, and decisions. Since they refer to cases of noncompliance with EU legal acts, they are reported as consecutive infringements of these legal acts, adding another stage to the infringement proceedings.

4. Thomson Reuters, CELEX, http://data.ellispub.com/ojolplus/help/celex.htm, last accessed 26 April 2020.

5. European Commission, Single Market Scoreboard, http://ec.europa.eu/internal_market/scoreboard/performance_by_governance_tool/transposition/index_en.htm#main contentSec4, last accessed 26 April 2020.

6. According to the doctrine of the *éffet utile*, developed by the ECJ, member states have to choose the most effective means, however (Case C-8/55 *Fédéchar v. High Authority* [1956] ECLI:EU:C:1956:11; C-26/62 *Van Gend en Loos* [1963] ECLI:EU:C:1963:1; cf. Dimitrakopoulos 2001).

7. The original title of the reports was *Annual Report to the European Parliament on Commission Monitoring of the Application of Community Law.*

8. See, e.g., Case C-29/59 *Knutange v. ECSC High Authority* [1960] ECR-00001.

9. See, e.g., Case C-294/83 *Les Verts v. European Parliament* [1986] ECR-01339.

10. The possibility of imposing financial penalties was dropped in the Treaty of Rome (1957) and only reintroduced by the Maastricht Treaty (1992). For the history of the infringement proceedings see Prete 2017.

11. Note, however, that, according to the view of the ECJ, the letter defines the object at issue in any subsequent court proceedings. As a result, the Commission is not allowed to include additional points during subsequent stages, even if it later discovers new infringements.

12. Case T-191/99 *Petrie and Others v. Commission* [2001] ECR II-3677: 67–68, drawing on Case T-105/95 *WWF UK v. Commission* [1997] ECR II-313.

13. The European Court of Justice is increasingly referred to as the Court of Justice of the European Union (CJEU). However, the CJEU denotes the entire court system of the EU, which includes the ECJ but also the General Court. Since the ECJ adjudicates infringement proceedings, I keep using ECJ.

14. Case T-191/99 *Petrie and Others v. Commission* [2001] ECR II-3677, drawing on Case T-105/95 *WWF UK v. Commission* [1997] ECR II-313 and Case T-309/97 *Bavarian Lager Company v. Commission* [1999] ECR II-3217.

15. The fine's basic amount of €640 per day is multiplied by a factor n, taking into account the GDP of a member state and its number of votes in the Council. The factor n for Luxembourg, for instance, is 1 and for Germany 21.12 (Commission of the European Communities 2012b).

16. For a similar argument on the ECJ as strategic enforcer see Blauberger and Schmidt 2017; Carrubba 2005; Carrubba, Gabel, and Hankla 2008; Fjelstul and Carrubba 2018; and Larsson and Naurin 2016. Their findings demonstrate that the ECJ is selective in its rulings but do not reveal that this results in a bias toward certain member states or policy sectors.

17. Commission official, interview with the author, Berlin, 30 May 2013.

18. The questionnaires and the results of the two surveys are available from the author on request.

19. Eszter Zalan, "Juncker Rebukes Hungary's EU Commissioner," EUobserver, 2 December 2015, https://euobserver.com/institutional/131353, last accessed 29 August 2020.

20. Case C-6/64 *Flaminio Costa v. E.N.E.L.* [1964] ECR 614.

21. Case C-26/62 *Van Gend en Loos* [1962] ECR 001.

22. Case 43/75 *Defrenne v. Sabena* [1976] ECR 455.

23. Case C-144/04 *Mangold v. Rudiger Helm* [2005] ECR I-9981.

24. I owe this term to Beth Simmons.

25. EUR-Lex, "About EUR Lex," http://eur-lex.europa.eu/content/welcome/about.html?locale=en, last accessed 27 August 2020.

26. Dimiter Toshkov, "Data and Replication Materials," http://www.dimiter.eu/Data.html, last accessed 29 April 2017.

27. From 1984 until 2010, data in the annual reports accounted only for any "new steps" taken in infringement proceedings in that year. Since 2011, annual reports have been limited to presenting aggregate data on selected topics. Finally, the newly introduced search engine on infringement decisions by the Commission is limited to a period starting in 2002 and, similarly, only provides for separate accounts of single decisions ("new steps")—which often precede the official issuing of the corresponding act within the infringement proceeding, as compared to the dates provided in earlier annual reports or on the ECJ's website CURIA.

28. The first year for which the Commission comprehensively collected and published infringement data was 1978; the most recent update of the BID was 7 March 2019. Since it takes on average two years for the Commission to send a reasoned opinion, I made the cut for asserted infringements in 2017.

29. EUR-Lex, "Access to European Union Law," http://eur-lex.europa.eu/homepage.html, last accessed 24 April 2020.

30. Pre-Lex does not exist anymore. The data was integrated in EUR-Lex, http://eur-lex.europa.eu/collection/legislative-procedures.html?locale=en, last accessed 18 July 2017.

31. Cf. Case T-309/97 *Bavarian Lager Company v. Commission* [1999] ECR II-3217: 40.

32. In one particular case it took France about twenty years to comply with Council Regulation No. 2057/82 establishing certain control measures for fishing activities.

33. The graph shows the ratio of average annual infringements (1978–2012) to average annual adopted directives (1978–2009), according to policy sector. For infringements, the categorization of policy sectors is based on the Directorate-General of the European Commission leading the infringement proceeding. For directives, the policy indicator was hand coded on the basis of "directory code" data in the EUR-Lex database. However, the European Commission has undergone numerous changes in its internal structure,

reflecting developments in both the nature and focus of EU policymaking over time. These changes have become more significant in recent years and thus present challenges to the continuation of the policy categories at hand. A notable example can be seen in the rearrangement of Directorate-General (DG) Health & Consumers (SANCO) and DG Justice & Home Affairs (JAIN) into the newly formed DGs for Health & Food Safety (DG SANTE), Justice & Consumers (DG JUST), and Migration & Home Affairs (DG HOME). In most of these cases, the continued existence of similar configurations in other EU institutions—including both the Justice and Home Affairs Council (JHA) and the European Parliament's Committee on Civil Liberties, Justice and Home Affairs (LIBE)—as well as continued cooperation among the corresponding internal services of the Commission (cf. "Area of Freedom, Security and Justice") may justify keeping the original categorization of policy sectors. As opposed to former policy sectors being split at some point in time, however, the incremental integration of the long-standing Directorate-Generals for Internal Market and Services (DG MARKT) and Enterprise & Industry (DG ENTR) constitutes a change in the available data (especially from 2014 onward), which cannot be easily resolved in the coding process. Accordingly, a continuation will either require strict indicators for the division of new infringements and directives into existing policy categories, or a fusion of both categories in line with the newly formed Directorate-General for Internal Market, Industry, Entrepreneurship and SMEs (DG GROW), which would in turn significantly reduce the degree of differentiation in an analysis of policy sectors. I have thus refrained from any further continuation of these statistics for the time being, instead only presenting secure data based on the original version of the Berlin Infringement Database (1978–2012).

2. POWER, CAPACITY, AND POLITICIZATION

1. Council Directive 91/271/EEC of 21 May 1991 concerning urban waste water treatment.

2. European Commission, "Commission Takes Italy Back to the Court and Proposes Fines," press release, 8 December 2016, http://europa.eu/rapid/press-release_IP-16-4212_en.htm, last accessed 11 March 2019.

3. For the distinction between preferences over outcomes versus preferences over strategies in the literature on international cooperation see Stein 1983; Axelrod 1984; Oye 1986; Frieden 1999. Theories of international cooperation tend to refer to cooperation and defection rather than compliance and noncompliance as the two main strategies states can pursue to achieve their most preferred policy outcome.

4. Fearon refers to the two stages as the bargaining versus the enforcement phase (Fearon 1998). Shaping and taking go beyond his distinction most importantly by systematically incorporating domestic actors in both the bargaining and the enforcement of international and EU law.

5. The votes in the Council of Ministers are weighted according to a member state's population. Even though the system has been skewed in favor of smaller member states, France, Germany, Italy, and the UK as the four most populous member states have had almost ten times more votes than Malta, whose population is less than 0.05 percent of the German population. Under the double majority rule introduced by the Lisbon Treaty's ordinary legislative procedure, population size still matters. Each member state has only one vote now. However, majority decisions require 55 percent of member states representing at least 65 percent of the EU population (Article 238 TFEU).

6. A blocking minority requires three of the larger member states to join forces with one of the smaller member states. After Brexit, Spain and Poland have enough weight to substitute for the UK.

7. The Lisbon Treaty summarizes the consultative, cooperation, and assent procedures under special legislative procedures and made the former co-decision procedure the ordinary legislative procedure (Article 294 of the Treaty on the Functioning of the EU).

3. WHY SOME STATES COMPLY LESS THAN OTHERS

1. Bergman 2000, Falkner et al. 2005, and Falkner, Hartlapp, and Treib 2007 put the UK and the Netherlands in the middle group. Lampinen and Uusikylä 1998, Haverland, Steunenberg, and van Waarden 2011, Haverland and Romeijn 2007, and König and Luetgert 2009 concur with regard to the Netherlands. Yet almost all these studies focus on timely transposition only.

2. The graph shows the annual ratio between new member states' infringements (according to reasoned opinions) and the mean number of infringements on behalf of the old member states during their first ten years of membership. As opposed to the average annual number of infringements per member state displayed in other statistics, the graph at hand also includes the year of accession, which has often been marked by a certain "grace period" and is clearly visible in the statistical outliers among countries such as Greece, Portugal, Spain, Malta, or Croatia.

3. The International Country Risk Guide, provided by the World Bank, has an indicator on rule of law or "law and order tradition," but it does not cover the full time period of my analysis (Kaufmann, Kraay, and Mastruzzi 2003). James L. Gibson and Gregory A. Caldeira's opinion poll survey retrieved data at only one point in time, 1992–1993 (Gibson and Caldeira 1996).

4. "Selon la Commission européenne, la Clause Molière est une 'discrimination,'" *Le Figaro*, 19 March 2017, https://www.lefigaro.fr/conjoncture/2017/03/19/20002-20170319ART FIG00054-la-clause-moliere-est-une-discrimination-estime-la-commission-europeenne.php, last accessed 28 August 2020.

5. Countries that receive funding from the Cohesion Fund, the EU established in 1993 have a gross national income per inhabitant of less than 90 percent of the EU average. After eastern enlargement, the only EU-15 member states that still qualify are Greece and Portugal.

6. Directive 2006/24/EC of the European Parliament and of the Council of 15 March 2006 on the retention of data generated or processed in connection with the provision of publicly available electronic communications services or of public communications networks and amending Directive 2002/58/EC.

7. BVerfG, Judgment of the First Senate of 02 March 2010–1 BvR 256/08—paras. (1–345).

8. See https://www.bmu.de/fileadmin/Daten_BMU/Download_PDF/Umweltin formation/aarhus_umsetzungsbericht_2013_korrektur_bf.pdf, last accessed 3 August 2020.

9. See chapter 4 for more details on the directive.

10. While EU opposition has been rather stable for most member states, Denmark and Italy have seen some substantial changes. In Italy, opposition more than tripled since 1999 (from 5 to 17 percent in 2010). In Denmark, it halved during the same period (from 24 to 12 percent). Greece saw a recent rise from 13 to 21 percent, probably due to the euro crisis.

4. WHY THERE IS NO GROWING NONCOMPLIANCE

1. The EU adopted "unity in diversity" as its official motto in 2000, https://europa.eu/ european-union/about-eu/symbols/motto_en, last accessed 3 September 2017.

2. Commission Communication on "A Europe of Results—Applying Community Law," COM(2007)502 final, p. 1.

3. On the following see also Börzel and Buzogány 2019.

4. Once an infringement is "confirmed," a letter of formal notice is sent.

5. Suspected infringements were initially broken down into "complaints" and "cases detected by the Commission" by inquiries on its own initiative. In 1988, "parliamentary questions" and "petitions" were added to "cases detected by the Commission." In 1998, "cases detected by the Commission" became the overall category for "petitions," "parliamentary questions," and a residual category, which may refer to the Commission's own investigations. From 2006 to 2010, "cases detected by the Commission" were renamed as "own initiative cases." In 1996, the Annual Reports included a third category, next to complaints and cases detected by the Commission / own-initiative cases: the noncommunication of national measures transposing EU directives. Since 2011, the Commission only reports data on complaints and own initiatives as a total as done before 1988. Noncommunication is relabeled as late transposition. Petitions and parliamentary questions are no longer listed separately. Finally, the Commission introduced "enquiries" as a separate category next to complaints. These changes take effect gradually, since old cases are recoded and partly recounted under the newly introduced categories. I therefore limit the analysis to data available for the years 1982–2010. Data on own investigations and noncommunication are available only since 1988 and 1996, respectively.

6. Commission Communication on Effective Problem Solving in the Internal Market ("SOLVIT") COM(2001) 702 final.

7. European Commission, "Internal Market Information System," http://ec.europa.eu/internal_market/imi-net/about/index_en.htm#maincontentSec1, last accessed 31 January 2020.

8. Commission Communication on "A Europe of Results—Applying Community Law," COM(2007) 502 final.

9. Internal document of the Commission, unpublished but available from the author on request.

10. Commission official, interview with the author, Berlin, 30 May 2013.

11. The treaty establishing the European Coal and Steel Community had provided for the possibility of imposing financial penalties (Article 89). Articles 169–171 of Treaty of Rome dropped these provisions.

12. Case C-387/97 *Commission v. Greece* [*2000*] ECR I-5047.

13. The Commission closed the case on the Greek landfill in 2001—only to discover that Greece had not fully complied with the ECJ ruling. Instead of reopening the case, the Commission launched an infringement proceeding against a second illegal landfill close by (Hedemann-Robison 2015: 186, 199; *Case C-112/06 Commission v. Greece* [2006] OJ C121/4).

14. Commission Communication on the Application of Article 260 of the Treaty on the Functioning of the European Union. Updating of data used to calculate lump sum and penalty payments to be proposed by the Commission to the Court of Justice in infringement proceedings SEC(2010) 1371; cf. Peers 2012.

15. Commission Communication: Action Plan for the Single Market CSE(97)1 final.

16. For 1988–2005, tov_2 and tov_3 follow similar trajectories as their aggregates.

17. European Commission, Single Market Scoreboard, SOLVIT, http://ec.europa.eu/internal_market/scoreboard/performance_by_governance_tool/solvit/index_en.htm#maincontentSec4, last accessed 8 September 2020.

18. Ibid.

19. European Commission, Single Market Scoreboard, EU Pilot, http://ec.europa.eu/internal_market/scoreboard/performance_by_governance_tool/eu_pilot/index_en.htm#maincontentSec4, last accessed 8 September 2020.

20. For 1978–2008 see EU Budget 2008 Financial Report, http://ec.europa.eu/budget/library/biblio/publications/2008/fin_report/fin_report_08_en.pdf, last accessed 10 December 2019. For 2008–2013, EU Commission Budget in Figures, http://ec.europa.eu/budget/figures/index_en.cfm, last accessed 10 December 2019.

21. "Reinforcing the Effectiveness of the Internal Market. Working Document of the Commission on a Strategic Programme on the Internal Market" (Sutherland Report) COM (93) 256 final, Section IV, Enforcing the rules through partnership.

22. "A New Strategy for the Single Market: At the Service of Europe's Economy and Society," Report to the President of the European Commission José Manuel Barroso, 9 May 2010, https://www.kfw.de/migration/Weiterleitung-zur-Startseite/Homepage/KfW-Group/Research/PDF-Files/Monti_Report.pdf, last accessed 31 August 2020.

23. ECHA, European Chemicals Agency, "Enforcement Forum," http://echa.europa.eu/about-us/who-we-are/enforcement-forum, last accessed 27 August 2020.

24. Case 138/79 *Roquette Frères S.A. v. Council* [1980] ECR-03333.

25. The Treaty of Maastricht mentioned the role of national parliaments within the European Union in the nonbinding Declaration No. 13 (Declaration on the role of national Parliaments in the European Union [1992] OJ C191/1). The Amsterdam Treaty included a Protocol on the Role of National Parliaments in the European Union [1997] OJ C340/1.

26. Article 7 of Protocol No. 2 to the Lisbon Treaty on the application of the principles of subsidiarity and proportionality.

27. OE (Open Europe), "National Democracy Pushing Back: European Commission Shown Its Second Ever 'Yellow Card,'" 29 October 2013, http://openeuropeblog.blogspot.com/2013/10/european-commission-shown-its-second.html, last accessed 28 March 2020.

28. Unfortunately, there is no corresponding data on the directives in force. However, with an average transposition deadline of eighteen to twenty-four months, and another eighteen to twenty-four months it takes for an infringement to reach the official stage of a reasoned opinion, the cutoff points for directives adopted (2009) and reasoned opinions sent (2012) match.

29. Council Directive 92/43/EEC of 21 May 1992 on the conservation of natural habitats and of wild fauna and flora.

30. Council Directive 2006/112/EC of 28 November 2006 on the common system of value added tax.

31. EUR-Lex, Legal Acts, https://eur-lex.europa.eu/collection/eu-law/legislation/recent.html, last accessed 6 March 2020.

32. Council Directive 92/43/EEC of 21 May 1992 on the conservation of natural habitats and of wild fauna and flora.

33. Council Directive 79/409/EEC of 2 April 1979 on the conservation of wild birds.

34. Council Directive 91/271/EEC of 21 May 1991 concerning urban waste water treatment.

35. Council Directive 85/337/EEC of 27 June 1985 on the assessment of the effects of certain public and private projects on the environment.

36. Council Directive 2006/112/EC of 28 November 2006 on the common system of value added tax.

37. Council Directive 92/50/EEC of 18 June 1992 relating to the coordination of procedures for the award of public service contracts.

38. Council Directive 93/37/EEC of 14 June 1993 concerning the coordination of procedures for the award of public works contracts.

39. Directive 2004/18/EC of the European Parliament and of the Council of 31 March 2004 on the coordination of procedures for the award of public works contracts, public supply contracts, and public service contracts.

40. Council Directive 83/189/EEC of 28 March 1983 laying down a procedure for the provision of information in the field of technical standards and regulations.

41. Council Directive 88/182/EEC of 22 March 1988 amending Directive 83/189/EEC laying down a procedure for the provision of information in the field of technical standards and regulations.

42. Directive 2005/36/EC of the European Parliament and of the Council of 7 September 2005 on the recognition of professional qualifications.

43. EUR-Lex, http://eur-lex.europa.eu/legal-content/en/ALL/?uri=CELEX:31992L0043, last accessed 7 April 2020.

44. *Directive* 2006/123/EC of the European Parliament and of the Council of 12 December 2006 on services in the Internal Market.

45. "European Commission Shelves Olive Oil Jug Ban after Outcry," Euronews, updated 23 May 2013, https://www.euronews.com/search?query=European%20Commission%20Shelves%20Olive%20Oil%20Jug%20Ban%20after%20Outcry, last accessed 28 August 2020.

5. WHY NONCOMPLIANCE IS SECTOR SPECIFIC

1. Directive 2004/38/EC of the European Parliament and of the Council of 29 April 2004 on the right of citizens of the Union and their family members to move and reside freely within the territory of the Member States, amending Regulation (EEC) No 1612/68 and repealing Directives 64/221/EEC, 68/360/EEC, 72/194/EEC, 73/148/EEC, 75/34/EEC, 75/35/EEC, 90/364/EEC, 90/365/EEC and 93/96/EEC.

2. For the purpose of identifying most infringed legal acts per policy sector, the number of infringements per legal act was calculated differently from identifying the most infringed directives in chapter 4 (table 4.4). Each infringement proceeding was attributed to a single legal act, namely the most recent directive. This method was employed in order to avoid double counting of one infringement proceeding, particularly with a view to the data used in the (directive-based) regression analysis. However, the method fails to take into account those infringements against a legal act where the proceeding concerned several acts and another CELEX number took precedence in the coding process. In identifying the most infringed legal acts per policy sector, this disadvantage becomes more significant, as all legal acts are considered (instead of directives only), and the single-counting method would leave several infringed legal acts seem "untouched." For this reason, all CELEX numbers mentioned in an infringement proceeding (amounting to up to thirty different legal acts) were listed and counted, allowing us to account for all legal acts ever infringed, as well as the entire volume of infringements against a single legal act. However, it should be kept in mind that this method includes multi-counting, thus rendering any accumulation of the number of infringements against a certain "complex" of legal acts (e.g., consisting of several interconnected, supplementary, and amending directives; or of one treaty article changing its CELEX number over time) extremely problematic. At the same time, any double counting between policy sectors is precluded, as each ranking exclusively counts infringements in that same policy sector. For this purpose, the policy sector was identified on the basis of the infringement proceeding, not the legal act in question.

3. Directive 2006/24/EC of the European Parliament and of the Council of 15 March 2006 on the retention of data generated or processed in connection with the provision of publicly available electronic communications services or of public communications networks and amending Directive 2002/58/EC.

4. Directive 2008/99/EC of the European Parliament and of the Council of 19 November 2008 on the protection of the environment through criminal law.

5. Council Directive 79/409/EEC of 2 April 1979 on the conservation of wild birds.

6. Directive 2009/147/EC of the European Parliament and of the Council of 30 November 2009 on the conservation of wild birds.

7. Council Directive 92/43/EEC of 21 May 1992 on the conservation of natural habitats and of wild fauna and flora.

8. The initial Directive of 1985 (85/337/EEC) and its three amendments have been codified by Directive 2011/92/EU of 13 December 2011. Directive 2011/92/EU was amended in 2014 by Directive 2014/52/EU.

9. Council Directive 91/271/EEC of 21 May 1991 concerning urban waste water treatment.

10. INSO was renamed Communications Networks, Content and Technology in 2016.

11. Directive 2002/22/EC of the European Parliament and of the Council of 7 March 2002 on universal service and users' rights relating to electronic communications networks and services.

12. Directive 2009/136/EC of the European Parliament and of the Council of 25 November 2009 amending Directive 2002/22/EC on universal service and users' rights relating to electronic communications networks and services, Directive 2002/58/EC concerning the processing of personal data and the protection of privacy in the electronic communications sector, and Regulation (EC) No 2006/2004 on cooperation between national authorities responsible for the enforcement of consumer protection laws.

13. Council Directive 93/13/EEC of 5 April 1993 on unfair terms in consumer contracts.

14. Directive 2005/29/EC of the European Parliament and of the Council of 11 May 2005 concerning unfair business-to-consumer commercial practices in the internal market and amending Council Directive 84/450/EEC, Directives 97/7/EC, 98/27/EC and 2002/65/EC of the European Parliament and of the Council and Regulation (EC) No 2006/2004 of the European Parliament and of the Council ("Unfair Commercial Practices Directive").

15. Council Directive 1999/74/EC of 19 July 1999 laying down minimum standards for the protection of laying hens.

16. Somewhat similar to the scope is the concept of specializations (or the lack thereof), which is described by Steunenberg and Kaeding 2009 as "the extent to which directives regulate rather technical issues, which are intended to be implemented uniformly by national administrations" (11).

17. The dependent variable is the number of infringements per member state per year.

18. The dependent variable is the number of infringements per directive.

19. EU Vocabularies, https://op.europa.eu/en/web/eu-vocabularies/, last accessed 8 May 2020.

20. Council Directive 83/189/EEC of 28 March 1983 laying down a procedure for the provision of information in the field of technical standards and regulations.

21. Regulation (EU) 2015/2120 of the European Parliament and of the Council of 25 November 2015 laying down measures concerning open internet access and amending Directive 2002/22/EC on universal service and users' rights relating to electronic communications networks and services and Regulation (EU) No 531/2012 on roaming on public mobile communications networks within the Union.

22. Since the Maastricht Treaty and the Lisbon Treaty entered in force at the end of 1993 and 2009, respectively, we took the following year as reference point for calculating the age of a sector.

23. Customs Union falls under the exclusive competence of the EU, i.e., has the highest score in terms of level and scope. Taxation is exactly the opposite. Since it is hard to infringe on the EU's external tariffs, and all infringements in the sector concern Taxation, we drop Customs Union.

24. Until 6 September 2017, Germany accepted only 7,852 refugees of the 27,536 (2.5 percent) it had agreed to in September 2015. For Sweden, it was 1,903 out of 3,766 (50.5 percent). *Report from the Commission to the European Parliament, the European*

Council, and the Council: Fifteenth Report on Relocation and Resettlement, COM(2017) 465 final, annex 3.

25. Ibid.

26. Peter Teffer, "Czechs, Hungarians, and Poles Have One Month to Start Taking Migrants," EUobserver, 26 July 2017, https://euobserver.com/migration/138619, last accessed 29 August 2020. Poland and Hungary have hosted none, the Czech Republic twelve (0.4 percent), and Slovakia sixteen (3.5 percent). The Commission has spared Austria despite its government also refusing to receive any of the 1,953 refugees it was supposed to take in under the relocation scheme. Yet Austria had accepted more than 130,000 refugees in 2015 and 2016. Moreover, it did not join Hungary and Slovakia in challenging the legality of the Council decision on the temporary relocation scheme and pledged to make places available instead. The Czech Republic and Poland, in contrast, supported Hungary and Slovakia in their lawsuit and refused to comply until the ECJ would rule on the issue. The ECJ decided on 7 September 2017 that the Council had had the authority to adopt temporary measures in emergency situations. Since the four Visegrád countries continue to defy openly the relocation decision of the Council, refusing to comply, they are likely to face financial sanctions (Börzel 2020).

27. To help Greece and other member states struggling with the influx of refugees, in March 2016 the Commission unveiled plans for a refugee emergency fund of €700 million to be disbursed over the next three years. The EU and the other member states have promised to provide twenty-three hundred experts and to foot most of the €300 million for Greece to establish the necessary administrative and legal procedures for registering refugees and processing their asylum request, as well as to turn its already ill-equipped hot spots (asylum processing facilities) into proper reception facilities and detention centers (Börzel 2020).

28. After a five-year suspension, Germany restarted sending back migrants to Greece in August 2017, https://euobserver.com/migration/138700, last accessed 28 August 2020.

29. Council Decision (EU) 2015/1601 of 22 September 2015 establishing provisional measures in the area of international protection for the benefit of Italy and Greece.

30. "International Protection: Provisional Measures for the Benefit of Italy and Greece," Legislative Observatory, European Parliament, http://www.europarl.europa.eu/oeil/popups/ficheprocedure.do?lang=en&reference=2015/0209(NLE), last accessed 10 June 2020.

31. Compare the amendments the European Parliament had proposed, http://www.europarl.europa.eu/sides/getDoc.do?type=REPORT&reference=A8-2016-0236&language=EN (last accessed 24 July 2020), with the Council Decision (EU) 2016/1754 of 29 September 2016 amending Decision (EU) 2015/1601 establishing provisional measures in the area of international protection for the benefit of Italy and Greece.

32. Nikolaj Nielsen, "Computer to Make EU Asylum Decisions," EUobserver, 4 May 2016, https://euobserver.com/migration/133341, last accessed 28 August 2020.

33. Ursula von der Leyen, *A Union That Strives for More: My Agenda for Europe*, https://ec.europa.eu/commission/sites/beta-political/files/political-guidelines-next-commission_en.pdf, last accessed 30 March 2020.

34. Standard Eurobarometer 87—Wave EB87.3—TNS opinion & social, http://ec.europa.eu/commfrontoffice/publicopinion/index.cfm/Survey/getSurveyDetail/instruments/STANDARD/surveyKy/2142, p. 35, last accessed 3 August 2020.

CONCLUSION. THE LIMITS OF REGULATORY GOVERNANCE

1. In 2003, however, Regulation 1/2003 abolished the Commission's previous monopoly on applying many of the EU competition rules, with the aim of sharing the enforcement activities and responsibilities with the member states' national competition authorities and national courts.

2. "State Aid: Commission Refers Ireland to Court for Failure to Recover Illegal Tax Benefits from Apple Worth up to €13 Billion," European Commission press release,

Brussels, 4 October 2017, http://europa.eu/rapid/press-release_IP-17-3702_en.htm. The Commission withdrew the case in September 2018 after Apple had repaid the fiscal payments plus interest.

3. "European Commission Withdraws ECJ Case against Ireland after €13.1 Billion Apple Tax Is Recovered," thejournal.ie, 18 October 2018, https://www.thejournal.ie/euro pean-commission-apple-tax-court-case-4293555-Oct2018/.

4. European Commission, "Excessive Deficit Procedures—Overview," https://ec.europa. eu/info/business-economy-euro/economic-and-fiscal-policy-coordination/eu-economic-governance-monitoring-prevention-correction/stability-and-growth-pact/corrective-arm-excessive-deficit-procedure/excessive-deficit-procedures-overview_en, last accessed 8 September 2019.

5. "Q&A: Excessive Deficit Procedure without Fines?," Hertie School, Jacques Delors Centre, 29 July 2016, http://www.delorsinstitut.de/2015/wp-content/uploads/2016/07/20160729_Excessive-deficit-Brinke-AB.pdf.

6. European Commission, "A New EU Framework to Strengthen the Rule of Law," COM(2014)158.

7. European Commission, "Upholding the Rule of Law," http://ec.europa.eu/justice/effective-justice/rule-of-law/index_en.htm, last accessed 12 June 2017.

8. European Commission, "Commission Presents European Pillar of Social Rights and Launches Reflection on the Social Dimension of Europe by 2025," press release, 26 April 2017, http://europa.eu/rapid/press-release_MEX-17-1116_en.htm.

9. A few months later, the ECJ confirmed that the Polish retirement provisions for the supreme court as well as ordinary judges broke EU law: see Eszter Zalan, "Commission Takes Poland to Court on Eve of Election," 11 October 2019, http://euobserver.com/political/146234, last accessed 28 August 2020.

10. Eszter Zalan, "EU Action of Hungary and Poland Drowns in Procedure," EUobserver, 13 November 2018, http://euobserver.com/political/143359, last accessed 28 August 2020.

11. Eszter Zalan, "Commission Takes Poland to Court on Eve of Election," EUobserver, 11 October 2019, http://euobserver.com/political/146234, last accessed 28 August 2020.

12. Andrew Rettmann, "EU Court Blocks Poland's Bid to 'Frighten' Judges," 9 April 2020, https://euobserver.com/justice/148033, last accessed 28 August 2020.

13. Sam Morgan, "EU Bans Logging in Poland's Primeval Forest," Euractiv, 31 July 2017, https://www.euractiv.com/section/energy-environment/news/eu-court-bans-logging-in-polands-primeval-forest/, last accessed 28 August 2020.

14. Jack Ewing, "E.U. Commission Approves Billions in Aid for 2 Italian Banks," *New York Times*, 25 June 2017, https://www.nytimes.com/2017/06/25/business/eu-italy-banks-popolare-veneto.html, last accessed 28 August 2020.

References

Abbott, Kenneth W., Robert O. Keohane, Andrew Moravcsik, Anne Marie Slaughter, and Duncan Snidal. 2000. "The Concept of Legalization." *International Organization* 54 (3): 401–419.

Acharya, Amitav. 2016. "Regionalism beyond EU-Centrism." In *The Oxford Handbook of Comparative Regionalism*, edited by T. A. Börzel and T. Risse, 109–130. Oxford: Oxford University Press.

Ademmer, Esther, and Tanja A. Börzel. 2013. "Migration, Energy and Good Governance in the EU's Eastern Neighbourhood." *Europe Asia Studies* 65 (4): 581–608.

Aguilar Fernández, Susana. 1994. "Spanish Pollution Control Policy and the Challenge of the European Union." *Regional Politics and Policy* 4 (1, special issue): 102–117.

Aksoy, Deniz. 2010. "Who Gets What, When, and How Revisited: Voting and Proposal Powers in the Allocation of the EU Budget." *European Union Politics* 11 (2): 171–194.

Alcaro, Riccardo. 2018. "Contestation and Transformation. Final Thoughts on the Liberal International Order." *International Spectator* 53 (1): 152–167.

Alesina, Alberto, and Howard Rosenthal. 1995. *Partisan Politics, Divided Government, and the Economy*. Cambridge: Cambridge University Press.

Alter, Karen J. 2000. "The European Union's Legal System and Domestic Policy: Spillover or Backlash?" *International Organization* 54 (3): 489–517.

Alter, Karen J. 2001. *Establishing the Supremacy of European Law: The Making of an International Rule of Law in Europe*. Oxford: Oxford University Press.

Alter, Karen J. 2014. *The New Terrain of International Law: Courts, Politics, Rights*. Princeton, NJ: Princeton University Press.

Alter, Karen J., and Liesbet Hooghe. 2016. "Regional Dispute Settlement." In *The Oxford Handbook of Comparative Regionalism*, edited by T. A. Börzel and T. Risse, 538–558. Oxford: Oxford University Press.

Alter, Karen J., and Sophie Meunier-Aitsahalia. 1994. "Judicial Politics in the European Community: European Integration and the Pathbreaking Cassis de Dijon Decision." *Comparative Political Studies* 26 (4): 535–561.

Alter, Karen J., and Jeannette Vargas. 2000. "Explaining Variation in the Use of European Litigation Strategies: European Community Law and British Gender Equality Policy." *Comparative Political Studies* 33 (4): 452–482.

Andersen, Mikael Skou, and Duncan Liefferink, eds. 1997. *European Environmental Policy: The Pioneers*. Manchester: Manchester University Press.

Angelova, Mariyana, Tanja Dannwolf, and Thomas König. 2012. "How Robust Are Compliance Findings? A Research Synthesis." *Journal of European Public Policy* 19 (8): 1269–1291.

Audretsch, H. A. H., ed. 1986. *Supervision in European Community Law: Observance by the Member States of Their Treaty Obligations; A Treatise on International and Supra-National*. New York: Elsevier.

Auel, Katrin. 2007. "Democratic Accountability and National Parliaments: Redefining the Impact of Parliamentary Scrutiny in EU Affairs." *European Law Journal* 13 (4): 487–504.

Auel, Katrin, Olga Eisele, and Lucy Kinski. 2016. "From Constraining to Catalysing Dissensus? The Impact of Political Contestation on Parliamentary Communication in EU Affairs." *Comparative European Politics* 14 (2): 154–176.

Auel, Katrin, and Oliver Höing. 2015. "National Parliaments and the Eurozone Crisis: Taking Ownership in Difficult Times?" *West European Politics* 38 (2): 375–395.

Auel, Katrin, and Tapio Raunio. 2014. "Introduction: Connecting with the Electorate? Parliamentary Communication in EU Affairs." *Journal of Legislative Studies* 20 (1): 1–12.

Auer, Astrid, Christoph Demmke, and Robert Polet. 1996. *Civil Services in the Europe of the Fifteen: Current Situation and Prospects*. Maastricht: European Institute of Public Administration.

Avdeyeva, Olga A. 2010. "States' Compliance with International Requirements: Gender Equality in EU Enlargement Countries." *Political Research Quarterly* 63 (1): 203–217.

Axelrod, Robert A. 1984. *The Evolution of Cooperation*. New York: Basic Books.

Bailer, Stefanie, and Gerald Schneider. 2006. "Nash and Shelling: Legislative Bargaining with and without Domestic Constraints." In *The European Union Decides*, edited by R. Thomson, F. N. Stokman, C. Achen, and T. König, 153–177. Cambridge: Cambridge University Press.

Baldwin, David A. 2013. "Power and IR." In *Handbook of International Relations*, edited by W. Carlsnaes, T. Risse, and B. A. Simmons, 273–297. London: Sage.

Baldwin, David A. 2016. *Power and International Relations: A Conceptual Approach*. Princeton, NJ: Princeton University Press.

Barnett, Michael N., and Raymond Duvall. 2005. "Power in International Politics." *International Organization* 59 (1): 39–75.

Batory, Agnes. 2012. "Why Do Anti-corruption Laws Fail in Central Eastern Europe? A Target Compliance Perspective." *Regulation and Governance* 6 (1): 66–82.

Baun, Michael, and Dan Marek. 2008. "EU Cohesion Policy and Sub-national Authorities in the New Member States." *Contemporary European Studies* (2): 5–20.

Beach, Derek. 2005. "Why Governments Comply: An Integrative Compliance Model That Bridges the Gap between Instrumental and Normative Models of Compliance." *Journal of European Public Policy* 12 (1): 113–142.

Berglund, Sara, Ieva Grange, and Frans van Waarden. 2006. "Mass Production of Law: Routinization in Transposition of European Directives; A Sociological-Institutionalist Account." *Journal of European Public Policy* 13 (5): 692–716.

Bergman, Torbjörn. 2000. "The European Union as the Next Step of Delegation and Accountability." *European Journal of Political Research* 37 (3): 415–429.

Bergström, Carl-Fredrik, Henry Farrell, and Adrienne Héritier. 2007. "Legislate or Delegate? Bargaining over Implementation and Legislative Authority in the EU." *West European Politics* 30 (2): 338–366.

Bernauer, Thomas. 1995. "The Effect of International Environmental Institutions: How We Might Learn More." *International Organization* 49 (2): 351–377.

Bickerton, Christopher J. 2012. *European Integration: From Nation-States to Member States*. Oxford: Oxford University Press.

Biesenbender, Jan. 2011. "The Dynamics of Treaty Change: Measuring the Distribution of Power in the European Union?" *European Integration Online Papers* 15 (5). http://eiop.or.at/eiop/texte/2011-005a.htm, last accessed 29 August 2020.

Blauberger, Michael. 2009a. "Compliance with Rules of Negative Integration: State Aid Control in the New Member States." *Journal of European Public Policy* 16 (7): 1030–1046.

Blauberger, Michael. 2009b. "Of 'Good' and 'Bad' Subsidies: European State Aid Control through Soft and Hard Law." *West European Politics* 32 (4): 719–737.

Blauberger, Michael, and Susanne K. Schmidt. 2017. "The European Court of Justice and Its Political Impact." *West European Politics* 40 (4): 907–918.

Blom-Hansen, Jens. 2011. "The EU Comitology System: Taking Stock before the New Lisbon Regime." *Journal of European Public Policy* 18 (4): 607–617.

Bomberg, Elizabeth, and John Peterson. 2000. *Policy Transfer and Europeanization: Passing the Heineken Test?* Belfast: Queen's University.

Borghetto, Enrico, and Fabio Franchino. 2010. "The Role of Subnational Authorities in the Implementation of EU Directives." *Journal of European Public Policy* 17 (6): 759–780.

Borghetto, Enrico, Fabio Franchino, and Daniela Giannetti. 2006. "Complying with the Transposition Deadlines of EU Directives: Evidence from Italy." *Rivista Italiana di Politiche Pubbliche* 1 (1): 7–38.

Börzel, Tanja A. 2000a. "Improving Compliance through Domestic Mobilisation? New Instruments and the Effectiveness of Implementation in Spain." In *Implementing EU Environmental Policy: New Approaches to an Old Problem*, edited by C. Knill and A. Lenschow, 221–250. Manchester: Manchester University Press.

Börzel, Tanja A. 2000b. "Why There Is No Southern Problem: On Environmental Leader and Laggards in the EU." *Journal of European Public Policy* 7 (1): 141–162.

Börzel, Tanja A. 2001a. "Europeanization and Territorial Institutional Change: Towards Cooperative Regionalism in Europe?" In *Transforming Europe: Europeanization and Domestic Change*, edited by M. G. Cowles, J. A. Caporaso, and T. Risse, 137–158. Ithaca, NY: Cornell University Press.

Börzel, Tanja A. 2001b. "Non-compliance in the European Union: Pathology or Statistical Artefact?" *Journal of European Public Policy* 8 (5): 803–824.

Börzel, Tanja A. 2002a. "Pace-Setting, Foot-Dragging, and Fence-Sitting: Member State Responses to Europeanization." *Journal of Common Market Studies* 40 (2): 193–214.

Börzel, Tanja A. 2002b. *States and Regions in the European Union: Institutional Adaptation in Germany and Spain*. Cambridge: Cambridge University Press.

Börzel, Tanja A. 2003a. *Environmental Leaders and Laggards in Europe: Why There Is (Not) a Southern Problem*. Aldershot, UK: Ashgate.

Börzel, Tanja A. 2003b. "Guarding the Treaty: The Compliance Strategies of the European Commission." In *The State of the European Union VI: Law, Politics, and Society*, edited by T. A. Börzel and R. Cichowski, 197–220. Oxford: Oxford University Press.

Börzel, Tanja A. 2003c. *Shaping and Taking EU Policies: Member State Responses to Europeanization*. Belfast: Queen's University.

Börzel, Tanja A. 2005. "Mind the Gap! European Integration between Level and Scope." *Journal of European Public Policy* 12 (2): 1–20.

Börzel, Tanja A. 2006. "Participation through Law Enforcement: The Case of the European Union." *Comparative Political Studies* 39 (1): 128–152.

Börzel, Tanja A., ed. 2009a. *Coping with Accession to the European Union: New Modes of Environmental Governance*. Houndmills, Basingstoke, UK: Palgrave Macmillan.

Börzel, Tanja A. 2009b. "New Modes of Governance and Accession: The Paradox of Double Weakness." In *Coping with Accession to the European Union: New Modes of Environmental Governance*, edited by T. A. Börzel, 7–31. Houndmills, Basingstoke, UK: Palgrave Macmillan.

Börzel, Tanja A. 2010. "European Governance—Negotiation and Competition in the Shadow of Hierarchy." *Journal of Common Market Studies* 48 (2): 191–219.

Börzel, Tanja A. 2013. "Comparative Regionalism: European Integration and Beyond." In *Handbook of International Relations*, edited by W. Carlsnaes, T. Risse, and B. A. Simmons, 503–530. London: Sage.

Börzel, Tanja A. 2016. "From EU Governance of Crisis to Crisis in EU Governance: Regulatory Failure, Redistributive Conflict, and Eurosceptic Publics." *Journal of Common Market Studies: The JCMS Annual Review of the European Union in 2015* 54 (S1): 8–23.

Börzel, Tanja A. 2018. "Researching the EU (Studies) into Demise?" *Journal of European Public Policy* 25 (3): 475–485.

Börzel, Tanja A. 2020. "Contesting the EU Refugee Regime." SCRIPTS Working Paper, Cluster of Excellence 2055 "Contestations of the Liberal Script (SCRIPTS)." Freie Universität Berlin (5).

Börzel, Tanja A., and Aron Buzogány. 2010. "Environmental Organizations and the Europeanization of Public Policy in Central and Eastern Europe: The Case of Biodiversity Governance." *Environmental Politics* 19 (5): 708–735.

Börzel, Tanja A., and Aron Buzogány. 2019. "Compliance with EU Environmental Law. The Iceberg Is Melting." *Environmental Politics* 28 (2): 315–341.

Börzel, Tanja A., Meike Dudziak, Tobias Hofmann, Diana Panke, and Carina Sprungk. 2007. "Recalcitrance, Inefficiency and Support for European Integration: Why Member States Do (Not) Comply with European Law." CES Working Paper, Harvard University (151).

Börzel, Tanja A., and Tobias Hofmann. 2010. "Shaping and Taking Environmental Policies in the European Union." Unpublished manuscript.

Börzel, Tanja A., Tobias Hofmann, and Diana Panke. 2009. "Opinions, Referrals, and Judgements: Analyzing Longitudinal Patterns of Non-compliance." Berlin Working Paper on European Integration, Berlin Center for European Integration, Freie Universität Berlin (13).

Börzel, Tanja A., Tobias Hofmann, and Diana Panke. 2011. "Policy Matters But How? Explaining Non-compliance Dynamics in the EU." KFG Working Papers, Research College. The Transformative Power of Europe. Freie Universität Berlin (24).

Börzel, Tanja A., Tobias Hofmann, and Diana Panke. 2012. "Caving In or Sitting It Out? Longitudinal Patterns of Non-compliance in the European Union." *Journal of European Public Policy* 19 (4): 454–471.

Börzel, Tanja A., Tobias Hofmann, Diana Panke, and Carina Sprungk. 2010. "Obstinate and Inefficient: Why Member States Do Not Comply with European Law." *Comparative Political Studies* 43 (11): 1363–1390.

Börzel, Tanja A., Tobias Hofmann, and Carina Sprungk. 2003. "Einhaltung von Recht jenseits des Nationalstaats. Zur Implementationslogik marktkorrigierender Regelungen in der EU." *Zeitschrift für Internationale Beziehungen* 10 (2): 247–286.

Börzel, Tanja A., and Moritz Knoll. 2013. "Compliance with EU Directives: From Union Law to Law of the Land." Paper presented at the Thirteenth Biennial Conference of the European Union Studies Association, Baltimore, May 9–11.

Börzel, Tanja A., and Moritz Knoll. 2015. "The Depoliticization of EU Law: Explaining Non-compliance with EU Directives." Paper presented at the Fourteenth Biennial Conference of the European Union Studies Association, Boston, March 5–7.

Börzel, Tanja A., and Yasemin Pamuk. 2012. "Pathologies of Europeanization: Fighting Corruption in the Southern Caucasus." *West European Politics* 35 (1): 79–97.

Börzel, Tanja A., and Thomas Risse. 2000. "When Europe Hits Home: Europeanization and Domestic Change." *European Integration Online Papers* 4 (15), http://eiop. or.at/eiop/pdf/2000-015.pdf, last accessed 29 August 2020.

Börzel, Tanja A., and Thomas Risse. 2003. "Conceptualising the Domestic Impact of Europe." In *The Politics of Europeanisation*, edited by K. Featherstone and C. Radaelli, 55–78. Oxford: Oxford University Press.

Börzel, Tanja A., and Thomas Risse. 2018. "From the Euro to the Schengen Crisis: European Integration Theories, Politicization, and Identity Politics." *Journal of European Public Policy* 25 (1): 83–108.

Börzel, Tanja A., and Frank Schimmelfennig. 2017. "Coming Together or Driving Apart? The EU's Political Integration Capacity in Eastern Europe." *Journal of European Public Policy* 24 (2): 278–296.

Börzel, Tanja A., and Ulrich Sedelmeier. 2017. "Larger and More Law Abiding? The Impact of Enlargement on Compliance in the European Union." *Journal of European Public Policy* 24 (2): 197–217.

Börzel, Tanja A., and Carina Sprungk. 2009. "The Goodness of Fit and the Democratic Deficit in Europe: A Review of Vivien A. Schmidt, *Democracy in Europe; The EU and National Polities*." *Comparative European Politics* 7 (3): 364–373.

Börzel, Tanja A., and Vera van Hüllen. 2014. "State-Building and the European Union's Fight against Corruption in the Southern Caucasus: Why Legitimacy Matters." *Governance* 27 (4): 613–634.

Bouckaert, Geert, B. Guy Peters, and Koen Verhoest. 2010. *The Coordination of Public Sector Organizations: Shifting Patterns of Public Management*. Houndmills, Basingstoke, UK: Palgrave Macmillan.

Boyle, Alan. 1991. "Saving the World? Implementation and Enforcement of International Law through International Institutions." *Journal of Environmental Law* 3 (2): 229–245.

Brautigam, Deborah. 1996. *State Capacity and Effective Governance, Agenda for Africa's Economic Renewal*. Washington, DC: Transaction.

Bronckers, Marco, and Freya Baetens. 2013. "Reconsidering Financial Remedies in WTO Dispute Settlement." *Journal of International Economic Law* 16 (2): 281–311.

Bruszt, Laszlo. 2008. "Multi-level Governance—the Eastern Versions: Emerging Patterns of Regional Development Governance in the New Member States." *Regional and Federal Studies* 18 (5): 607–627.

Bruszt, Laszlo, and Julia Langbein. 2017. "Varieties of Dis-embedded Liberalism: EU Integration Strategies in the Eastern Peripheries of Europe." *Journal of European Public Policy* 24 (2): 297–315.

Bruszt, Laszlo, and Gerald A. McDermott. 2009. "Transnational Integration Regimes as Development Programs." In *The Transnationalization of Economies, States, and Civil Societies—New Modes of Governance in Europe*, edited by L. Bruszt and R. Holzhacker, 23–59. New York: Springer.

Bruszt, Laszlo, and Visnja Vukov. 2018. "Governing Market Integration and Development—Lessons from Europe's Eastern and Southern Peripheries: Introduction to the Special Issue." *Studies in Comparative Development Studies* 53 (2): 153–168.

Brysk, Alison. 1993. "From Above and from Below: Social Movements, the International System, and Human Rights in Argentina." *Comparative Political Studies* 26 (3): 259–285.

Bugdahn, Sonja. 2005. "Of Europeanization and Domestication: The Implementation of the Environmental Information Directive in Ireland, Great Britain and Germany." *Journal of European Public Policy* 12 (1): 177–199.

Bulmer, Simon, and Christian Lequesne, eds. 2005. *Member States and the European Union*. Oxford: Oxford University Press.

Burley, Anne-Marie, and Walter Mattli. 1993. "Europe before the Court: A Political Theory of Legal Integration." *International Organization* 47 (1): 41–76.

Bursens, Peter. 2002. "Why Denmark and Belgium Have Different Implementation Records: On Transposition Laggards and Leaders in the EU." *Scandinavian Political Studies* 25 (2): 173–195.

Bursens, Peter, and Kristof Geeraerts. 2006. "EU Environmental Policy-Making in Belgium: Who Keeps the Gate?" *Journal of European Integration* 28 (2): 157–179.

Buzogány, Aron. 2009. "Romania: Environmental Governance—Form without Substance." In *Coping with Accession to the European Union: New Modes of Environmental Governance*, edited by T. A. Börzel, 169–191. Houndmills, Basingstoke, UK: Palgrave Macmillan.

Callanan, Mark, and Michaël Tatham. 2014. "Territorial Interest Representation in the European Union: Actors, Objectives and Strategies." *Journal of European Public Policy* 21 (2): 188–210.

Caporaso, James A. 1997. "Does the European Union Represent an *n* of 1?" *ECSA Review* 10 (3): 1–5.

Cappelletti, Mauro, Monica Seccombe, and Joseph H. H. Weiler, eds. 1986. *Integration through Law*. Vol. 1. New York: Walter de Gruyter.

Carrubba, Clifford J. 2005. "Courts and Compliance in International Regulatory Regimes." *Journal of Politics* 67 (3): 669–689.

Carrubba, Clifford J., and Matthew J. Gabel. 2015. *International Courts and the Performance of International Agreements: A General Theory with Evidence from the European Union*. Cambridge: Cambridge University Press.

Carrubba, Clifford J., and Matthew J. Gabel. 2017. "International Courts: A Theoretical Assessment." *Annual Review of Political Science* 20:55–73.

Carrubba, Clifford J., Matthew J. Gabel, and Charles Hankla. 2008. "Judicial Behavior under Political Constraints: Evidence from the European Court of Justice." *American Political Science Review* 102 (4): 435–452.

Cerych, Ladislav, and Paul Sabatier. 1986. *Great Expectations and Mixed Preferences: The Implementation of European Higher Education Reforms*. Stoke on Trent, UK: Trentham Books.

Chalmers, Damian. 1997. "Judicial Preferences and the Community Legal Order." *Modern Law Review* 60 (2): 164–199.

Chalmers, Damian, and Mariana Chaves. 2012. "The Reference Points of EU Judicial Politics." *Journal of European Public Policy* 19 (1): 25–42.

Chalmers, Damian, Markus Jachtenfuchs, and Christian Joerges, eds. 2016. *The End of the Eurocrats' Dream: Adjusting to European Diversity*. Cambridge: Cambridge University Press.

Charron, Nicholas, Lewis Dijkstra, and Victor Lapuente. 2010. "Mapping Quality of Government in the European Union: A Study of National and Sub-national Variation." QoG Working Paper Series 2010 (22).

Chayes, Abram, and Antonia Handler Chayes. 1991. "Compliance without Enforcement: State Behavior under Regulatory Treaties." *Negotiation Journal* 7 (2): 311–331.

Chayes, Abram, and Antonia Handler Chayes. 1993. "On Compliance." *International Organization* 47 (2): 175–205.

Chayes, Abram, and Antonia Handler Chayes. 1995. *The New Sovereignty: Compliance with International Regulatory Agreements*. Cambridge, MA: Harvard University Press.

Chayes, Abram, Antonia Handler Chayes, and Ronald B. Mitchell. 1998. "Managing Compliance: A Comparative Perspective." In *Engaging Countries: Strengthening Compliance with International Environmental Accords*, edited by E. B. Weiss and H. K. Jacobsen, 39–62. Cambridge, MA: MIT Press.

Checkel, Jeffrey T. 2001. "Why Comply? Social Learning and European Identity Change." *International Organization* 55 (3): 553–588.

Ciavarini Azzi, Giuseppe. 1988. "What Is This New Research into the Implementation of Community Legislation Bringing Us?" In *Making European Policies Work: The Implementation of Community Legislation in the Member States*, edited by H. Siedentopf and J. Ziller, 190–201. London: Sage.

Ciavarini Azzi, Giuseppe. 2000. "The Slow March of European Legislation: The Implementation of Directives." In *European Integration after Amsterdam*, edited by K. Neunreither and A. Wiener, 52–68. Oxford: Oxford University Press.

Cichowski, Rachel A. 2007. *The European Court and Civil Society*. Cambridge: Cambridge University Press.

Cioffi-Revilla, Claudio, and Harvey Starr. 1995. "Opportunity, Willingness and Political Uncertainty: Theoretical Foundations of Politics." *Journal of Theoretical Politics* 7 (4): 447–476.

Cirtautas, Arista Maria, and Frank Schimmelfennig. 2010. "Europeanisation before and after Accession: Conditionality, Legacies and Compliance." *Europe Asia Studies* 62 (3): 421–441.

Clark, Ann Marie, and Kathryn Sikkink. 2013. "Information Effects and Human Rights Data: Is the Good News about Increased Human Rights Information Bad News for Human Rights Measures?" *Human Rights Quarterly* 35 (3): 539–568.

Coen, David, and Mark Thatcher. 2008. "Network Governance and Multi-level Delegation: European Networks of Regulatory Agencies." *Journal of Public Policy* 28 (1): 49–71.

Commission of the European Communities. 1984. *First Annual Report to the European Parliament on Commission Monitoring of the Application of Community Law (1983)*. Brussels.

Commission of the European Communities. 1990. *Seventh Annual Report to the European Parliament on Commission Monitoring of the Application of Community Law (1989)*. Brussels.

Commission of the European Communities. 2000. *Seventeenth Annual Report on Monitoring the Application of Community Law (1999)*. Brussels.

Commission of the European Communities. 2001. "European Governance." White Paper, edited by European Commission. COM(2001) 428 final. Brussels.

Commission of the European Communities. 2002. "Commission Communication on Better Monitoring of the Application of Community Law." COM(2002) 725 final. Brussels.

Commission of the European Communities. 2007. "Commission Communication on 'A Europe of Results—Applying Community Law.'" COM(2007) 502 final. Brussels.

Commission of the European Communities. 2011. *28th Annual Report on Monitoring the Application of EU Law (2010)*. COM(2011) 588 final. Brussels.

Commission of the European Communities. 2012a. "Commission Communication on Better Governance for the Single Market." COM(2012) 259 final. Brussels.

Commission of the European Communities. 2012b. "Communication from the Commission: Updating of Data Used to Calculate Lump Sum and Penalty Payments to be Proposed by the Commission to the Court of Justice in Infringement Procedures." C(2012) 6106 final. Brussels.

Commission of the European Communities. 2013. *30th Annual Report on Monitoring the Application of EU Law*. COM(2013) 726 final. Brussels.

Commission of the European Communities. 2014. *31st Annual Report on Monitoring the Application of EU Law*. COM(2014) 612 final. Brussels.

Commission of the European Communities. 2016. *33rd Annual Report on Monitoring the Application of European Union Law (2015)*. COM(2016) 463 final. Brussels.

Conant, Lisa J. 2001. "Europeanization and the Courts: Variable Patterns of Adaptation among National Judiciaries." In *Transforming Europe: Europeanization and Domestic Change*, edited by M. G. Cowles, J. A. Caporaso, and T. Risse, 97–115. Ithaca, NY: Cornell University Press.

Conant, Lisa J. 2002. *Justice Contained: Law and Politics in the European Union*. Ithaca, NY: Cornell University Press.

Cooper, Ian. 2015. "A Yellow Card for the Striker: National Parliaments and the Defeat of EU Legislation on the Right to Strike." *Journal of European Public Policy* 22 (10): 1406–1425.

Cowles, Maria Green, and Thomas Risse. 2001. "Transforming Europe: Conclusions." In *Transforming Europe: Europeanization and Domestic Change*, edited by M. G. Cowles, J. A. Caporaso, and T. Risse, 217–238. Ithaca, NY: Cornell University Press.

Coyle, Carmel. 1994. "Administrative Capacity and the Implementation of EU Environmental Policy in Ireland." In *Protecting the Periphery*, edited by S. Baker, K. Milton, and S. Yearley, 62–79. London: Frank Cass.

Craig, Paul P. 1993. "Francovitch: Remedies and the Scope for Damages Liability." *Law Quarterly Review* 109:595–621.

Craig, Paul P. 1997. "Once More unto the Breach: The Community, the State and Damages Liability." *Law Quarterly Review* 113:67–94.

Crawford, Beverly, and Arend Lijphart. 1997. "Explaining Political and Economic Change in Post-Communist Eastern Europe: Old Legacies, New Institutions, Hegemonic Norms, and International Pressures." *Comparative Political Studies* 28 (2): 171–199.

Cremona, Marise, ed. 2012. *Compliance and the Enforcement of EU Law*. Oxford: Oxford University Press.

Crespy, Armandine. 2012. *Qui a peur de Bolkestein? Conflit, résistances et démocratie dans l'Union européenne*. Paris: Economica.

Crombez, Christophe. 1997. "The Co-decision Procedure in the European Union." *Legislative Studies Quarterly* 22 (1): 97–119.

Dai, Xinyuan. 2005. "Why Comply? The Domestic Constituency Mechanism." *International Organization* 59 (02): 363–398.

Dai, Xinyuan. 2007. *International Institutions and National Policies*. Cambridge: Cambridge University Press.

Dehousse, Renaud. 1997. "Regulation by Networks in the European Community: The Role of European Agencies." *Journal of European Public Policy* 4 (2): 246–261.

De la Fuente, Angel, and Rafael Doménech. 2000. *The Redistributive Effect of the EU Budget: An Analysis and a Proposal for Reform*. La Coruña, Spain: Fundación Caixa Galicia.

de Rynk, Stefaan. 2016. "Banking on a Union: The Politics of Changing Eurozone Banking Supervision." *Journal of European Public Policy* 23 (1): 119–135.

DeSombre, Elizabeth R. 2006. *Flagging Standards: Globalization and Environmental, Safety, and Labor Regulations at Sea*. Cambridge, MA: MIT Press.

De Ville, Ferdi, and Gabriel Siles-Brügge. 2016. "Why TTIP Is a Game-Changer and Its Critics Have a Point." *Journal of European Public Policy* 24 (10): 1–15.

De Wilde, Pieter, Anna Leupold, and Henning Schmidtke. 2016. "Introduction: The Differentiated Politicisation of European Governance." *West European Politics* 39 (1): 3–22.

De Wilde, Pieter, and Michael Zürn. 2012. "Can the Politicization of European Integration Be Reversed?" *Journal of Common Market Studies* 50 (s1): 137–153.

Dimitrakopoulos, Dionyssis G. 2001. "The Transposition of EU Law: 'Post-Decisional Politics' and Institutional Autonomy." *European Law Journal* 7 (4): 442–458.

Dimitrova, Antoaneta L. 2002. "Enlargement, Institution-Building and the EU's Administrative Capacity Requirement." *West European Politics* 25 (4): 171–190.

Dimitrova, Antoaneta L. 2005. "Europeanization and Civil Service Reform in Central and Eastern Europe." In *The Europeanization of Central and Eastern Europe*, edited by F. Schimmelfennig and U. Sedelmeier, 71–91. Ithaca, NY: Cornell University Press.

Dimitrova, Antoaneta L. 2010. "The New Member States in the EU in the Aftermath of Accession: Empty Shells?" *Journal of European Public Policy* 17 (1): 137–148.

Dimitrova, Antoaneta L., and Aron Buzogány. 2014. "Post-accession Policy Making in Bulgaria and Romania: Can Non-state Actors Use EU Rules to Promote Better Governance?" *Journal of Common Market Studies* 52 (1): 139–156.

Dimitrova, Antoaneta L., and Bernard Steunenberg. 2000. "The Search for Convergence of National Policies in the European Union: An Impossible Quest." *European Union Politics* 1 (2): 201–226.

Dimitrova, Antoaneta L., and Bernard Steunenberg. 2013. "Living in Parallel Universes? Implementing European Movable Cultural Heritage Policy in Bulgaria." *Journal of Common Market Studies* 51 (2): 246–263.

Dimitrova, Antoaneta L., and Dimiter Toshkov. 2007. "The Dynamics of Domestic Co-ordination of EU Policy in the New and Candidate Member-States." *West European Politics* 35 (5): 961–986.

Dimitrova, Antoaneta L., and Dimiter Toshkov. 2009. "Post-accession Compliance between Administrative Co-ordination and Political Bargaining." *European Integration Online Papers* 13 (2), http://eiop.or.at/eiop/pdf/2009-019.pdf, last accessed 28 August 2020.

Dinan, Desmond. 2004. *Europe Recast: A History of European Union*. Houndmills, Basingstoke, UK: Macmillan.

Döring, Herbert. 1995. *Parliaments and Majority Rule in Western Europe*. New York: St. Martin's.

Dorn, A. Walter, and Andrew Fulton. 1997. "Securing Compliance with Disarmament Treaties: Carrots, Sticks, and the Case of North Korea." *Global Governance* 3 (1): 17–40.

Downs, George W., David M. Rocke, and Peter N. Barsoom. 1996. "Is the Good News about Compliance Good News about Cooperation?" *International Organization* 50 (3): 379–406.

Duina, Francesco G. 1997. "Explaining Legal Implementation in the European Union." *International Journal of the Sociology of Law* 25 (2): 155–179.

Duina, Francesco G., and Frank Blythe. 1999. "Nation-States and Common Markets: The Institutional Conditions for Acceptance." *Review of International Political Economy* 6 (4): 494–530.

Dworkin, Ronald. 1986. *Law's Empire*. Cambridge, MA: MIT Press.

Dyevre, Arthur, Monika Glavina, and Angelina Atanasova. 2019. "Who Refers Most? Institutional Incentives and Judicial Participation in the Preliminary Ruling System." *Journal of European Public Policy* 37 (6): 912–930.

Dyson, Kenneth. 1994. *Elusive Union: The Process of Economic and Monetary Union in Europe*. London: Longman.

Dyson, Kenneth, and Klaus H. Goetz, eds. 2004. *Germany, Europe, and the Politics of Constraint*. Oxford: Oxford University Press.

Eckert, Sandra. 2015. *The Social Face of the Regulatory State: Reforming Public Services in Europe*. Manchester: Manchester University Press.

Eder, Klaus, and Maria Kousis. 2001. *Environmental Politics in Southern Europe: Actors, Institutions, and Discourses in a Europeanizing Society*. Boston: Kluwer Academic.

Egeberg, Morten. 1999. "The Impact of Bureaucratic Structure on Policy Making." *Public Administration* 77 (1): 155–170.

Egeberg, Morten. 2001. "How Federal? The Organizational Dimension of Integration in the EU (and Elsewhere)." *Journal of European Public Policy* 8 (5): 728–746.

Egeberg, Morten. 2006. "Executive Politics as Usual: Role Behaviour and Conflict Dimensions in the College of European Commissioners." *Journal of European Public Policy* 13 (1): 1–15.

Egeberg, Morten. 2008. "European Government(s): Executive Politics in Transition?" *West European Politics* 31 (1): 235–257.

Egeberg, Morten, and Jarle Trondal. 2009. "National Agencies in the European Administrative Space: Government Driven, Commission Driven or Networked?" *Public Administration* 87 (4): 779–790.

Elster, Jon, Claus Offe, and Ulrich K. Preuss. 1998. *Institutional Design in Post-Communist Societies: Rebuilding the Ship at Sea*. Cambridge: Cambridge University Press.

Epstein, Rachel A. 2008. *In Pursuit of Liberalism: International Institutions in Postcommunist Europe*. Baltimore, MD: Johns Hopkins University Press.

Epstein, Rachel A., and Ulrich Sedelmeier, eds. 2009. *Beyond Conditionality: International Institutions in Postcommunist Europe after Enlargement*. London: Routledge.

European Commission. 2005. "Internal Market Scoreboard Update, no 14, July 2005." http://ec.europa.eu/internal_market/score/docs/score14/scoreboard14printed_en.pdf, last accessed 29 August 2020.

European Commission. 2016. "Communication from the Commission to the European Parliament and the Council on the State of Play of Implementation of the Priority Actions under the European Agenda on Migration." COM(2016) 85 final. Brussels.

European Parliament / European Council. 2013. "Regulation No 604/2013 [. . .] establishing the criteria and mechanisms for determining the Member State responsible for examining an application for international protection lodged in one of the Member States by a third-country national or a stateless person." OJ L 180, 29.6.2013, pp. 31–59.

Evans, Peter B. 1993. "Building an Integrative Approach to International and Domestic Politics." In *Double-Edged Diplomacy: International Bargaining and Domestic Politics*, edited by P. B. Evans, H. K. Jacobsen, and R. D. Putnam, 397–430. Berkeley, CA: University of California Press.

Evans, Peter B. 1995. *Embedded Autonomy: States and Industrial Transformation*. Princeton, NJ: Princeton University Press.

Evans, Peter B., Harold K. Jacobson, and Robert D. Putnam. 1993. *Double-Edged Diplomacy: International Bargaining and Domestic Politics*. Berkeley: University of California Press.

Evans, Peter B., Dietrich Rueschemeyer, and Theda Skocpol, eds. 1985. *Bringing the State Back In*. Cambridge: Cambridge University Press.

Fabbrini, Federico. 2014. "The Euro-Crisis and the Courts: Judicial Review and the Political Process in Comparative Perspective." *Berkeley Journal of International Law* 32 (1): 64–123.

Falkner, Gerda. 2010. "Institutional Performance and Compliance with EU Law: Czech Republic, Hungary, Slovakia and Slovenia." *Journal of Public Policy* 30 (1): 101–116.

Falkner, Gerda, Miriam Hartlapp, Simone Leiber, and Oliver Treib. 2004. "Non-compliance with EU Directives in the Member States: Opposition through the Backdoor?" *West European Politics* 27 (3): 452–473.

Falkner, Gerda, Miriam Hartlapp, and Oliver Treib. 2007. "Worlds of Compliance: Why Leading Approaches to European Union Implementation Are Only 'Sometimes-True Theories.'" *European Journal of Political Research* 46 (3): 395–416.

Falkner, Gerda, Oliver Treib, Miriam Hartlapp, and Simone Leiber. 2005. *Complying with Europe: EU Harmonization and Soft Law in the Member States*. Cambridge: Cambridge University Press.

Falkner, Gerda, Oliver Treib, and Elisabeth Holzleitner. 2008. *Compliance in the European Union: Living Rights or Dead Letters?* Aldershot, UK: Ashgate.

Fariss, Christopher. 2014. "Respect for Human Rights Has Improved over Time: Modeling the Changing Standard of Accountability." *American Political Science Review* 108 (2): 297–318.

Fearon, James D. 1994. "Domestic Political Audiences and the Escalation of International Disputes." *American Political Science Review* 88 (3): 577–592.

Fearon, James D. 1998. "Bargaining, Enforcement and International Cooperation." *International Organization* 52 (2): 269–305.

Finger, Matthias. 2011. "Towards a European Model of Regulatory Governance?" In *Handbook of the Politics of Regulation*, edited by D. Levi-Faur, 525–535. Cheltenham, UK: Edward Elgar.

Finke, Daniel, and Thomas König. 2009. "Why Risk Popular Ratification Failure? A Comparative Analysis of the Choice of the Ratification Instrument in the 25 Member States of the EU." *Constitutional Political Economy* 20 (3–4): 341–365.

Finnemore, Martha, and Kathryn Sikkink. 1998. "International Norm Dynamics and Political Change." *International Organization* 52 (4): 887–917.

Finnemore, Martha, and Stephen J. Toope. 2001. "Alternatives to 'Legalization': Richer Views of Law and Politics." *International Organization* 55 (3): 743–758.

Fjelstul, Joshua C., and Clifford J. Carrubba. 2018. "The Politics of International Oversight: Strategic Monitoring and Legal Compliance in the European Union." *American Political Science Review* 112 (3): 429–445.

Franck, Thomas M. 1990. *The Power of Legitimacy among Nations*. Oxford: Oxford University Press.

Frieden, Jeffry A. 1999. "Actors and Preferences in International Relations." In *Strategic Choice and International Relations*, edited by D. A. Lake and R. Powell, 39–76. Princeton, NJ: Princeton University Press.

From, Johan, and Per Stava. 1993. "Implementation of Community Law: The Last Stronghold of National Control." In *Making Policy in Europe: The Europeification of National Policy-Making*, edited by S. S. Andersen and K. A. Eliassen, 55–67. London: Sage.

Fukuyama, Francis. 2015. "Why Is Democracy Performing So Poorly?" *Journal of Democracy* 26 (1): 11–20.

Gajduschek, Gyorgy. 2003. "Bureaucracy: Is It Efficient? Is It Not? Is That the Question? Uncertainty Reduction: An Ignored Element of Bureaucratic Rationality." *Administration & Society* 34 (6): 700–723.

Garrett, Geoffrey, R. Daniel Kelemen, and Heiner Schulz. 1998. "The European Court of Justice, National Governments, and Legal Integration in the European Union." *International Organization* 52 (1): 149–176.

Gateva, Eli. 2010. "Post-accession Conditionality: Support Instrument for Continuous Pressure?" KFG Working Papers, Research College. The Transformative Power of Europe. Freie Universität Berlin (18).

Gaubatz, Kurt Taylor. 1996. "Democratic States and Commitment in International Relations." *International Organization* 50 (1): 109–139.

Gehring, Thomas, and Sebastian Krapohl. 2007. "Supranational Regulatory Agencies between Interdependence and Control: The EMEA and the Authorisation of Pharmaceuticals in the European Single Market." *Journal of European Public Policy* 14 (2): 208–266.

Genschel, Philipp, and Markus Jachtenfuchs. 2016. "More Integration, Less Federation: The European Integration of Core State Powers." *Journal of European Public Policy* 23 (1): 42–59.

Gibson, James L., and Gregory A. Caldeira. 1995. "The Legitimacy of Transnational Legal Institutions: Compliance, Support, and the European Court of Justice." *American Journal of Political Science* 39 (2): 459–489.

Gibson, James L., and Gregory A. Caldeira. 1996. "The Legal Cultures of Europe." *Law & Society Review* 30 (1): 55–85.

Giuliani, Marco. 2003. "Europeanization in Comparative Perspective: Institutional Fit and National Adaptation." In *The Politics of Europeanisation*, edited by K. Featherstone and C. Radaelli, 134–157. Oxford: Oxford University Press.

Goetz, Klaus H. 2001. "Making Sense of Post-Communist Central Administration: Modernization, Europeanization or Latinization." *Journal of European Public Policy* 8 (6): 1032–1051.

Goetz, Klaus H. 2005. "The New Member States and the EU: Responding to Europe." In *The Member States of the European Union*, edited by S. Bulmer and C. Lequesne, 254–280. Oxford: Oxford University Press.

Goldsmith, Jack L., and Eric A. Posner. 2005. *The Limits of International Law*. Oxford: Oxford University Press.

Goldstein, Judith L., Douglas Rivers, and Michael Tomz. 2007. "Institutions in International Relations: Understanding the Effects of the GATT and the WTO on World Trade." *International Organization* 61 (1): 37–67.

Grabbe, Heather. 2003. "Europeanization Goes East: Power and Uncertainty in the EU Accession Process." In *The Politics of Europeanization*, edited by K. Featherstone and C. M. Radaelli, 303–327. Oxford: Oxford University Press.

Grabbe, Heather. 2006. *The EU's Transformative Power: Europeanization through Conditionality in Central and Eastern Europe*. Houndmills, Basingstoke, UK: Palgrave Macmillan.

Groenleer, Martijn, Michael Kaeding, and Esther Versluis. 2010. "Regulatory Governance through Agencies of the European Union? The Role of the European Agencies for Maritime and Aviation Safety in the Implementation of European Transport Legislation." *Journal of European Public Policy* 17 (8): 1212–1230.

Gryzmala-Busse, Anna. 2007. *Rebuilding Leviathan: Party Competition and State Exploitation in Post-Communist Democracies*. Cambridge: Cambridge University Press.

Haas, Ernst B. 1958. *The Uniting of Europe: Political, Social, and Economic Forces, 1950–1957*. Stanford, CA: Stanford University Press.

Haas, Ernst B. 1998. "The Uniting of Europe." In *The European Union: Readings on Theory and Practice of European Integration*, edited by B. F. Nelsen and A. C.-G. Stubb, 139–144. Boulder, CO: Lynne Rienner.

Haas, Peter M. 1993. "Protecting the Baltic and the North Seas." In *Institutions for the Earth: Sources of Effective International Environmental Protection*, edited by P. M. Haas, R. O. Keohane, and M. A. Levy, 133–182. Cambridge, MA: MIT Press.

Haas, Peter M. 1998. "Compliance with EU Directives: Insights from International Relations and Comparative Politics." *Journal of European Public Policy* 5 (1): 17–37.

Habermas, Jürgen. 2013. "Democracy, Solidarity and the European Crisis." *Social Europe: The Journal of the European Left* 7 (2): 4–13.

Hafner-Burton, Emilie M. 2005. "Trading Human Rights: How Preferential Trade Agreements Influence Government Repression." *International Organization* 59 (3): 593–629.

Haftel, Yoram Z. 2012. *Regional Economic Institutions and Conflict Mitigation: Design, Implementation, and the Promise of Peace.* Ann Arbor: University of Michigan Press.

Häge, Frank. 2010. "Politicising Council Decisionmaking: The Effect of European Parliament Empowerment." *West European Politics* 34 (1): 18–47.

Hallstein, Walter Peter. 1972. *Europe in the Making.* London: Allen and Unwin.

Harfst, Philipp, and Kai-Uwe Schnapp. 2003. "Instrumente parlamentarischer Kontrolle der Exekutive in westlichen Demokratien." WZB Discussion Paper FS IV (03–201).

Hartlapp, Miriam. 2009. "Implementation of EU Social Policy Directives in Belgium: What Matters in Domestic Politics?" *Journal of European Integration* 31 (4): 467–488.

Hartlapp, Miriam, and Gerda Falkner. 2009. "Problems of Operationalisation and Data in EU Compliance Research." *European Union Politics* 10 (2): 281–304.

Hartlapp, Miriam, and Simone Leiber. 2010. "The Implementation of EU Social Policy: The 'Southern Problem' Revisited." *Journal of European Public Policy* 17 (4): 468–486.

Hauser, Christoph. 2004. *Das Vertragsverletzungsverfahren als Instrument des Europäischen Umweltrechts.* Frankfurt am Main: Peter Lang.

Haverland, Markus. 2000. "National Adaptation to European Integration: The Importance of Institutional Veto Points." *Journal of Public Policy* 20 (1): 83–103.

Haverland, Markus, and Marleen Romeijn. 2007. "Do Member States Make European Policies Work? Analysing the EU Transposition Deficit." *Public Administration* 85 (3): 757–778.

Haverland, Markus, Bernard Steunenberg, and Frans van Waarden. 2008. "Sectors at Different Speeds: Analyzing Transposition Deficits in the European Union." *Journal of Common Market Studies* 48 (1): 1–27.

Haverland, Markus, Bernard Steunenberg, and Frans van Waarden. 2011. "Sectors at Different Speeds: Analysing Transposition Deficits in the European Union." *Journal of Common Market Studies* 49 (2): 265–291.

Hayes-Renshaw, Fiona, Wim Van Aken, and Helen Wallace. 2006. "When and Why the EU Council of Ministers Votes Explicitly." *Journal of Common Market Studies* 44 (1): 161–194.

Hedemann-Robison, Martin. 2015. *Enforcement of European Union Environmental Law: Legal Issues and Challenges.* London: Routledge.

Heidbreder, Eva G. 2011. "Structuring the European Administrative Space: Policy Instruments of Multi-level Administration." *Journal of European Public Policy* 18 (5): 709–727.

Heidbreder, Eva G. 2014. "Horizontal Capacity Pooling: Direct, Decentralised, Joint Policy Execution." In *The Palgrave Handbook of the European Administrative System*, edited by M. W. Bauer and J. Trondal, 369–382. Houndmills, Basingstoke, UK: Palgrave.

Heipertz, Martin, and Amy Verdun. 2004. "The Dog That Would Never Bite? What We Can Learn from the Origins of the Stability and Growth Pact." *Journal of European Public Policy* 11 (5): 765–780.

Helfer, Laurence R., and Anne-Marie Slaughter. 1997. "Toward a Theory of Effective Supranational Adjudication." *Yale Law Journal* 107 (2): 273–391.

Henisz, Witold J. 2002. "The Institutional Environment for Infrastructure Investment." *Industrial and Corporate Change* 11 (2): 355–389.

Henkin, Louis. 1968. *How Nations Behave: Law and Foreign Policy*. New York: Columbia University Press.

Héritier, Adrienne. 1996. "The Accommodation of Diversity in European Policy-Making and Its Outcomes: Regulatory Policy as a Patchwork." *Journal of European Public Policy* 3 (2): 149–167.

Héritier, Adrienne. 2001. "Differential Europe: National Administrative Responses to Community Policy." In *Transforming Europe: Europeanization and Domestic Change*, edited by M. G. Cowles, J. A. Caporaso, and T. Risse, 44–59. Ithaca, NY: Cornell University Press.

Héritier, Adrienne, Christoph Knill, and Susanne Mingers. 1996. *Ringing the Changes in Europe: Regulatory Competition and the Redefinition of the State; Britain, France, Germany*. New York: De Gruyter.

Héritier, Adrienne, Catherine Moury, Carina S. Bischoff, and Carl Fredrik Bergström. 2013. *Changing Rules of Delegation: A Contest for Power in Comitology*. Oxford: Oxford University Press.

Héritier, Adrienne, Catherine Moury, and Katarzyna Granat. 2016. "The Contest for Power in Delegated Rulemaking." In *Rulemaking by the European Commission: The New System for Delegation of Powers*, edited by C. F. Bergström and D. Ritleng, 105–129. Oxford: Oxford University Press.

Héritier, Adrienne, Catherine Moury, Magnus G. Schoeller, Katharina L. Meissner, and Isabel Mota. 2015. *The European Parliament as a Driving Force of Constitutionalisation: EUDO Report 2015/09*. Florence: European University Institute.

Hilbe, Joseph M. 2007. *Negative Binomial Regression*. Cambridge: Cambridge University Press.

Hille, Peter, and Christoph Knill. 2006. "'It's the Bureaucracy, Stupid': The Implementation of the Acquis Communautaire in EU Candidate Countries, 1999–2003." *European Union Politics* 7 (4): 531–552.

Hix, Simon. 2008. *What's Wrong with the European Union and How to Fix It*. Cambridge: Polity.

Hix, Simon. 2015. "Democratizing a Macroeconomic Union in Europe." In *Democratic Politics in a European Union under Stress*, edited by O. Cromme and S. B. Hobolt, 180–198. Oxford: Oxford University Press.

Hobolth, Mogens, and Dorte Sindbjerg Martinsen. 2013. "Transgovernmental Networks in the European Union: Improving Compliance Effectively?" *Journal of European Public Policy* 20 (10): 1406–1424.

Hofmann, Andreas. 2018. "Is the Commission Levelling the Playing Field? Rights Enforcement in the European Union." *Journal of European Integration* 40 (6): 737–751.

Hofmann, Andreas. 2019. "Left to Interest Groups? On the Prospects for Enforcing Environmental Law in the European Union." *Environmental Politics* 28 (2): 342–364.

Hollyer, James R. 2010. "Conditionality, Compliance, and Domestic Interests: State Capture and EU Accession Policy." *Review of International Organizations* 5 (4): 387–431.

Holzinger, Katharina, and Frank Schimmelfennig. 2012. "Differentiated Integration in the European Union: Many Concepts, Sparse Theory, Few Data." *Journal of European Public Policy* 19 (2): 292–305.

Hooghe, Liesbet. 2003. "Europe Divided? Elites vs. Public Opinion on European Integration." *European Union Politics* 4 (3): 281–304.

Hooghe, Liesbet, Tobias Lenz, and Gary Marks. 2019. *Community, Scale and International Organization*. Oxford: Oxford University Press.

Hooghe, Liesbet, and Gary Marks. 2001. *Multi-level Governance and European Integration*. Lanham, MD: Rowman & Littlefield.

Hooghe, Liesbet, and Gary Marks. 2007. "Sources of Euroscepticism." *Acta Politica* 42 (2–3): 119–127.

Hooghe, Liesbet, and Gary Marks. 2009. "A Postfunctionalist Theory of European Integration: From Permissive Consensus to Constraining Dissensus." *British Journal of Political Science* 39 (1): 1–23.

Hooghe, Liesbet, and Gary Marks. 2018. "Cleavage Theory Meets Europe's Crises: Lipset, Rokkan, and the Transnational Cleavage." *Journal of European Public Policy* 25 (1): 109–135.

Hooghe, Liesbet, Gary Marks, Tobias Lenz, Jeanine Bezuijen, Besir Ceka, and Svet Derderyan. 2017. *Measuring International Authority: A Postfunctionalist Theory of Governance*. Vol. 3. Oxford: Oxford University Press.

Hooghe, Liesbet, Gary Marks, Arjan H. Schakel, Sandi Chapman Osterkatz, Sara Niedzwiecki, and Sarah Shair-Rosenfield. 2016. *Measuring Regional Authority: A Postfunctionalist Theory of Governance*. Vol. 1. Oxford: Oxford University Press.

Horne, Christine, and Anna Cutlip. 2002. "Sanctioning Costs and Norm Enforcement." *Rationality and Society* 14 (3): 285–307.

Hosli, Madeleine O., and Ben Soetendorp. 2001. "The Hidden Dynamics of EU Council Decision-Making." *Acta Politica* 36 (3): 252–287.

Houghton, Tim. 2014. "Money, Margins, and the Motors of Politics: The EU and the Development of Party Politics in Central and Eastern Europe." *Journal of Common Market Studies* 52 (1): 71–87.

Hübner, Denise Carolin. 2018. "The Decentralized Enforcement of European Law: National Court Decisions on EU Directives with and without Preliminary Reference Submissions." *Journal of European Public Policy* 25 (12): 1817–1834.

Huelshoff, Micheal G., James Sperling, and Michael Hess. 2005. "Is Germany a 'Good European'? German Compliance with EU Law." *German Politics* 14 (3): 354–370.

Hug, Simon, and Thomas König. 2002. "In View of Ratification: Governmental Preferences and Domestic Constraints at the Amsterdam Intergovernmental Conference." *International Organization* 56 (2): 447–476.

Hughes, James, Gwendolyn Sasse, and Claire Gordon. 2004. *Europeanization and Regionalization in the EU's Enlargement to Central and Eastern Europe: The Myth of Conditionality*. Houndmills, Basingstoke, UK: Palgrave Macmillan.

Hurd, Ian. 1999. "Legitimacy and Authority in International Politics." *International Organization* 53 (2): 379–408.

Hurrell, Andrew. 1995. "International Society and the Study of Regimes: A Reflective Approach." In *Regime Theory and International Relations*, edited by V. Rittberger, 49–72. Oxford: Clarendon.

Hutter, Swen, Edgar Grande, and Hanspeter Kriesi, eds. 2016. *Politicising Europe: Integration and Mass Politics*. Cambridge: Cambridge University Press.

Iankova, Elena A., and Peter J. Katzenstein. 2003. "European Enlargement and Institutional Hypocrisy." In *The State of the European Union*, vol. 6, *Law, Politics and Society*, edited by T. A. Börzel and R. A. Cichowski, 269–290. Oxford: Oxford University Press.

Ikenberry, G. John. 2018. "The End of Liberal International Order?" *International Affairs* 94 (1): 7–23.

Immergut, Ellen M. 1990. "Institutions, Veto Points, and Policy Results: A Comparative Analysis of Health Care." *Journal of Public Policy* 10 (4): 391–416.

Immergut, Ellen M. 1998. "The Theoretical Core of the New Institutionalism." *Politics and Society* 26 (1): 5–34.

Ingram, Helen, and Anne Schneider. 1990. "Improving Implementation through Framing Smarter Statutes." *Journal of Public Policy* 10 (1): 67–88.

Innes, Abby. 2014. "The Political Economy of State Capture in Central Europe." *Journal of Common Market Studies* 52 (1): 88–104.

Jachtenfuchs, Markus. 2018. "From Market Integration to Core State Powers: The Eurozone Crisis, the Refugee Crisis and Integration Theory." *Journal of Common Market Studies* 56 (1): 178–196.

Jacobsen, Harold K., and Edith Weiss Brown. 1995. "Strengthening Compliance with International Environmental Accords: Preliminary Observations from a Collaborative Project." *Global Governance* 1 (2): 119–148.

Jacoby, Wade. 2004. *The Enlargement of the European Union and NATO: Ordering from the Menu in Central Europe*. Cambridge: Cambridge University Press.

Jakab, András, and Dimitry Kochenov, eds. 2016. *The Enforcement of EU Law and Values*. Oxford: Oxford University Press.

Jensen, Christian B. 2007. "Implementing Europe: A Question of Oversight." *European Union Politics* 8 (4): 451–477.

Joerges, Christian. 1996. "Taking the Law Seriously: On Political Science and the Role of Law in the Process of European Integration." *European Law Journal* 2 (2): 105–135.

Joerges, Christian. 2016. "Integration through Law and the Crisis of Law in Europe's Emergency." In *The End of the Eurocrats' Dream: Adjusting to European Diversity*, edited by D. Chalmers, M. Jachtenfuchs, and C. Joerges, 299–338. Cambridge: Cambridge University Press.

Jones, Alison, and Brenda Sufrin. 2016. *EU Competition Law: Text, Cases, and Materials*. Oxford: Oxford University Press.

Jordan, Andrew. 1999. "The Implementation of EU Environmental Policy: A Policy Problem without a Political Solution." *Environment and Planning C: Government and Policy* 17 (1): 69–90.

Jung, Jai Kwan. 2008. "Growing Supranational Identities in a Globalising World? A Multilevel Analysis of the World Values Surveys." *European Journal of Political Research* 47 (5): 578–609.

Junge, Dirk, Thomas König, and Bernd Luig. 2015. "Legislative Gridlock and Bureaucratic Politics in the European Union." *British Journal of Political Science* 45 (4): 777–797.

Kaeding, Michael. 2006. "Determinants of Transposition Delay in the European Union." *Journal of Public Policy* 26 (3): 229–253.

Kaeding, Michael. 2008. "Lost in Translation or Full Steam Ahead: The Transposition of EU Transpost Directives across Member States." *European Union Politics* 9 (1): 115–143.

Kaeding, Michael, and Alan Hardacre. 2013. "The European Parliament and the Future of Comitology after Lisbon." *European Law Journal* 19 (3): 382–403.

Kaeding, Michael, and Esther Versluis. 2014. "EU Agencies as a Solution to Pan-European Implementation Problems." In *European Agencies in between Institutions and Member States*, edited by M. Everson, C. Monda, and E. Vos, 73–85. Alphen aan de Rijn, Netherlands: Wolters Kluwer.

Kahler, Miles. 2000. "Conclusion: The Causes and Consequences of Legalization." *International Organization* 54 (3): 661–683.

Kardasheva, Raya. 2009. "The Power to Delay: The European Parliament's Influence in the Consultation Procedure." *Journal of Common Market Studies* 47 (2): 385–409.

Kassim, Hussein, Anand Menon, B. Guy Peters, and Vincent Wright. 2000. *The National Co-ordination of EU Policy: The Domestic Level.* Oxford: Oxford University Press.

Kassim, Hussein, Anand Menon, B. Guy Peters, and Vincent Wright. 2001. *The National Co-ordination of EU Policy: The European Level.* Oxford: Oxford University Press.

Katzenstein, Peter J., ed. 1978. *Between Power and Plenty: Foreign Economic Policies of Advanced Industrial States.* Madison: University of Wisconsin Press.

Kaufmann, Daniel, Aart Kraay, and Massimo Mastruzzi. 2003. "Governance Matters III: Governance Indicators for 1996–2002." World Bank Policy Research Working Paper.

Keck, Margaret E., and Kathryn Sikkink. 1998. *Activists beyond Borders: Advocacy Networks in International Politics.* Ithaca, NY: Cornell University Press.

Keleman, R. Daniel. 2006. "Suing for Europe: Adversarial Legalism and European Governance." *Comparative Political Studies* 39 (1): 101–127.

Kelemen, R. Daniel. 2011. *Eurolegalism: The Transformation of Law and Regulation in the European Union.* Cambridge, MA: Harvard University Press.

Keleman, R. Daniel. 2017. "Europe's Other Democratic Deficit: National Authoritarianism in Europe's Democratic Union." *Government and Opposition* 52 (2): 211–238.

Keohane, Robert O. 1984. *After Hegemony: Cooperation and Discord in the World Political Economy.* Princeton, NJ: Princeton University Press.

Keohane, Robert O. 1989. *International Institutions and State Power: Essays in International Relations Theory.* Boulder, CO: Westview.

Keohane, Robert O., and Stanley Hoffmann. 1990. "Conclusions: Community Politics and Institutional Change." In *The Dynamics of European Integration*, edited by W. Wallace, 276–300. London: Pinter.

Keohane, Robert O., Andrew Moravcsik, and Anne-Marie Slaughter. 2000. "Legalized Dispute Resolution: Interstate and Transnational." *International Organization* 54 (3): 457–488.

Keohane, Robert O., and Joseph S. Nye. 1977. *Power and Interdependence: World Politics in Transition.* Boston: Little, Brown.

Keulen, Mendeltje van. 2006. *Going Europe or Going Dutch: How the Dutch Government Shapes European Union Policy.* Amsterdam: Amsterdam University Press.

Kim, Soo Yeon, Edward D. Mansfield, and Helen V. Millner. 2016. "Regional Trade Governance." In *The Oxford Handbook of Comparative Regionalism*, edited by A. T. Börzel and T. Risse, 323–350. Oxford: Oxford University Press.

Kleine, Mareike O. 2013. *Informal Governance in the European Union: How Governments Make International Organizations Work.* Ithaca, NY: Cornell University Press.

Knill, Christoph. 1998. "Implementing European Policies: The Impact of National Administrative Traditions." *Journal of Public Policy* 18 (1): 1–28.

Knill, Christoph. 2001. *The Europeanisation of National Administrations: Patterns of Institutional Change and Persistence.* Cambridge: Cambridge University Press.

Knill, Christoph. 2015. "Implementation." In *European Union: Power and Policy-Making*, edited by J. J. Richardson and S. Mazey, 371–395. London: Routledge.

Knill, Christoph, and Jale Tosun. 2009. "Post-accession Transposition of EU Law in the New Member States: A Cross-Country Comparison." *European Integration Online Papers*, Special Issue 2 (13). http://eiop.or.at/eiop/pdf/2009-018.pdf, last accessed 29 August 2020.

Knoll, Moritz. 2016. "A Two-Level Model of Compliance: Non-compliance with EU Directives across Policy Sectors." Berlin: Dissertationsschrift zur Erlangung des Doktor Phil. an der Freien Universitat Berlin.

Knudsen, Ann-Christina L. 2009. *Farmers on Welfare: The Making of Europe's Common Agricultural Policy*. Ithaca, NY: Cornell University Press.

Kochenov, Dimitry, and Laurent Pech. 2016. "Better Late Than Never? On the European Commission's Rule of Law Framework and Its First Activation." *Journal of Common Market Studies* 54 (5): 1062–1074.

Koh, Harold H. 1996. "Transnational Legal Process." *Nebraska Law Review* 75:181–206.

Koh, Harold H. 1997. "Why Do Nations Obey International Law?" *Yale Law Journal* 106 (8): 2599–2659.

Kohler-Koch, Beate. 2000. "Framing the Bottleneck of Constructing Legitimate Institutions." *Journal of European Public Policy* 7 (4): 513–531.

Kölliker, Alkuin. 2005. *Flexibility and European Unification: The Logic of Differentiated Integration*. Lanham, MD: Rowman & Littlefield.

König, Thomas. 2007. "Discontinuity: Another Source of the EU's Democratic Deficit?" *European Union Politics* 8 (3): 411–432.

König, Thomas, and Thomas Bräuninger. 2004. "Accession and Reform of the European Union." *European Union Politics* 5 (4): 419–439.

König, Thomas, and Brooke Luetgert. 2009. "Troubles with Transposition: Explaining Trends in Member-State Notification and the Delayed Transposition of EU Directives." *British Journal of Political Science* 39 (1): 163–194.

König, Thomas, Brooke Luetgert, and Tanja Dannwolf. 2006. "Quantifying European Legislative Research." *European Union Politics* 7 (4): 553–574.

König, Thomas, and Bernd Luig. 2014. "Ministerial Gatekeeping and Parliamentary Involvement in the Implementation Process of EU Directives." *Public Choice* 160 (3–4): 501–519.

König, Thomas, and Lars Mäder. 2013. "Non-conformable, Partial and Conformable Transposition: A Competing Risk Analysis of the Transposition Process of Directives in the EU 15." *European Union Politics* 14 (1): 46–69.

König, Thomas, and Lars Mäder. 2014a. "Enforcing Compliance: A Quantitative Study of the Member States' Transposition and the European Commission's Infringement Activities: A Comprehensive Overview." Paper presented at the American Political Science Association meeting, Washington, DC, August 27–31.

König, Thomas, and Lars Mäder. 2014b. "The Strategic Nature of Compliance: An Empirical Evaluation of Law Implementation in the Central Monitoring System of the European Union." *American Journal of Political Science* 58 (1): 246–263.

Kono, Daniel Y. 2007. "Making Anarchy Work: International Legal Institutions and Trade Cooperation." *Journal of Politics* 69 (3): 746–759.

Koops, Catharina E. 2011. "EU Compliance Mechanisms: The Interaction between the Infringement Procedures, IMS, SOLVIT and EU-Pilot." Amsterdam Law School Legal Studies, Research Paper No. 2011–42.

Kopecky, Petr, and Gerardo Scherlis. 2008. "Party Patronage in Contemporary Europe." *European Review* 16 (3): 355–371.

Kreppel, Amie. 1999. "What Affects the European Parliament's Legislative Influence? An Analysis of the Success of EP Amendments." *Journal of Common Market Studies* 37 (3): 521–537.

Kreppel, Amie. 2002. "Moving beyond Procedure: An Empirical Analysis of European Parliament Legislative Influence." *Comparative Political Studies* 35 (7): 784–813.

Krislov, Samuel, Claus-Dieter Ehlermann, and Joseph H. H. Weiler. 1986. "The Political Organs and the Decision-Making Process in the United States and the European Community." In *Integration through Law, Methods, Tools and Institutions: Political Organs, Integration Techniques and Judicial Process*, edited by M. Cappelletti, M. Seccombe, and J. H. H. Weiler, 3–112. Berlin: Gruyter.

Kriszan, Andrea. 2009. "From Formal Adoption to Enforcement: Post-accession Shifts in EU Impact on Hungary in the Equality Policy Field." *European Integration Online Papers* 2 (13). http://eiop.or.at/eiop/texte/2009-022a.htm, last accessed 29 August 2020.

Kronsell, Annica. 2002. "Can Small States Influence EU Norms? Insights from Sweden's Participation in the Field of Environmental Politics." *Scandinavian Studies* 74 (3): 287–304.

Kuzio, Taras. 2001. "Transition in Post-Communist States: Triple or Quadruple?" *Politics* 21 (3): 168–177.

La Spina, Antonio, and Giuseppe Sciortino. 1993. "Common Agenda, Southern Rules: European Integration and Environmental Change in the Mediterranean States." In *European Integration and Environmental Policy*, edited by J. D. Liefferink, P. D. Lowe, and A. P. J. Mol, 217–236. London: Belhaven.

Laffan, Brigid. 1989. "Putting European Law into Practice: The Irish Experience." *Administration* 37 (3): 203–217.

Laffan, Brigid, Rory O'Donnell, and Michael Smith. 2000. *Europe's Experimental Union: Rethinking Integration*. London: Routledge.

Laffan, Brigid, and Jane O'Mahony. 2008. *Ireland and the European Union*. Houndmills, Basingstoke, UK: Palgrave Macmillan.

Lake, David. 2009. *Hierarchy in International Relations*. Ithaca, NY: Cornell University Press.

Lake, David, Lisa L. Martin, and Thomas Risse, eds. 2021. Challenges to Liberal World Order: 75th Anniversary Issue of *International Organization*.

Lampinen, Risto, and Petri Uusikylä. 1998. "Implementation Deficit: Why Member States Do Not Comply with EU Directives?" *Scandinavian Political Studies* 21 (3): 231–251.

Larsson, Olof, and Daniel Naurin. 2016. "Judicial Independence and Political Uncertainty: How the Risk of Override Affects the Court of Justice of the EU." *International Organization* 70 (2): 377–408.

Lebovic, James H., and Erik Voeten. 2009. "The Cost of Shame: International Organizations and Foreign Aid in the Punishing of Human Rights Violators." *Journal of Peace Research* 46 (1): 79–97.

Leiber, Simone. 2007. "Transposition of EU Social Policy in Poland: Are There Different 'Worlds of Compliance' in East and West?" *Journal of European Social Policy* 17 (4): 349–360.

Lenz, Tobias, and Gary Marks. 2016. "Regional Institutional Design." In *The Oxford Handbook of Comparative Regionalism*, edited by T. A. Börzel and T. Risse, 513–537. Oxford: Oxford University Press.

Leuffen, Dirk, Frank Schimmelfennig, and Berthold Rittberger. 2013. *Differentiated Integration: Explaining Variation in the European Union*. Basingstoke, UK: Palgrave.

Levitz, Philip, and Grigore Pop-Eleches. 2009. "Why No Backsliding? The European Union's Impact on Democracy and Governance before and after Accession." *Comparative Political Studies* 43 (4): 457–485.

Levitz, Philip, and Grigore Pop-Eleches. 2010. "Monitoring, Money and Migrants: Countering Post-accession Backsliding in Bulgaria and Romania." *Europe-Asia Studies* 62 (3): 461–479.

Levy, Marc A., Oran R. Young, and Michael Zürn. 1995. "The Study of International Regimes." *European Journal of International Relations* 1 (3): 267–330.

Liefferink, Duncan, and Mikael Skou Andersen. 1998. "Strategies of the 'Green' Member States in EU Environmental Policy-Making." *Journal of European Public Policy* 5 (2): 254–270.

Lindberg, Leon N., and Stuart A. Scheingold. 1970. *Europe's Would-Be Polity*. Englewood Cliffs, NJ: Prentice-Hall.

Linden, Robert, ed. 2002. *Norms and Nannies: The Impact of International Organizations on the Central and Eastern European States*. Lanham, MD: Rowman & Littlefield.

Linos, Katerina. 2007. "How Can International Organizations Shape National Welfare States? Evidence from Compliance with European Union Directives." *Comparative Political Studies* 40 (5): 547–5470.

Lipsky, Michael. 1980. *Street-Level Bureaucracy*. New York: Russell Sage.

Loughlin, John, Frank Hendriks, and Anders Lidström, eds. 2012. *The Oxford Handbook of Local and Regional Democracy in Europe*. Oxford: Oxford University Press.

Lowi, Theodore J. 1972. "Four Systems of Policy, Politics and Choice." *Public Administration Review* 32 (4): 298–310.

Luetgert, Brooke, and Tanja Dannwolf. 2009. "Mixing Methods: A Nested Analysis of EU Transposition Patterns." *European Union Politics* 10 (3): 307–334.

Maggetti, Martino, and Fabrizio Gilardi. 2014. "Network Governance and the Domestic Adoption of Soft Rules." *Journal of European Public Policy* 21 (9): 1293–1310.

Majone, Giandomenico. 1993. "The European Community between Social Policy and Social Regulation." *Journal of Common Market Studies* 11 (1): 79–106.

Majone, Giandomenico. 1994. "The Rise of the Regulatory State in Europe." *West European Politics* 17 (3): 77–101.

Majone, Giandomenico, ed. 1996. *Regulating Europe*. London: Routledge.

Majone, Giandomenico. 2005. *Dilemmas of European Integration: The Ambiguities and Pitfalls of Integration by Stealth*. Oxford: Oxford University Press.

March, James G., and Johan P. Olsen. 1989. *Rediscovering Institutions. The Organizational Basics of Politics*. New York: Free Press.

Marks, Gary, Liesbet Hooghe, and Arjan Schakel. 2010. *The Rise of Regional Authority: A Comparative Study of 42 Countries*. London: Routledge.

Martin, Lisa L. 1992. *Coercive Cooperation: Explaining Multilateral Economic Sanctions*. Princeton, NJ: Princeton University Press.

Mastenbroek, Ellen. 2003. "Surviving the Deadline: The Transposition of EU Directives in the Netherlands." *European Union Politics* 4 (4): 371–396.

Mastenbroek, Ellen, Stijn van Voorst, and Anne Meuwese. 2015. "Closing the Regulatory Cycle? A Meta Evaluation of Ex-post Legislative Evaluations by the European Commission." *Journal of European Public Policy* 23 (9): 1329–1348.

Maurer, Andreas, and Wolfgang Wessels, eds. 2001. *National Parliaments on Their Ways to Europe: Losers or Latecomers?* Baden-Baden: Nomos.

Mazmanian, Daniel A., and Paul A. Sabatier, eds. 1981. *Effective Policy Implementation*. Lexington: Lexington Books.

Mbaye, Heather A. D. 2001. "Why National States Comply with Supranational Law: Explaining Implementation Infringements in the European Union, 1972–1993." *European Union Politics* 2 (3): 259–281.

McLaren, Lauren M. 2006. *Identity, Interests and Attitudes to European Integration*. Houndmills, Basingstoke, UK: Palgrave.

Mendrinou, Maria. 1996. "Non-compliance and the European Commission's Role in Integration." *Journal of European Public Policy* 3 (1): 1–22.

Merlingen, Michael, Cas Mudde, and Ulrich Sedelmeier. 2001. "The Right and the Righteous? European Norms, Domestic Politics and the Sanctions against Austria." *Journal of Common Market Studies* 39 (1): 59–77.

Milward, Alan S. 1992. *The European Rescue of the Nation-State*. Berkeley, CA: University of California Press.

Mitchell, Ronald B. 1996. "Compliance Theory: An Overview." In *Improving Compliance with International Environmental Law*, edited by J. Cameron, J. Werksman, and P. Roderick, 3–28. London: Earthscan.

Mitchell, Ronald B. 2003a. "Of Course International Institutions: But When and How? Global Environment Change and the Nation State." In *How Institutions Change: Perspectives on Social Learning in Global and Local Environmental Context*, edited by H. Breit, A. Engels, T. Moss, and M. Troja, 35–52. Leverkusen, Germany: Leske+Budrich.

Mitchell, Ronald B. 2003b. "Regime Design Matters: Intentional Oil Pollution and Treaty Compliance." *International Organization* 48 (3): 425–458.

Moravcsik, Andrew. 1993. "Preferences and Power in the European Community: A Liberal Intergovernmental Approach." *Journal of Common Market Studies* 31 (4): 473–524.

Moravcsik, Andrew. 1994. *Why the European Community Strengthens the State: Domestic Politics and International Cooperation*. Cambridge, MA: Harvard University Press.

Moravcsik, Andrew. 1997a. "Taking Preferences Seriously: A Liberal Theory of International Politics." *International Organization* 51 (4): 513–553.

Moravcsik, Andrew. 1997b. "Warum die Europäische Union die Exekutive stärkt: Innenpolitik und internationale Kooperation." In *Projekt Europa im Übergang? Staat und Demokratie in der Europäischen Union*, edited by K. D. Wolf, 211–269. Baden-Baden: Nomos.

Moravcsik, Andrew. 1998. *The Choice for Europe: Social Purpose and State Power from Messina to Maastricht*. Ithaca, NY: Cornell University Press.

Moravcsik, Andrew, and Milada Anna Vachudova. 2003. "National Interests, State Power, and EU Enlargement." *East European Politics and Societies* 17 (1): 42–57.

Morrow, James D. 1999. "The Strategic Setting of Choices: Signaling, Commitment, and Negotiation in International Politics." In *Strategic Choice and International Relations*, edited by D. A. Lake and R. Powell, 77–114. Princeton, NJ: Princeton University Press.

Morrow, James D. 2007. "When Do States Follow the Laws of War?" *American Political Science Review* 101 (3): 559–572.

Mungiu-Pippidi, Alina. 2006. "Corruption: Diagnosis and Treatment." *Journal of Democracy* 17 (3): 86–99.

Mungiu-Pippidi, Alina. 2014. "The Legacies of 1989: The Transformative Power of Europe Revisited." *Journal of Democracy* 25 (1): 20–32.

Mungiu-Pippidi, Alina. 2015. *The Quest for Good Governance: How Societies Develop Control of Corruption*. Cambridge: Cambridge University Press.

Nachmias, David, and David H. Rosenbloom. 1978. *Bureaucratic Culture: Citizens and Administrators in Israel*. London: Taylor & Francis.

Nanou, Kyriaki, Galina Zapryanova, and Fanni Toth. 2017. "An Ever Closer Union? Measuring the Expansion and Ideological Content of European Union Policy-Making through an Expert Survey." *European Union Politics* 18 (4) 678–693.

Nijenhuis, Albert. 2013. "Electronic Communications and the EU Consumer." In *Services and the EU Citizen*, edited by F. S. Benyon, 47–74. Oxford: Hart.

Nollkämper, André. 1992. "On the Effectiveness of International Rules." *Acta Politica* 27 (1): 49–70.

Nordlinger, Eric A. 1981. *On the Autonomy of the Democratic State*. Cambridge: Cambridge University Press.

Norris, Pippa. 2000. "Global Governance and Cosmopolitan Citizens." In *Governance in a Globalizing World*, edited by J. S. Nye and E. Kamarck, 155–177. Washington, DC: Brookings Institution.

North, Douglass C. 1990. *Institutions, Institutional Change, and Economic Performance*. New York: Cambridge University Press.

Noutcheva, Gergana, and Dimitar Bechev. 2008. "The Successful Laggards: Bulgaria and Romania's Accession to the EU." *East European Politics and Society* 22 (1): 114–144.

Nugent, Neil. 2016. "Enlargements and Their Impact on EU Governance and Decision-Making." *Journal of Contemporary European Research* 12 (1): 424–439.

Offe, Claus. 1991. "Capitalism by Democratic Design? Democratic Theory Facing the Triple Transition in East Central Europe." *Social Research* 58 (4): 865–892.

Oye, Kenneth A., ed. 1986. *Cooperation under Anarchy*. Princeton, NJ: Princeton University Press.

Panara, Carlo. 2015. *The Sub-national Dimension of the EU: A Legal Study of Multilevel Governance*. New York: Springer.

Panke, Diana. 2007. *Talking States into Compliance: Explaining the Differential Success of the European Court of Justice*. Berlin: Dissertationsschrift zur Erlangung des Doktor Phil. an der Freien Universität Berlin.

Panke, Diana. 2010a. *Small States in the European Union: Coping with Structural Disadvantages*. London: Ashgate.

Panke, Diana. 2010b. "Why (Big) States Cannot Do What They Want: International Legalization at Work." *International Politics* 47 (2): 186–209.

Peers, Steve. 2012. "Sanctions for Infringement of EU Law after the Treaty of Lisbon." *European Public Law* 18 (1): 33–64.

Pelc, Krzysztof J. 2009. "Seeking Escape: The Use of Escape Clauses in International Trade Agreements." *International Studies Quarterly* 53 (2): 349–368.

Pelkmans, Jacques, and L. Alan Winters. 1988. *Europe's Domestic Market*. Chatham House Papers. London: Routledge.

Perkins, Richard, and Eric Neumayer. 2007. "Do Membership Benefits Buy Regulatory Compliance?" *European Union Politics* 8 (2): 180–206.

Peters, Anne. 2003. "International Dispute Settlement: A Network of Cooperational Duties." *European Journal of International Law* 14 (1): 1–34.

Pichler, Florian. 2012. "Cosmopolitanism in a Global Perspective: An International Comparison of Open-Minded Orientations and Identity in Relation to Globalization." *International Sociology* 27 (1): 21–50.

Pinder, John. 1968. "Positive Integration and Negative Integration: Some Problems of Economic Union in the EEC." *World Today* 24 (3): 88–110

Plechanovová, Béla. 2011. "The European Council Enlarged: North-South-East or Core-Periphery?" *European Union Politics* 12 (1): 87–106.

Pollack, Mark A. 1997a. "Delegation, Agency, and Agenda Setting in the European Community." *International Organization* 51 (1): 99–134.

Pollack, Mark A. 1997b. "Representing Diffuse Interests in EC Policy-Making." *Journal of European Public Policy* 4 (4): 572–590.

Polyakova, Alina, and Neil Fligstein. 2016. "Is European Integration Causing Europe to Become More Nationalist? Evidence from the 2007–9 Financial Crisis." *Journal of European Public Policy* 23 (1): 60–83.

Pressman, Jeffrey L., and Aaron B. Wildavsky. 1973. *Implementation: How Great Expectations in Washington Are Dashed in Oakland*. Berkeley: University of California Press.

Prete, Luca. 2017. *Infringement Proceedings in EU Law*. Amsterdam: Wolters Kluwer.

Pridham, Geoffrey. 1994. "National Environmental Policy-Making in the European Framework: Spain, Greece and Italy in Comparison." *Regional Politics and Policy* 4 (1, special issue): 80–101.

Pridham, Geoffrey. 1996. "Environmental Policies and Problems of European Legislation in Southern Europe." *South European Society and Politics* 1 (1): 47–73.

Pridham, Geoffrey. 2007. "Romania and EU Membership in Comparative Perspective: A Postaccession Compliance Problem? The Case of Political Conditionality." *Perspectives on European Politics and Society* 8 (2): 166–188.

Pridham, Geoffrey. 2008. "The EU's Political Conditionality and Post-accession Tendencies: Comparisons from Slovakia and Latvia." *Journal of Common Market Studies* 46 (2): 365–387.

Pridham, Geoffrey, and Michelle Cini. 1994. "Enforcing Environmental Standards in the European Union: Is There a Southern Problem?" In *Environmental Standards in the EU in an Interdisciplinary Framework*, edited by M. Faure, J. Vervaele, and A. Waele, 251–277. Antwerp: Maklu.

Przeworski, Adam. 1990. *East-South System Transformation*. Chicago: Chicago University Press.

Putnam, Robert D. 1988. "Diplomacy and Domestic Politics: The Logic of Two-Level Games." *International Organization* 42 (3): 427–460.

Rauch, James, and Peter B. Evans. 2000. "Bureaucratic Structure and Bureaucratic Performance in Less Developed Countries." *Journal of Public Economics* 75 (1): 49–71.

Rauh, Christian, and Pieter De Wilde. 2017. "The Opposition Deficit in EU Accountability: Evidence from Over 20 Years of Plenary Debate in Four Member States." *European Journal of Political Research* 57 (1): 194–216.

Raunio, Tapio, and John O'Brennan. 2007. *National Parliaments within the Enlarged European Union: From Victims of Integration to Competitive Actors?* London: Routledge.

Raustiala, Kal, and Anne Marie Slaughter. 2002. "International Law, International Relations and Compliance." In *Handbook of International Relations*, edited by W. Carlsnaes, T. Risse, and B. A. Simmons, 538–558. London: Sage.

Reinhardt, Eric. 2001. "Adjudication without Enforcement in GATT Disputes." *Journal of Conflict Resolution* 45 (2): 174–195.

Risse, Thomas. 2010. *A Community of Europeans? Transnational Identities and Public Spheres*. Ithaca, NY: Cornell University Press.

Risse, Thomas. 2015a. "European Public Spheres, the Politicization of EU Affairs, and Its Consequences." In *European Public Spheres: Politics Is Back*, edited by T. Risse, 141–164. Cambridge: Cambridge University Press.

Risse, Thomas, ed. 2015b. *European Public Spheres: Politics Is Back*. Cambridge: Cambridge University Press.

Risse, Thomas, Stephen C. Ropp, and Kathryn Sikkink, eds. 1999. *The Power of Human Rights: International Norms and Domestic Change*. Cambridge: Cambridge University Press.

Risse, Thomas, Stephen C. Ropp, and Kathryn Sikkink, eds. 2013. *The Persistent Power of Human Rights: From Commitment to Compliance*. Cambridge: Cambridge University Press.

Rodden, Jonathan. 2002. "Strength in Numbers? Representation and Redistribution in the European Union." *European Union Politics* 3 (2): 151–175.

Rogowski, Ronald. 1989. *Commerce and Coalitions: How Trade Affects Domestic Political Alignments*. Princeton, NJ: Princeton University Press.

Romeu, Francisco Ramos. 2006. "Law and Politics in the Application of EC Law: Spanish Courts and the ECJ, 1986–2000." *Common Market Law Review* 43:395–421.

Rosendorff, B. Peter, and Helen V. Milner. 2001. "The Optimal Design of International Trade Institutions: Uncertainty and Escape." *International Organization* 55 (4): 829–857.

Rothstein, Bo. 2011. *The Quality of Government: Corruption, Social Trust, and Inequality in International Perspective*. Chicago: University of Chicago Press.

Rothstein, Bo, and Jan A. Teorell. 2008. "What Is Quality of Government? A Theory of Impartial Government Institutions." *Governance* 21 (2): 165–190.

Sadurski, Wojciech. 2006. "Introduction: The Law and Institutions of New Member States in Year One." In *Après Enlargement: Legal and Political Responses in Central and Eastern Europe*, edited by W. Sadurski, J. Ziller, and K. Zurek, 3–18. Florence: European University Institute.

Sadurski, Wojciech. 2012. *Constitutionalism and the Enlargement of Europe*. Oxford: Oxford University Press.

Sánchez-Cuenca, Ignacio. 2000. "The Political Basis of Support for European Integration." *European Union Politics* 1 (2): 147–171.

Sandholtz, Wayne, and Alec Stone Sweet, eds. 1998. *European Integration and Supranational Governance*. Oxford: Oxford University Press.

Sbragia, Alberta. 1994. "From 'Nation-State' to 'Member-State': The Evolution of the European Community." In *Europe after Maastricht: American and European Perspectives*, edited by P. M. Lützeler, 69–87. Providence: Berghahn Books.

Scharpf, Fritz W. 1996. "Negative and Positive Integration in the Political Economy of European Welfare States." In *Governance in the European Union*, edited by G. Marks, F. W. Scharpf, P. C. Schmitter, and W. Streeck, 15–39. London: Sage.

Scharpf, Fritz W. 1997a. "Economic Integration, Democracy and the Welfare State." *Journal of European Public Policy* 4 (4): 18–36.

Scharpf, Fritz W. 1997b. "Introduction: The Problem-Solving Capacity of Multi-level Governance." *Journal of European Public Policy* 4 (4): 520–538.

Scharpf, Fritz W. 1999. *Governing Europe: Effective and Legitimate?* Oxford: Oxford University Press.

Scharpf, Fritz W. 2001a. "European Governance: Common Concerns vs. the Challenge of Diversity." In *Symposium: Responses to the European Commission's White Paper on Governance*, edited by C. Joerges, Y. Mény, and J. H. H. Weiler. Florence: European University Institute, Robert Schuman Centre for Advanced Studies.

Scharpf, Fritz W. 2001b. "Notes toward a Theory of Multilevel Governing in Europe." *Scandinavian Political Studies* 24 (1): 1–26.

Scharpf, Fritz W. 2003. "Problem-Solving Effectiveness and Democratic Accountability in the EU." MPIfG Working Papers 3 (1).

Scharpf, Fritz W. 2015. "Political Legitimacy in a Non-optimal Currency Area." In *Democratic Politics in a European Union under Stress*, edited by O. Cromme and S. B. Hobolt, 19–47. Oxford: Oxford University Press.

Scharpf, Fritz W. 2016a. "The Costs of Non-disintegration: The Case of EMU." In *The End of the Eurocrats' Dream: Adjusting to European Diversity*, edited by D. Chalmers, M. Jachtenfuchs, and C. Joerges, 29–49. Cambridge: Cambridge University Press.

Scharpf, Fritz W. 2016b. "De-constitutionalization and Majority Rule: A Democratic Vision for Europe." MPIfG Discussion Paper 16 (14).

Schelling, Thomas C. 1960. *The Strategy of Conflict*. Cambridge, MA: Harvard University Press.

Schenk, Angelika, and Susanne K. Schmidt. 2018. "Failing on the Social Dimension: Judicial Law-Making and Student Mobility in the EU." *Journal of European Public Policy* 25 (10): 1522–1540.

Scherpereel, John A. 2007. "Sub-national Authorities in the EU's Post-Socialist States: Joining the Multi-level Polity?" *Journal of European Integration* 29 (1): 23–46.

Schimmelfennig, Frank. 2010. "The Normative Origins of Democracy in the European Union: Toward a Transformationalist Theory of Democratization." *European Political Science Review* 2 (2): 211–233.

Schimmelfennig, Frank. 2014a. "EU Enlargement and Differential Integration: Discrimination or Equal Treatment?" *Journal of European Public Policy* 21 (5): 681–698.

Schimmelfennig, Frank. 2014b. "European Integration in the Euro Crisis: The Limits of Postfunctionalism." *Journal of European Integration* 36 (3): 321–337.

Schimmelfennig, Frank, Stefan Engert, and Heiko Knobel. 2003. "Costs, Commitment and Compliance: The Impact of EU Democratic Conditionality on Latvia, Slovakia and Turkey." *Journal of Common Market Studies* 41 (3): 495–518.

Schimmelfennig, Frank, and Ulrich Sedelmeier. 2004. "Governance by Conditionality: EU Rule Transfer to the Candidate Countries of Central and Eastern Europe." *Journal of European Public Policy* 11 (4): 661–679.

Schimmelfennig, Frank, and Ulrich Sedelmeier. 2005. "Conclusions: The Impact of the EU on the Accession Countries." In *The Europeanization of Central and Eastern Europe*, edited by F. Schimmelfennig and U. Sedelmeier, 210–228. Ithaca, NY: Cornell University Press.

Schimmelfennig, Frank, and Florian Trauner, eds. 2010. "Post-accession Compliance in the EU's New Member States." *European Integration Online Papers*, Special Issue 2 (1): https://www.ies.be/files/issue.pdf.

Schimmelfennig, Frank, and Thomas Winzen. 2014. "Instrumental and Constitutional Differentiation in the European Union." *Journal of Common Market Studies* 52 (2): 354–370.

Schimmelfennig, Frank, and Thomas Winzen. 2017. "Eastern Enlargement and Differentiated Integration: Towards Normalization." *Journal of European Public Policy* 24 (2): 239–258.

Schlipphak, Bernd, and Oliver Treib. 2016. "Playing the Blame Game on Brussels: The Domestic Political Effects of EU Interventions against Democratic Backsliding." *Journal of European Public Policy* 24 (3): 352–365.

Schmidt, Susanne K. 2018. *The European Court of Justice and the Policy Process*. Oxford: Oxford University Press.

Schmidt, Susanne K., and R. Daniel Kelemen, eds. 2014. *The Power of the European Court of Justice*. London: Routledge.

Schmidt, Susanne K., and Arndt Wonka. 2012. "European Commission." In *The Oxford Handbook of the European Union*, edited by E. Jones, A. Menon, and S. Weatherill, 336–349. Oxford: Oxford University Press.

Schmidt, Vivien A. 2006. *Democracy in Europe: The EU and National Polities*. Oxford: Oxford University Press.

Schneider, Gerald, Daniel Finke, and Stefanie Bailer. 2010. "Bargaining Power in the European Union: An Evaluation of Competing Game-Theoretic Models." *Political Studies* 58 (1): 85–103.

Scholten, Miroslava. 2017. "Mind the Trend! Enforcement of EU Law Has Been Moving to 'Brussels.'" *Journal of European Public Policy* 24 (9): 1348–1366.

Schumann, Wolfgang. 1991. "EG-Forschung und Policy-Analyse: Zur Notwendigkeit, den ganzen Elefanten zu erfassen." *Politische Vierteljahresschrift* 32 (2): 232–257.

Schwellnus, Guido. 2009. "It Ain't Over When It's Over: The Adoption and Sustainability of Minority Protection Rules in New EU Member States." *European Integration Online Papers* 13 (24). http://eiop.or.at/eiop/texte/2009-024a.htm.

Scully, Roger, Simon Hix, and David M. Farrell. 2012. "National or European Parliamentarians? Evidence from a New Survey of the Members of the European Parliament." *Journal of Common Market Studies* 50 (4): 670–683.

Sedelmeier, Ulrich. 2005. *Constructing the Path to Eastern Enlargement: The Uneven Policy Impact of EU Identity*. Manchester: Manchester University Press.

Sedelmeier, Ulrich. 2006. "Pre-accession Conditionality and Post-accession Compliance in the New Member States: A Research Note." In *Après Enlargement: Legal and Political Responses in Central and Eastern Europe*, edited by W. Sadurski, J. Ziller, and K. Zurek, 145–160. Florence: European University Institute.

Sedelmeier, Ulrich. 2008. "After Conditionality: Post-accession Compliance with EU Law in East Central Europe." *Journal of European Public Policy* 15 (6): 806–825.

Sedelmeier, Ulrich. 2009. "Post-accession Compliance with EU Gender Equality Legislation in Post-Communist New Member States." *European Integration Online Papers* 13 (23). http://eiop.or.at/eiop/texte/2009-023a.htm.

Sedelmeier, Ulrich. 2012. "Is Europeanization through Conditionality Sustainable? Lock-In of Institutional Change after EU Accession." *West European Politics* 35 (1): 20–38.

Sedelmeier, Ulrich. 2014. "Anchoring Democracy from Above: The European Union's Measures against Democratic Backsliding in Hungary and Romania after Accession." *Journal of Common Market Studies* 52 (1): 105–121.

Selck, Torsten J., and Bernard Steunenberg. 2004. "Between Power and Luck: The European Parliament in the EU Legislative Process." *European Union Politics* 5 (1): 25–46.

Seleny, Anna. 2007. "Communism's Many Legacies in East-Central Europe." *Journal of Democracy* 18 (3): 156–170.

Senden, Linda. 2004. *Soft Law in the European Community*. Portland, OR: Hart.

Shapley, Lloyd S., and Martin Shubik. 1954. "A Method for Evaluating the Distribution of Power in a Committee System." *American Political Science Review* 48 (3): 787–792.

Siedentopf, Heinrich, and Christoph Hauschild. 1988. "The Implementation of Community Legislation by the Member States." In *Making European Policies Work: The Implementation of Community Legislation in the Memeber States*, edited by H. Siedentopf and J. Ziller, 1–87. London: Sage.

Siedentopf, Heinrich, and Jacques Ziller, eds. 1988. *Making European Policies Work: The Implementation of Community Legislation in the Member States*. Vol. 1, *Comparative Syntheses*. London: Sage.

Siegel, Scott N. 2011. *The Political Economy of Noncompliance: Adjusting to the Single European Market*. London: Routledge.

Simmons, Beth A. 1998. "Compliance with International Agreements." *Annual Review of Political Science* 1:75–93.

Simmons, Beth A. 2009. *Mobilizing for Human Rights: International Law in Domestic Politics*. Cambridge: Cambridge University Press.

Simon, Herbert A. 1962. "The Architecture of Complexity." *Proceedings of the American Philosophical Society* 106 (6): 467–482.

Sion-Tzidkiyahu, Maya. 2012. "Europe à la Carte: Comparing the Paths of Opt-Outs in the European Union." PhD diss. Department of Political Science, Hebrew University, Jerusalem.

Sissenich, Beate. 2005. "The Transfer of EU Social Policy Transfer of EU Social Policy to Poland and Hungary." In *The Europeanization of Central and Eastern Europe*, edited by F. Schimmelfennig and U. Sedelmeier, 156–177. Ithaca, NY: Cornell University Press.

Sissenich, Beate. 2007. *Building States without Society: European Union Enlargement and the Transfer of EU Social Policy to Poland and Hungary*. Lanham, MD: Lexington Books.

Slapin, Jonathan B. 2015. "How European Union Membership Can Undermine the Rule of Law in Emerging Democracies." *West European Politics* 38 (3): 627–648.

Slaughter, Anne-Marie. 1995. "International Law in a World of Liberal States." *European Journal of International Law* 6 (4): 504–538.

Slaughter, Anne-Marie. 2004. *A New World Order*. Princeton, NJ: Princeton University Press.

Smith, James McCall. 2000. "The Politics of Dispute Settlement Design: Explaining Legalism in Regional Trade Pacts." *International Organization* 54 (1): 137–180.

Snyder, Francis. 1993. "The Effectiveness of European Community Law: Institutions, Processes, Tools and Techniques." *Modern Law Review* 56 (1): 19–54.

Sotiropoulos, Dimitri A. 2004. "Southern European Public Bureaucracies in Comparative Perspective." *West European Politics* 27 (3): 405–422.

Spendzharova, Aneta, and Milada Anna Vachudova. 2012. "Catching-Up? Consolidating Liberal Democracy in Bulgaria and Romania." *West European Politics* 35 (1): 39–58.

Sprungk, Carina. 2010. "Ever More or Ever Better Scrutiny? Analysing the Conditions of Effective National Parliamentary Involvement in EU Affairs." *European Integration Online Papers* 14 (2). http://eiop.or.at/eiop/texte/2010-002a.htm.

Sprungk, Carina. 2011. "How Policy-Shaping Might (Not) Affect Policy-Taking: The Case of National Parliaments in the European Union." *Journal of European Integration* 33 (3): 323–340.

Sprungk, Carina. 2013. "Legislative Transposition of Directives: Exploring the Other Role of National Parliaments in the European Union." *Journal of Common Market Studies* 51 (2): 298–315.

Starr, Harvey. 1978. "'Opportunity' and 'Willingness' as Ordering Concepts in the Study of War." *International Interactions* 4 (4): 363–387.

Staton, Jeffrey K., and Will H. Moore. 2011. "Judicial Power in Domestic and International Politics." *International Organization* 65 (3): 553–587.

Stein, Arthur A. 1983. "Coordination and Collaboration: Regimes in an Anarchic World." In *International Regimes*, edited by S. D. Krasner, 115–140. Ithaca, NY: Cornell University Press.

Steinberg, Richard H. 2002. "In the Shadow of Law or Power? Consensus-Based Bargaining and Outcomes in the GATT/WTO." *International Organization* 56 (2): 339–374.

Steunenberg, Bernard. 2006. "Turning Swift Policy-Making into Deadlock and Delay: National Policy Coordination and the Transposition of EU Directives." *European Union Politics* 7 (3): 293–319.

Steunenberg, Bernard. 2007. "A Policy Solution to the EU Directives' Transposition Puzzle: Interactions of Interests in Different Domestic Arenas." *West European Politics* 30 (1): 23–49.

Steunenberg, Bernard. 2010. "Is Big Brother Watching? Commission Oversight on the National Implementation of Directives." *European Union Politics* 11 (3): 359–380.

Steunenberg, Bernard, and Antoaneta Dimitrova. 2007. "Compliance in the EU Enlargement Process: The Limits of Conditionality." *European Integration Online Papers* 11 (5). http://eiop.or.at/eiop/texte/2007-005a.htm

Steunenberg, Bernard, and Michael Kaeding. 2009. "'As Time Goes By': Explaining the Transposition of Maritime Directives." *European Journal of Political Research* 48 (3): 432–454.

Steunenberg, Bernard, and Mark Rhinard. 2010. "The Transposition of European Law in EU Member States: Between Process and Politics." *European Political Science Review* 2 (3): 495–520.

Steunenberg, Bernard, and Dimiter Toshkov. 2009. "Comparing Transposition in 27 Member States of the EU: The Impact of Discretion and Legal Fit." *Journal of European Public Policy* 16 (7): 951–970.

Streeck, Wolfgang, and Lea Elsässer. 2016. "Monetary Disunion: The Domestic Politics of Euroland." *Journal of European Public Policy* 23 (1): 1–24.

Sverdrup, Ulf. 2004. "Compliance and Conflict Management in the European Union: Nordic Exceptionalism." *Scandinavian Political Studies* 27 (1): 23–43.

Taggart, Paul, and Aleks Szczerbiak. 2004. "Contemporary Euroscepticism in the Party Systems of the European Union Candidate States of Central and Eastern Europe." *European Journal of Political Research* 43 (1): 1–27.

Tallberg, Jonas. 2000a. "The Anatomy of Autonomy: An Institutional Account of Variation in Supranational Influence." *Journal of Common Market Studies* 38 (5): 843–864.

Tallberg, Jonas. 2000b. "Supranational Influence in EU Enforcement: The ECJ and the Principle of State Liability." *Journal of European Public Policy* 7 (1): 104–121.

Tallberg, Jonas. 2002. "Paths to Compliance: Enforcement, Management, and the European Union." *International Organization* 56 (3): 609–643.

Tallberg, Jonas. 2003. *European Governance and Supranational Institutions: Making States Comply*. London: Routledge.

Tatham, Michaël. 2018. "The Rise of Regional Influence in the EU: From Soft Policy Lobbying to Hard Vetoing." *Journal of Common Market Studies* 56 (3): 672–686.

Thomann, Eva. 2015. "Customizing Europe: Transposition as Bottom-Up Implementation." *Journal of European Public Policy* 22 (10): 1368–1387.

Thomson, Robert. 2007. "Time to Comply: National Responses to Six EU Labour Market Directives Revisited." *West European Politics* 30 (5): 987–1008.

Thomson, Robert. 2010. "Opposition through the Back Door in the Transposition of EU Directives." *European Union Politics* 11 (4): 577–96.

Thomson, Robert, Frans N. Stokman, Thomas König, and Christopher Achen, eds. 2006. *The European Union Decides: Testing Theories of European Decision Making*. Cambridge: Cambridge University Press.

Thomson, Robert, René Torenvield, and Javier Arregui. 2007. "The Paradox of Compliance: Infringements and Delays in Transposing European Union Directives." *British Journal of Political Science* 37 (4): 685–709.

Thucydides. 2009. *The Peloponnesian War*. Translated by Martin Hammond. Oxford World's Classics. Oxford: Oxford University Press.

Toshkov, Dimiter. 2007a. "In Search of the Worlds of Compliance: Culture and Transposition Performance in the European Union." *Journal of European Public Policy* 14 (6): 933–954.

Toshkov, Dimiter. 2007b. "Transposition of EU Social Policy in the New Member States." *Journal of European Social Policy* 17 (4): 335–348.

Toshkov, Dimiter. 2008. "Embracing European Law: Compliance with EU Directives in Central and Eastern Europe." *European Union Politics* 9 (3): 379–402.

Toshkov, Dimiter. 2010. "Taking Stock: A Review of Quantitative Studies of Transposition and Implementation of EU Law." eif Working Paper 01/2010.

Toshkov, Dimiter. 2012. "Compliance with EU Law in Central and Eastern Europe." *L'Europe en Formation* (2): 91–109.

Tosun, Jale. 2011. "When the Grace Period Is Over: Assessing the New Member States' Compliance with EU Requirements for Oil Stockholding." *Energy Policy* 39:7156–7164.

Trauner, Florian. 2009. "Post-accession Compliance with EU Law in Bulgaria and Romania: A Comparative Perspective." *European Integration Online Papers* 13 (21). http://eiop.or.at/eiop/texte/2009-021a.htm.

Treib, Oliver. 2008. "Implementing and Complying with EU Governance Outputs." *Living Reviews in European Governance* 3 (5): 1–13.

Trondal, Jale. 2010. *An Emergent European Executive Order*. Oxford: Oxford University Press.

Tsebelis, George. 2002. *Veto Players: How Political Institutions Work*. Princeton, NJ: Princeton University Press.

Vachudova, Milada Anna. 2005. *Europe Undivided: Democracy, Leverage and Integration after Communism*. Oxford: Oxford University Press.

van Hüllen, Vera, and Tanja A. Börzel. 2015. "Why Being Democratic Is Just Not Enough: The EU's Governance Transfer." In *Governance Transfer by Regional Organizations: Patching Together a Global Script*, edited by T. A. Börzel and V. van Hüllen, 227–244. Houndmills, Basingstoke, UK: Palgrave Macmillan.

Verheijen, Tony. 2007. "Administrative Capacity in the New EU Member States: The Limits of Innovation?" World Bank Working Paper No. 115.

Versluis, Esther. 2004. "Explaining Variations in Implementation of EU Directives." *European Integration Online Papers* 8 (19). http://eiop.or.at/eiop/texte/2004-019a.htm.

Versluis, Esther. 2007. "EU Law: Even Rules, Uneven Practices." *West European Politics* 30 (1): 50–67.

Versluis, Esther, and Erika Tarr. 2013. "Improving Compliance with European Union Law via Agencies: The Case of the European Railway Agency." *Journal of Common Market Studies* 51 (2): 316–333.

von Bogdandy, Armin, and Pál Sonnevend. 2015. *Constitutional Crisis in the European Constitutional Area: Theory, Law and Politics in Hungary and Romania*. Oxford: Hart.

Wallace, Helen. 1971. "The Impact of the European Communities on National Policy-Making." *Government and Opposition* 6 (4): 520–538.

Wallace, Helen. 2005. "An Institutional Anatomy and Five Policy Modes." In *Policy-Making in the European Union*, edited by H. Wallace, W. Wallace, and M. A. Pollack, 49–90. Oxford: Oxford University Press.

Wallace, William. 1983. "Less Than a Federation, More Than a Regime: The Community as a Political System." In *Policy-Making in the European Community*, edited by H. Wallace, W. Wallace, and C. Webb, 43–80. Chichester: John Wiley.

Weiler, Joseph H. H. 1981. "The Community System: The Dual Character of Supranationalism." *Yearbook of European Law* 1:268–306.

Weiler, Joseph H. H. 1988. "The White Paper and the Application of Community Law." In *1992: One European Market?*, edited by R. Bieber, R. Dehousse, J. Pinder, and J. H. H. Weiler, 337–358. Baden-Baden: Nomos.

Weiler, Joseph H. H. 1999. *The Constitution of Europe*. Cambridge: Cambridge University Press.

Weiss, Edith Brown, and Harold K. Jacobsen, eds. 1998. *Engaging Countries: Strengthening Compliance with International Environmental Accords*. Cambridge, MA: MIT Press.

Wiener, Antje, Tanja A. Börzel, and Thomas Risse, eds. 2019. *European Integration Theory*. 3rd ed. Oxford: Oxford University Press.

Williams, Rhiannon. 1994. "The European Commission and the Enforcement of Environmental Law: An Invidious Position." *Yearbook of European Law* 14:351–400.

Wilson, James Q., ed. 1980. *The Politics of Regulation*. New York: Basic Books.

Wind, Marlene. 2010. "The Nordics, the EU and the Reluctance towards Supranational Judicial Review." *Journal of Common Market Studies* 48 (4): 1039–1063.

Wind, Marlene, Dorte Sindbjerg Martinsen, and Gabriel Pons Rotger. 2009. "The Uneven Legal Push for Europe: Questioning Variation When National Courts Go to Europe." *European Union Politics* 10 (1): 63–88.

Winzen, Thomas. 2013. "European Integration and National Parliamentary Oversight Institutions." *European Union Politics* 14 (2): 297–323.

Wolf, Klaus Dieter. 2000. *Die neue Staatsräson—Zwischenstaatliche Kooperation als Demokratieproblem in der Weltgesellschaft*. Baden-Baden: Nomos.

Wright, Vincent. 1999. "The National Co-ordination of European Policy-Making: Negotiating the Quagmire." In *European Union: Power and Policy-Making*, edited by J. J. Richardson, 148–169. London: Routledge.

Yesilkagit, Kutsal. 2011. "Institutional Compliance, European Networks of Regulation and the Bureaucratic Autonomy of National Regulatory Authorities." *Journal of European Public Policy* 18 (7): 962–979.

Young, Oran R. 1979. *Compliance and Public Authority: A Theory with International Applications*. Baltimore: Johns Hopkins University Press.

Young, Oran R. 1992. "The Effectiveness of International Institutions: Hard Cases and Critical Variables." In *Governance without Government: Order and Change in World Politics*, edited by J. N. Rosenau and E.-O. Czempiel, 160–194. Cambridge: Cambridge University Press.

Zeff, Eleanor E., and Ellen B. Pirro, eds. 2001. *The European Union and the Member States: Cooperation, Coordination, and Compromise*. Boulder, CO: Lynne Rienner.

Zhelyazkova, Asya, Tanja A. Börzel, Frank Schimmelfennig, and Ulrich Sedelmeier. 2015. "Beyond Uniform Integration? Researching the Effects of Enlargement on the EU's Legal System." MAXCAP Working Paper. Berlin: Freie Universität (8).

Zhelyazkova, Asya, Cansarp Kaya, and Reini Schrama. 2016. "Decoupling Practical and Legal Compliance: Analysis of Member States' Implementation of EU Policy." *European Journal of Political Research* 55 (4): 827–846.

Zhelyazkova, Asya, Cansarp Kaya, and Reini Schrama. 2017. "Notified and Substantive Compliance with EU Law in Enlarged Europe: Evidence from Four Policy Areas." *Journal of European Public Policy* 24 (2): 216–238.

Zhelyazkova, Asya, and René Torenvlied. 2009. "The Time-Dependent Effect of Conflict in the Council on Delays in the Transposition of EU Directives." *European Union Politics* 10 (1): 35–62.

Zhelyazkova, Asya, and René Torenvlied. 2011. "The Successful Transposition of European Provisions by Member States: Application to the Framework Equality Directive." *Journal of European Public Policy* 18 (5): 690–708.

Zhelyazkova, Asya, and Nikoleta Yordanova. 2015. "Signalling 'Compliance': The Link between Notified EU Directive Implementation and Infringement Cases." *European Union Politics* 16 (3): 408–428.

Zubek, Radoslaw. 2005. "Complying with Transposition Commitments in Poland: Collective Dilemmas, Core Executive and Legislative Outcomes." *West European Politics* 28 (3): 592–619.

Zubek, Radoslaw. 2011. "Core Executives and Coordination of EU Law Transposition: Evidence from New Member States." *Public Administration* 89 (2): 433–450.

Zubek, Radoslaw, and Klaus H. Goetz. 2010. "Performing to Type? How State Institutions Matter in East Central Europe." *Journal of Public Policy* 30 (1): 1–22.

Zürn, Michael. 1997. "'Positives Regieren' jenseits des Nationalstaates." *Zeitschrift für Internationale Beziehungen* 4 (1): 41–68.

Zürn, Michael. 2002. "Societal Denationalization and Positive Governance." In *Towards a Global Polity*, edited by M. Ougaard and R. A. Higgott, 98–124. London: Routledge.

Zürn, Michael. 2012. "The Politicization of World Politics and Its Effects: Eight Propositions." *European Political Science Review* 61 (1): 47–71.

Zürn, Michael. 2018. *A Theory of Global Governance: Authority, Legitimation and Contestation*. Oxford: Oxford University Press.

Zürn, Michael, Martin Binder, and Matthias Ecker-Ehrhardt. 2012. "International Authority and Its Politicization." *International Theory* 4 (1): 69–106.

Zürn, Michael, and Christian Joerges, eds. 2005. *Law and Governance in Postnational Europe: Compliance beyond the Nation-State*. Cambridge: Cambridge University Press.

Index

Lightning Source UK Ltd.
Milton Keynes UK
UKHW010927150121
377088UK00004B/120